LISA SHARA HALL & ROGER J. PORTER

THE FOOD LOVER'S COMPANION TO
PORTLAND

CHRONICLE BOOKS

SAN FRANCISCO

To Ann Levy, who gave me life, unlimited love, and a passion for food;
and to Kirk Hall, who sustains it all.
—L.S.H.

For Howard Wolf, who cannot tell a miso soup from a soupy tiramisu,
but who has been a loyal and supportive friend for four decades.
—R.J.P.

Printed in the United States of America.

Library of Congress Cataloging-in-Publication Data:
Hall, Lisa Shara.
  The food lover's companion to Portland / by Lisa Shara Hall and
Roger J. Porter.
    p.   cm.
  Includes index.
  ISBN 0-8118-1192-1 (pb.)
  1. Food—Guidebooks. 2. Grocery trade—Oregon—Portland—
Guidebooks. 3. Restaurants—Oregon—Portland—Guidebooks.
I. Porter, Roger J.   II Title.
TX354.5.H35   1996
381'.45641'02579549—dc20   96-14256
                        CIP

Book and cover design: Margery Cantor
Composition: Margery Cantor
Cover illustration: Jeff Foster
Illustration: Karen Smith

Distributed in Canada by Raincoast Books
8680 Cambie Street
Vancouver, BC V6P 6M9

10 9 8 7 6 5 4 3 2 1

Chronicle Books
275 Fifth Street
San Francisco, CA 94103

CONTENTS

Acknowledgments

We wish to express our appreciation to Patty Merrill, who helped make Powell's Books for Cooks such a magnificent store, for her belief in and support of this book; and Patti Hill, former chef at Bread and Ink, who chimed in with useful suggestions; but no one more than Karen Brooks, our great companion for many years, whose unerring taste and editorial acumen kept us right on track. Howard Waskow's adept counsel eased a number of rough moments.

We especially wish to thank Karen Silver and Sharilyn Hovind, our editors at Chronicle Books, for generously and smartly shepherding this book through the publishing labyrinths.

Lisa Hall has been Roger's inspiring companion for food shopping and food schmoozing, and an enduring and endearing companion at Portland restaurants of all stripes. She has made working on this book a challenging and lively experience for him.

Over the years Roger has eaten his way around Portland with a number of other friends who have made countless dinners both pleasurable and instructive. The regulars include Joan Peck, whose "saveur faire" contributed to numerous splendid meals; Joan Strouse and Bill Greenfield, pals at many a feast; Joanna Goff, who is always on, whether on the boards or at the groaning boards; and of late especially Bija Gutoff, whose savvy palate detects culinary pretense and prowess with equal aplomb, and who always provides good copy to match her great company.

Rebecca Crighton finally fulfilled a long-standing promise to cook with Roger, and brought her impressive knowledge to that meal as she had to precious others. David Schiff delivers restaurant news from everywhere, and can always be counted on to talk a good food game. For sheer hedonism and joy of the table, Roger is grateful to Amy Godine, remembering from among hundreds a riotous duck dinner in Montauk and a dicey gypsy supper in Istanbul. His several editors at *Oregon* magazine and *Willamette Week* have given him comfortable venues for writing about food, and he is appreciative for their encouragement.

This book has allowed Lisa to package the twenty-five years of food research, cooking, and ingredient hunting she's enjoyed in Portland. Food has always been a primary focus in her life, falling only slightly behind love.

Roger was a wonderful co-author; his love of words complements his food obsessions. His food sensibilities and palate are a perfect match for Lisa's, making the *Food Lover's Companion* an ideal joint project.

Lisa is indebted to Patricia Wells for her model of a successful marriage between love of food and pride of place, exemplified in the extraordinary book *The Food Lover's Guide to Paris*. Portland may not be so glorious a subject, but Wells's book was the inspiration for Lisa and Roger to treat their own city with the same respect and love.

Most of all Lisa wants to thank her husband, who each day quietly teaches her what it means to be a partner.

PORTLAND:
A FOOD TOWN COME OF AGE

Everyone in Portland realizes that in the past decade remarkable changes have occurred on the food scene. Talk to cooks, restaurant enthusiasts, importers, caterers, and shopkeepers–all will agree that Portland has undergone an immense transformation in its culinary consciousness. When we came to Portland from the New York metropolitan area (Roger in the early 1960s, Lisa in 1970), we thought we were in gastronomic hell. Restaurants served concoctions like Cheese Bings, Lobster Flambéed in a Pineapple Boat, and *jambon en croûte*, a.k.a. Canned Ham Wrapped in Frozen Pie Dough. Hostesses served Stuffed Cheese Balls rolled in chopped pecans, Tuna Casserole, and Baked Beans à Glow-Glow. And there were scarcely any food shops other than the blandly uniform supermarkets (Pierri's Italian Delicatessen and Strohecker's were two rare exceptions). Of course there were spectacular ingredients about—we lived in a paradise of farm produce and amidst a bounty from the Pacific Ocean and Oregon rivers—but it seemed as if few people paid much attention to this richness. As for wine, it came in two flavors: Burgundy and Chablis.

The local changes concurred with shifts on the national scene, though at first Portland marched to a slower drummer. Restaurants led the way, with L'Auberge, Genoa, and Uncle Chen spearheading an interest in serious French, Northern Italian, and regional Chinese cuisines, respectively. Millie Howe's Indian cooking at Indigine exemplified the highly personal recipes starting to be seen in town. New Orleans chef Paul Prudhomme consulted on the launching of the successful Cajun Café. And the amazing influx of Southeast Asian refugees made the cuisines of Vietnam and Thailand almost commonplace. Portlanders demonstrated an increasing awareness of ethnic foods and demanded authenticity in their French and Italian restaurants, not satisfied with the ostentation of what Calvin Trillin calls "La Casa de la Maison Gourmet House."

As the city's culinary sophistication and responsiveness to food fashions has grown, the interest in home cooking has blossomed and excellent food stores have begun sprouting like chanterelles after a fall rain. People have become curious about such ingredients as balsamic vinegar, fresh pasta, blue corn, and ahi tuna. Purveyors now scour the forests of Mt. Hood for wild mushrooms—chanterelles, morels, and lobster mushrooms—that were almost unheard of previously, and local makers of goat cheese have appeared on the scene. By the mid-1970s, Oregon vineyards, with their Pinot Noir and Chardonnay grapes, were in full crush; ten years later, an enterprising distiller sought to replicate the great European eaux-de-vie with Oregon pears from the Hood River area; today, Oregon microbreweries lead the nation in hand-made beers and ales.

Likewise Northwest cooks have discovered new uses for marionberries: in Pinot Noir marinades for alder wood-grilled Chinook salmon and as flavoring for local microbrews. Oyster and mussel breeders on the coast have begun sending their shellfish to Portland markets. Oregon greens have come to mean more than romaine, let alone iceberg lettuce, now implying arugula, mustard greens, and the wild bunch called mesclun. As Portlanders' eating habits became not just more sophisticated but healthier, the long-dormant farmers' markets revived, and numerous small growers now bring their wares morning-fresh from the surrounding rural belt: huckleberries, raspberries, wild plums, kiwis, hazelnuts, shiitake mushrooms, purple bell peppers, radicchio, and baby artichokes. We don't want to suggest that until recently no one in Portland knew how to make use of this great abundance—after all, Portland was James Beard's gastronomical training ground. But only of late have most people appreciated just what he meant and how we can learn his lessons.

Both of us are serious and devoted cooks, as well as writers and reviewers of Portland's food scene. We search tirelessly for the ultimate bagel, the undiscovered cheese shop, the Platonically perfect poussin. We spend a good part of many days on passionate food prowls, seeking devoted sausage-makers, organic farmers, and expert coffee roasters. A while ago, we realized that our friends and readers were asking us not only about the best restaurants but where they could find ingredients, whether Spanish spices or the city's freshest feta. It occurred to us that Portland was ready for a guide to its increasingly impressive foods. Wouldn't it be useful to let others know who we think has the most interesting breads, the best selection of olive oils, the hottest salsas?

While working on *The Food Lover's Companion to Portland* we've discovered little out-of-the-way places and learned that some of our favorite haunts had far more offerings than we realized. We found that some of the best cookware in town is not at trendy kitchenware boutiques but at hotel and restaurant supply houses; that among the dozens of Asian markets in the area some specialize in Korean, some in Filipino food; and that a small local café brings in *pain Polaine*, the most famous bread in the world, weekly from Paris. We've also talked to numerous people who have made a difference in Portland's food world—chocolate designers, importers of Italian cheeses, and local creators of new teas—and we introduce them to you.

A word about our collaboration: Both of us know all of the stores that we write about in this book, but we do have certain "specialties" and have taken primary responsibility for reporting and writing on those places and categories. Lisa, connoisseur of cutlets, can be found more often at Portland's butcher shops; Roger, aficionado of Asian spices, haunts Vietnamese groceries. Inevitably authors of a jointly composed book bring different strengths to the project. While each of us is intimately familiar with the market world of Portland, Lisa is more deeply immersed in the food scene, and, partly because of her reviewing and food writing in *The Oregonian*, she spends a lot of time scouting out the latest food establishments around town. Roger, who for fifteen years has been a restaurant critic and food writer for *Oregon Magazine* and *Willamette Week*, is an inveterate food shopper, but his strength centers more in the writing about the food itself. Furthermore, we have quite different voices and have not sought to blend them into a single homogeneous tone. Ultimately, however, this is one book by two dedicated Portlanders who have come to love what their city offers for table and palate.

Although this is not a restaurant guide, we have included a chapter describing a selected number of our favorite local dining places—those spots we return to again and again for sheer pleasure, when we're not doing a working dinner with either *Willamette Week* or *The Oregonian* footing the bill. The book's coverage is almost exclusively of Portland, with some attention paid to Beaverton, Tigard, Milwaukie, Gresham, and Vancouver, Washington, as well as some of the outlying countryside. This is a city book, but of course Portland's suburbs have provided a goodly share of the region's new consciousness about food. All phone numbers, unless otherwise noted, have 503 as their area code.

At the end of many chapters you will notice a section entitled "And Keep in Mind…" Here we list shops or food services that we do not feel merit as full a discussion as the others, though they are certainly worthy of attention and provide an interesting supplement to the places about which we write at greater length.

We have long wished for a guide such as this, and we hope it will be your companion in the kitchen and in the market as you stock your larder, plan a dinner party, or seek out the most interesting places in town to shop and eat.

Part 1

FOOD SHOPS AND SPECIALTY STORES

Chapter 1

BREAD

Everything about bread is sensual. Of course we love the taste and texture, but a great loaf is so much more than that. All of the senses get involved with the wonderfully heady aroma, the chewy texture, the sound of a crisp, crackling crust. We love to handle bread, to get a sense of its density and to feel the imprints of the baker's hands.

Texture, aroma, and flavor sound simple enough, but defining good bread is elusive. How do you know a good loaf from a bad? What makes a loaf legendary? As with fine wines and cheeses—the perfect partners to a great bread—the ingredients must be of high quality and it's the technique that defines results.

As recently as five years ago, good bread in Portland was a dream, a myth, or a major home project. For good bread fixes, we headed for the legendary bakeries in Paris, New York, and San Francisco, wandering in and out of yeast-perfumed shops, nibbling on fresh products we knew we couldn't find in Portland unless we tried to make them ourselves. The few wonderful breads in town were baked on a small scale, including (the dearly departed) Le Panier's classic, crusty baguettes; sour, round loaves of levain bread from Zefiro; and the Greek country loaf baked by (and still served at) Alexis restaurant but sadly no longer sold through retailers. These are simple breads made with few ingredients, given care and love: slow rising and hand crafting make the difference.

By the early 1990s Portland had developed a food sophistication that allowed a bakery like the Seattle-based Grand Central Baking to move in and claim the market. Their yeasty loaves—made by traditional Italian methods, using natural, slow fermentation and baked in complicated deck ovens—have a signature crust, chewy texture, and earthy flavor.

The proliferation of bakeries is as evident as the variety of loaves. Bagel places are rising up on each block, much the way that coffee shops have moved into so many neighborhoods. Croissants, baguettes, rustic breads, and sour loaves can now be purchased from a range of bakeries, allowing us to shop for breads in our own neighborhoods rather than making a pilgrimage to one grand temple of yeast. Portland's rich ethnic communities have also contributed to the bread scene. Freshly baked pita bread is commonplace, Chinese steamed buns are a staple of the many dim sum shops in Old Town, and fresh tortillas are easy to find in many Hispanic groceries.

Portland doesn't have everything. A good Jewish rye bread is nonexistent, and old-fashioned dinner rolls are still best made at home or consumed at a restaurant like L'Etoile, where one of us once ate four of the flour-dusted bread pillows instead of our appetizer. And good, crusty sandwich rolls—called Italian rolls or Portuguese rolls in some communities—aren't in big demand here. For most sandwiches, portions of baguettes or ciabatta bread work just fine, although a good meatball sandwich deserves a bona fide Italian roll as its casing. We'll keep looking and testing.

The Bagel Basket

2800 S.W. Cedar Hills Boulevard, phone: 644-2245; 9140-A S.W. Hall Boulevard,
Tigard, phone: 639-0890; 408–410 N.W. 23rd Avenue, phone: 241-1191;
15350 S.W. Sequoia Parkway, #100, Tigard, phone: 684-1739;
and other locations around the Portland area.
Open Monday through Saturday, 6:30 a.m.–6 p.m.; Sunday, 8 a.m.–5p.m.

This source for credible bagels didn't get us too excited until a branch opened in Northwest Portland. It wasn't so long ago that Portland Bagel Baking had a lock on the market, distributing the chewy rounds fresh through its restaurants (Kornblatt's and Murray's) and in plastic bags in area grocery stores. So when the first Bagel Basket opened in Beaverton, driving out to the burbs for another decent bagel didn't have us rushing to our cars.

But the appearance of The Bagel Basket closer in town makes bagel comparisons easier and more fun. Bagel Basket products are at least as good as the Portland Bagel Baking standard. One distinctive flavor—chocolate chip—is a Bagel Basket-only flavor and it's a knockout. We can say that because we are really bagel purists who prefer a salted or seeded bagel over the more trendy and often silly alternatives. No jalapeño bagels for us. No cinnamon raisin. But the chocolate chip bagel at The Bagel Basket wowed us. Who would have thought a couple of foodies from New Jersey would fall for something so unorthodox?

The physical spaces and the feel of the stores don't thrill us: not one of their outlets makes you think of a deli. No smells perfume the air. The ambience in each shop is a bit too antiseptic for our taste. Still, The Bagel Basket is a find, especially for people who live in the suburbs, since most of their locations are pretty far out of Portland's core. For folks in town, it will be interesting to see how Kornblatt's fares with a Bagel Basket just up the street.

Bagel Sphere

1200 N.E. Broadway, phone: 335-8816. Open Monday through Friday, 7 a.m.–8 p.m.; Saturday and Sunday, 7 a.m.–6 p.m.

The bagel trend has been sweeping through Portland faster than Starbucks can open coffee shops. Anyone with an oven and a pot of boiling water seems to be turning them out, and new bagel vendors have been cropping up all over town. One recent newcomer that we like is Bagel Sphere—a Holladay Market vendor.

Bagel Sphere's product is solid. Their bagels' chewiness offers just enough jaw exercise, and the crusts have the right snap. Freshness is a big plus, as bagels are baked at least twice a day. Other bagel shops have made us frustrated when we've arrived to find our favorite varieties sold out. Bagel Sphere does a good job of keeping up with customer preferences.

B. Moloch / The Heathman Bakery & Pub

901 S.W. Salmon Street, phone: 227-5700. Open Sunday through Thursday, 8 a.m–11 p.m.; Friday and Saturday, 8 a.m.–12 midnight

While most of the well-prepared menu items at this crowded, restaurant-cum-brewpub are available to go, the real secret here is the bread.

The wood ovens that produce the pizzas and roasted meats are also used to bake a variety of creative breads. Every day, the solid selection of loaves includes an excellent Bier Brot in two sizes of rounds, as well as a baguette shape. The slightly fermented taste marries well with the dense crust.

Sourdough is also dominant in the crusty San Francisco–style sourdough breads; in big, round loaves; and in plump, baseball-sized rolls. Ciabatta bread—a flattened baguette with a mild flavor that suggests the addition of good olive oil—is also available flavored with artichoke, onion, olive, pesto, tomato, or goat cheese.

By 11 each morning, a specialty bread of the day is pulled from the ovens: on Monday you'll find a flavorful, sweet apricot and prune loaf; on Tuesday, Irish oatmeal; on Wednesday cheese and onion bread; on Thursday, pesto; and on Friday, either marble rye or Italian walnut.

Thick, puffy focaccia—heavily dimpled—has a crown of herbs and is so fluffy looking that you can imagine your teeth sinking down into a piece, as if you were biting into a cloud.

Treats are lined up in baskets along the top of the display case, beckoning you to succumb to desire: buttery croissants, properly layered like the leaves of a book; great pecan-studded sticky buns, each one tightly coiled like a spring and oozing rich, gooey glaze; and a variety of muffins that can please both the fat-phobic and guilt-free.

Elephants Delicatessen

13 N.W. 23rd Avenue, phone: 224-3955. Open Monday through
Friday, 7 a.m.–7 p.m.; Saturday, 7 a.m.–6 p.m.; Sunday, 10 a.m.–5:30 p.m.

Part of the fun of shopping at this busy, upscale, uptown delicatessen is the availability of samples: small baskets with pieces of bread are set out next to many of the varieties, easing selection while quieting a stomach made hungry by all the promising things to eat.

You'll find a rack containing baguettes, French loaves (both sliced and unsliced), and the breads of the day. On Monday, you'll find buttermilk bread, a homey white bread perfect for old-fashioned sandwiches. On other days a variety of rounds and loaves appear, including whole wheat walnut, English muffin bread, and cinnamon raisin. Friday is a bonanza: buttermilk bread, cheese onion bread, rounds of rustic peasant bread, and good braided challah loaves.

Every day, big and small Tuscan sourdough rounds sit in great mounds on a back table. Discs of salty Kalamata olive bread—black and heavy with the weight of olives—are nudged up against tomato-topped and plain focaccia, pocked with bubbles on the crust and as big and thick as tire wheels. (We always stop here for samples!)

Just when you think you're safe from bread temptation, you'll find, more bread lurking on the counter above the cookie case on your way to the cashier: buttery croissants and sturdy, seeded kaiser rolls with crisp crusts that shatter like glass.

Grand Central Baking

2230 S.E. Hawthorne Boulevard, phone: 232-0575; 3425 S.W. Multnomah Boulevard, phone: 977-2024. Open Monday through Saturday, 7 a.m.–7 p.m.; Sunday, 8 a.m.–5 p.m.

Bread in Portland was pretty ordinary until the day that Grand Central Baking opened its doors in 1993. Overnight, Portland entered the big leagues. Loaves of malty, rustic breads—hand crafted by the young, college-degreed staff that makes Grand Central seem like a halfway house to graduate school—appeared like magic, quelling the whines of desperation regularly heard from food lovers. Since then, nobody else in town has been able to match their quality and consistency, although many try. Grand Central simply ups the ante for everyone.

Grand Central bakes bread for many of the major restaurants in the area, and supplies loaves for other retail outlets. Their own retail business is not a primary focus— making superb bread is. (Word has it that the mother business in Seattle has taken second place to Portland in quality. The breads here keep winning awards, and not just local ones. National publications periodically hold bread competitions, and Portland's Grand Central always takes home ribbons.)

Grand Central's muse is Carol Field, whose book *The Italian Baker* practically revolutionized the art. Each variety of bread here has its loyalists. The Como is probably the signature loaf—a rustic football of crusty, slightly sour bread that comes in two sizes. The olive bread is marvelous as well—a perfumed, pocked, crackly loaf studded with big chunks of Kalamata. The baguette is our favorite in town, with a great fragile crust and a density that seems just right for dipping in olive oil or making sandwiches. And simple flour-dusted rustic buns are simply the best hamburger buns we've ever tried.

Be sure to check out the individual focaccia wheels with toppings: they're what good, personal-sized pizzas ought to be. The thin discs are offered with a choice of two or three toppings, the best variety to our taste sports thin slices of potatoes, caramelized onions, chunks of feta—creamy, sweet, and tart. Cut into quarters, these focaccia are perfect accompaniments to cocktails; or left whole, they make swell picnic fare.

Don't miss the flattened panini rolls, studded with raisins and fennel. Lisa eats them for breakfast, as a snack, with soup, and on any other occasion she can think of. Even the giant cinnamon rolls have a wonderful peasant quality. It's hard to imagine anything that Grand Central wouldn't do well.

Kornblatt's

628 N.W. 23rd Avenue, phone: 242-0055. Open Monday through Thursday, 7 a.m.–9 p.m.; Friday, 7 a.m.–10 p.m.; Saturday, 7:30 a.m.–10 p.m.; Sunday, 7:30 a.m.–9 p.m.

Bagel baron Josh Kornblatt owns and operates Portland Bagel Baking. The eponymous delicatessen he opened in the late 1980s also sells his bagels, as does Kornblatt's other deli venture, Murray's.

Kornblatt's bagels are close to the real New York thing. Many New Yorkers who know their bagels use as the ultimate standard the legendary H & H on the Upper West Side, and Kornblatt's bagels stand up to that model. They're a bit denser and chewier than the quintessential version, but somehow you can never find a perfect bagel outside of New York. Why is that? Is it the water? Another ingredient? Hand versus machine shaping? We've spent hours trying to analyze why a great bagel from one side of the country can't be made here.

Bagel flavors at Kornblatt's range from the simple and plain to salt, poppy, onion, super onion, sourdough, and all the wild tastes in vogue these days: cheese, cinnamon raisin, jalapeño.

The other bread wonders at Kornblatt's are the delicious onion buns. These oblong, doughy rolls are covered in minced onions and they are good warmed and filled with cream cheese or stuffed to make a dandy sandwich.

Marsee Baking

1323 N.W. 23rd Avenue, phone:295-4000; 645 S.W. 4th Avenue, phone: 226-9000; 1625 S.E. Bybee Avenue, phone: 232-0000; Portland International Airport. Open Monday through Friday, 6 a.m.–9 p.m.; Saturday, 7:30 a.m.–10 p.m.; Sunday, 7:30 a.m.–8 p.m.

Flavored baguettes, bagels, and Italian breads are the focus at this remarkable bakery. A major expansion of the production kitchen in 1995 caused a total revision of bread recipes and preparations—with spectacular results. Like Grand Central's stellar products, Marsee's breads are slow-risen with natural fermentation and baked in Bongard ovens (the Rolls Royces of the bread world). Crusts are taut and chewy; inside textures are elastic and dense. The slightly sour loaves exude a heady, malty scent. Marsee's deep-dish focaccia has been replaced with rustic crusty disks, shiny with olive oil and topped with olives, caramelized garlic, roasted, tomatoes, or peppers.

Rye bread is a new entry in the lineup, and Marsee's version comes pretty close to our idea of good Russian rye, with chewy crust and numerous caraway seeds. As with all other breads, the rye can be sliced for sandwiches if you ask. Chocolate rolls are another new discovery. Thick blocks of chocolaty-dark dough have chunks of bitter chocolate studded throughout. These rolls aren't too sweet and are more a bread than a pastry. Warmed for breakfast, one roll makes an indulgent morning wake-me-up, perfect with a cup of coffee.

Bagels here are credible, though they lack a certain snap. But the bialys— the flattened, chewy, bagel-like disk strewn with onion and poppy seeds or a pizza topping—give your jaws a good workout. (We feel that pizza bialy is sacrilegious, a gastronomic mixed metaphor.)

Other decent baked good include flay croissants and tender brioches. And on Friday, Marsee bakes a properly twisted and eggy challah bread.

Nature's Fresh Northwest

3016 S.E. Division Street, phone: 233-7374. Open daily 9 a.m. 10 p.m

5090 S.W. Corbett Street, phone: 244-3934. Open daily, 9 a.m.–8 p.m.

3449 N.E. 24th Avenue, phone: 288-3414. Open daily, 9 a.m.–9 p.m.

6344 S.W. Capitol Highway, phone: 244-3110. Open daily, 9 a.m.–10 p.m.

4000 S.W. 117th Avenue, Beaverton, phone: 646-3824. Open daily, 9 a.m.–9 P.m.

8024 E. Mill Plain Boulevard, Vancouver, phone: 360-695-8878. Open daily, 9 a.m.–10 p.m.

The profile of Nature's Fresh Northwest has been evolving over the last few years, inching its way toward broader market appeal. While still religiously believing in environmentally sound sustainable food resources, Nature's has been attracting serious eaters in addition to health food fans.

The bread offerings are a good example of their new approach. Not only does Nature's carry a broad selection of other vendors' breads (Grand Central Baking's and Kornblatt's among them), but also the bread marketed under Nature's own label is superb. (The tasty loaves are made by the Neighborhood Baking Company, a mostly wholesale operation that sells breads under the Delphina's and Alfredo's names as well, and bakes a wholly distinct line for Nature's.)

These crusty, flour-dusted loaves can compete with Grand Central's without embarrassment. The style is Italian peasant, and the bread is slow risen, with a slightly sour chew. Look for potato rolls, olive bread, wheat levain, walnut bread, and focaccia. Of course, really healthy grains are at home here, too. Nature's caters to every dietary need and proudly stocks gluten-free, dairy-free, and other wholesome varieties.

The newest of the Nature's (in Vancouver) bakes its own artisan loaves and rolls, with organic flours and biga sourdough starters. Varieties include ciabatta, Kalamata olive, seeded semolina, walnut, and yeasted corn. The Vancouver on-site bakery is small, and these breads are only available at that site.

Neighborhood Baking Company

3310 N.W. Yeon Street, phone: 221-1829.
Open Monday through Friday, 7a.m.–5 p.m.; Saturday, 8 a.m.–4 p.m.

Deep in the industrial maze of northwest Portland, this major baking operation offers a small retail outlet with a large selection of breads. Most of their inventory is sold directly to retailers or baked specifically for others to be sold under house labels, but here you can choose from the whole inventory.

The spare space is lined with bins and shelves of plastic-wrapped loaves of French breads, baguettes, Italian loaves, Hawaiian fruit braids, panettone, and a wonderful swirled rye loaf, plus all the up-market, hearth-baked Alfredo line of breads. What lures us here, though, are the baskets of fresh breads behind the counter: wonderful round rolls for sandwiches, different sizes of French baguettes, seed-encrusted rolls, small raisin-studded sweet rolls, potato levain rounds, and long thin Italian rolls that come closest to those we remember as the casing for the submarine and meatball sandwiches of our youth. Fresh croissants, scones, muffins, and cinnamon rolls are also for sale. Day-old bread is available at a substantial savings.

Pastaworks

Division Street Bakery, 4834 S.E. Division Street, phone: 236-1190. Open Tuesday through
Friday 8 a.m.–5:30 p.m.; Saturday and Sunday, 8 a.m.–3 p.m.
3735 S.E. Hawthorne Boulevard, phone: 232-1010; 735 N.W. 21st Avenue
(City Market), phone: 221-3002. Open Monday through Saturday, 9 a.m.–7 p.m.;
Sunday, 10 a.m.–6 p.m. (the 21st Avenue store stays open an hour later each day)

The variety and quality of the breads at these wonderful shops keep expanding like proofing bread. It seems that each visit turns up creative, new breads, but, happily, all the previous favorites are still available week after week.

The standouts include the best olive bread and rolls in town. So many olives are worked into the sour, chewy dough that the bread takes on a black cast. Try it with good, strong cheese: the combination of salty and savory tingles your tongue.

Make a trip to Pastaworks on the weekend and find the most remarkable raisin bread. Shiny oblong loaves of eggy bread are studded with moist raisins and flavored with orange rind. This bread makes terrific toast and heavenly sandwich bread: Lisa uses it for delicious chicken salad sandwiches. On Friday and Saturday look for great eggy challah, topped with your choice of sesame or poppy seeds. We've come to love this loaf for hand-sliced sandwich bread and, when it's a day old, for wonderful French toast.

The wheels of focaccia set the city's standard: about two inches thick and crusty, topped with huge cloves of roasted garlic and oozing olive oil. Pastaworks creates a range of rustic Italian breads, from crusty, sour round loaves to others made with wheat, flour, or rye. Baguettes come in two or three varieties, and many of the breads are also baked in sandwich-loaf form and sliced. Don't overlook the freshly made pita bread when it's available. Their breadsticks, standing in a display glass like staffs of curly willow, make an interesting, lighter alternative to bread.

Pazzoria Bakery & Cafe

621 S.W. Washington Street, phone: 228-1695.
Open Monday through Friday, 7 a.m.–6 A.M.; Saturday, 8 a.m.–5 p.m.

The large storefront windows cast bright ribbons of light into Pazzoria Bakery & Cafe, a spinoff of Pazzo Ristorante, the bustling Italian restaurant next door. Marble counters, a yellow ceiling, and warm woods cozy up the small space, which can seat forty people. Activity in the visible baking area provides entertainment and good smells: you can watch and savor the fresh breads as they come out of the ovens.

Pazzo pastry chef Lee Posey is in charge of the café. In the past few years, she has spent a great deal of time in Italy doing culinary research, and now she teaches Italian baking at various Portland venues.

For Pazzoria, Posey has developed a fine line of baked goods. The repertoire of daily breads includes a number of wonderfully fragrant focaccia, small potato rosemary rolls that are great for sandwiches, savory onion bread sticks (which would pair up wonderfully with soup), and a rotating selection of flavored loaves, from ciabatta to cornmeal sage with pancetta. Breakfast pastries are delicious, especially a grape focaccia that shimmers like colored glass and the breakfast brioche that comes filled with mascarpone and lox or smoked ham. Desserts include cookies, gelato, cheesecake, and fresh fruit pastries. Everything is available to eat here or take out.

Portland Pretzel Company

539 S.W. Broadway, phone: 223-5051; N.W. 23rd Avenue and Johnson Street (cart).
Open Monday through Friday, 8 A.M.–6 p.m.; Saturday, 10 A.M.–5 p.m.

Walk into this industrial-chic space and you'll find not only an eclectic selection of freshly made, soft, warm pretzels, but also an equally eclectic clientele waiting in line to purchase the yeasty twisters.

The different varieties are displayed in barrels that have been turned on their side and stacked on top of one another. Strong flavors like garlic parmesan or cinnamon sugar have never caught our fancy, but the sourdough and plain salt varieties are a purist's delight. Maybe that's because soft pretzels are first cousins to bagels. The basic dough is pretty much the same, just in a different shape. And we feel about funny flavors of pretzel the same as we do about bagels: simple, straight flavors, please.

Whatever your pretzel politics, your choice (except the cinnamon, of course) is sprinkled with salt and heated in a toaster oven while you wait. Three kinds of mustard are on hand to spread on the warm, chewy dough: beer, hot, and spicy.

Three Lions' Bakery

1138 S.W. Morrison Street, phone: 224-3429.
Open Monday through Friday, 7 a.m.–6 p.m.; Saturday, 7 a.m.–6 p.m.
135 N.W. Fifth Avenue, phone: 224-9039. Open Monday through Friday, 7 a.m.–5 p.m.
501 N. Graham Street (at Emanuel Hospital), phone: 287-9474.
Open Monday through Friday, 7 a.m.–6 p.m.; Saturday, 9 a.m.–3 p.m.

More than fifteen years ago, when the first of these bakeries opened, excitement filled the hearts of Portland food fans. The Three Lions' Bakery was the first shop in town to bake buttery fresh brioches and flaky croissants.

Many more bakeries turn out these same breads nowadays, but Three Lions' is still a reliable spot for baked goods. Their line has expanded over the years to include crumbly cheese bread sticks—long, flat wands of puff pastry that make great accompaniments to soup. Their sheepherder's bread is a simple, pleasant round loaf, sliced for sandwiches and toast.

The display cases are filled with pastries, muffins, Danish, coffee cakes, and decorated cakes—all well crafted but not extraordinary. We like to come here for the brioches and croissants, still reliable examples of the genre.

Zero

518 N.W. 23rd Avenue, phone: 226-3394.
Open Monday through Saturday, 8 a.m.–11 p.m.

Only four kinds of bread are sold at this tiny offspring of one of Portland's top restaurants, Zefiro. Of course their signature loaf is available, a great sour levain bread that is served at the restaurant, with butter and a cup of herb and oil-marinated olives. The other breads include a wonderfully grainy cornmeal-based loaf that's terrific toasted and a delicious walnut loaf studded with sweet raisins. Zero sells a different fourth loaf each week, depending on the whim of the Zefiro bakers.

AND KEEP IN MIND...

Bonjour Country French Bakery

1200 N.E. Broadway (inside Holladay Market), phone: 281-8508. Open Monday through
Friday, 7 a.m.–7:30 p.m.; Saturday 7 a.m.–7 p.m.; Sunday, 7 a.m.–6 p.m.
Look for classic French baguettes—crusty loaves that come in a number of sizes. Also good croissants, both filled and plain.

Gabriel's Bakery

2212 N.W. Kearney Street, phone: 227-4712; 1411 N.E. Broadway, phone: 287-9921.
Open Monday through Friday, 6:30 a.m.–5 p.m.;
Saturday, 7 a.m.–3 p.m.; Sunday, 8 a.m.–2 p.m.
Moist two-fisted muffins and scones—studded with everything from fruit to vegetables to chocolate, and packed with flavor.

Great Harvest Bread Company

810 S.W. Second Avenue, phone: 224-8583.

Open Monday through Friday, 7 A.M.–6 p.m.: Saturday, 8 A.M.–5 p.m.

All of the breads at this earnest bakery are made from its own milled flours, without dairy products or oil. Wheat breads of different types dominate the offerings, and everything has a good-for-you feel.

Ron Paul Charcuterie

1441 N.E. Broadway, phone: 284-5439.

Open Monday through Thursday, 8 a,m,–10:30 p.m.; Friday, 8 a,m,–12 midnight;

Saturday, 9 a,m,–12 midnight; Sunday, 9 a,m,–4 p.m.

6141 S.W. Macadam Avenue, phone: 977-0313.

Open Monday through Thursday, 7:30 a,m,–10 p.m.; Friday, 7:30 a,m,–11 p.m.;

Saturday, 9 a,m,–11 p.m.; Sunday, 9 a,m,–4 p.m.

8838 S.W. Hall Boulevard, Beaverton, phone: 646-3869.

Open Monday through Thursday, 9 a,m,–10 p.m.;

Friday and Saturday, 9 a,m,–11 p.m.; Sunday, 9 a,m,–4 p.m.

The standouts in the small selection include a lovely whole-wheat walnut baguette and a small, round flour-dusted levain loaf that's perfect for two people.

BULK FOOD

Chapter 2

T he past decade has seen a renewed interest in grains, legumes, and cereals, partly for health reasons, partly because we're discovering that such foods can taste wonderful. "Tastefully healthy" does not have to be oxymoronic. Every restaurant in town, it seems, has put risotto on the menu, and natural food buffs smile—they've known it all the while. There's never been a lack of places to purchase good bulk grains in Portland; Nature's Fresh Northwest and Food Front spearheaded this drive in the 1960s, and it has continued unabated. Now Bob's Red Mill has pushed the passion to new heights.

Take, for example, rice, many types of which are now available for bulk purchase. Basmati rice appeals to mainstream tastes, for everyone likes its fluffiness and fragrance, and it is de rigueur if you're cooking Indian foods at home. Risotto lovers tout the only rice that works well for this dish: *superfino arborio*, a grain that absorbs lots of liquid without turning to mush. Chinese glutinous rice is very good with fiery Asian spices, since it's so bland, and Valencia rice from Spain is the ideal grain for making paella.

The polenta craze has made bestsellers of maize from Northern Italy and cornmeal from the American South; you can also use this meal to form cornbread, cakes, muffins, dumplings, and even puddings. Bulgur has been popular for a while as the main ingredient in tabouli, the great Middle Eastern salad comprising the grain, chopped tomato, onion, mint, parsley, lemon juice, and olive oil. And you needn't have spent time in North Africa to have sampled couscous, another grain we're seeing a lot of these days. "New" powerhouse grains such as quinoa have come into prominence lately. This "supergrain" hails from the Andes, and is high in protein, good as a cold cereal, and excellent as a pilaf.

Bob's Red Mill Natural Foods

5209 S.E. International Way, Milwaukie, phone: 654-3215.
Open Monday through Saturday, 9 a.m.–5 p.m.

Bob's is at least four separate operations: an astonishing retail store, a stone mill-grinding operation, a huge packing plant, and a small restaurant. It occupies fifty thousand square feet on six acres. If you want the best and largest selection of dry goods available anywhere in the United States, this is your spot. It is a treasure house of flours, beans, lentils, peas, rice, oats, seeds, sugars, cereals and tapiocas, pancake and muffin mixes, and granola, and is absolutely worth a visit.

In the grinding room a pair of hundred-year-old quartz stone wheels quarried outside of Paris turn slowly on their modern wooden bases, starting the flour-making process. Bob's is dedicated to manufacturing natural foods with flint-hard stones employed by millers since Roman times. The old millstones not only make a finer grind, but also preserve the nutrients and oils of the grains better than mechanized methods.

The shop contains shelf after shelf of wonders, 350 products in all. Did you know that the Ethiopian grain teff is the world's smallest? Want something a tad more familiar but still unusual? How about rattlesnake beans, so named because the pods twist around like a snake as they grow? Or marrow beans, with a bacon flavor but minus the fat and nitrates? There's a delicious snack called wheat nuts; masa flour if you enjoy making your own tortillas; six kinds of wild rice; forty-three kinds of pasta; cornmeal in yellow, white, and blue; and, if you like lentils, your choice of petite crimson or petite French.

Hazelnut worshipers will be in their glory. Hazelnut pancake mix makes a good batter, and when the cakes are finished off with hazelnut butter and bathed in hazelnut syrup, the result is nirvana. Plain hazelnut flour is excellent for making all kinds of fruit breads, even for sprinkling on cooked cereal or cinnamon toast.

If you've got a hungry grain-loving family, you can seriously stock up, for, besides the 1- and 2-pound sacks, there are 25- and 50-pound bags of everything from pearl barley to dark rye flour to thirteen-bean soup mix. The store is a mine of information: handout sheets abound on the nature and history of wheat, the making of flour, tips on storage nutrition charts, and the like, and there's a book section as well. Bob's also houses a cooking school, with classes on polenta, cornbread, challah, pizza, and even on how to turn out a mean Hoppin' John and Barley Mushroom Casserole. The school is so hands-on you must bring your own rolling pin, whisk, mixing spoons, cup, and bowl.

You can find some of Bob's Red Mill products at Sheridan Fruit Company, Strohecker's, Wizers, Nature's Fresh Northwest, and in the Fred Meyer Nutrition Centers, but to see the full range, you must venture to the source.

Daily Grind Natural Foods

4026 S.E. Hawthorne Boulevard, phone: 233-5521. Open daily, 9 a.m.–9 p.m.

Daily Grind has a slightly dingy look, but it's a mecca for people who want to buy bulk grains, seeds, and cereals. Above each large bin, the store has placed packages of the same item, usually in 1-pound lots. The spices, herbs, and teas are decently, though conventionally, represented. One touch that sets Daily Grind apart is that they have numerous drums of pourable materials, such as olive and canola oils, tamari, and the stickier molasses, maple syrup, and honey. Bring your own containers and save.

Food Front Cooperative Grocery

2375 N.W. Thurmond Street, phone: 272-5658. Open daily, 9 a.m.–9 p.m.

Teas, herbs, and spices in two large cases are in frequent demand. Because of the rapid turnover, the supplies are fresh and retain their oils and thus their flavors. Across the aisle, there's a whole wall of grains, nuts, flours, and seeds in bins—hundreds of them. The store has plenty of bench strength in the granola department—thirteen different varieties, including something called New England Supernatural Cereal (and we thought cereal was *natural*). If you're contemplating hiking, there are seven different trail mixes. If you're a bean person, a dozen types—not counting dals and dried peas—should bring you comfort. And if you're seeking inexpensive bulk pasta, you'll find macaronis in rainbow colors.

Nature's Fresh Northwest

See listing on page 11 for locations and hours.

All the Nature's stores carry an impressive selection of bulk goods, with great depth in several areas. The rices are especially good, including black Japanese rice, sticky Kokuho (perfect for homemade sushi), scented Thai jasmine, an organic wild rice, and several organic brown rices. *Arborio* for risotto is available in boxes. Nature's is also an excellent source for dried fruits, nuts, and granola, as well as for dried pasta (including a quinoa elbow macaroni), though you should also examine their fine Italian imported pastas. Many mixes are available, as well as a small selection of Bob's Red Mill products, mostly flours and muffin mixes.

People's Food Store Co-op

3029 S.E. 21st Avenue, phone: 232-9051. Open daily, 9 a.m.–9 p.m.

People's blends easily into the neighborhood, lodged in a 1900-era house that was once a grain and feed store. Very little has been done to modernize the interior—an uneven wooden floor and very unfancy shelving recall its early days. People's is the only store in the city that refuses to carry non-organic produce. One of the bargains is the wild mushrooms, supplied by Forest Fruit: morels for around $10 a pound beats citywide prices hands down.

The bulk section comprises some 150 items; they, too, are largely organic. The bins look unchanged since the turn of the century, and the entire place has a ramshackle country store feel. The spices, herbs, and teas are strong-scented, a good sign. Bulk items lean toward serious back-to-earthers; thus, you'll find spelt flakes, oat groats, rye flakes, hummus mix, kelp, nori, yogi tea, and a few real oddities like gotu kola and ginkgo leaf mixed among more mainstream grains and nuts. The clientele is young and obviously dedicated to its principles.

Sheridan Fruit Company

408 S.E. 3rd Avenue, phone: 236-2113.
Open Monday through Saturday, 6 a.m.–8 p.m.; Sunday, 6 a.m.–6 p.m.

In a wing of the store stand barrel after wooden barrel of bulk foods in miscellaneous array. There are banana chips, yeast, vegetable broth powder, instant refried beans, yellow and white popcorn, and dry milk. Along the window ledge are glass cylinders of loose candies. Mojave ground seasonings are in abundance—virtually anything you could want to cook spicy Mexican—and there are plenty of large containers full of spices and herbs from the Oregon Spice Company.

Sheridan Fruit Company is especially well stocked with dried fruit: bins of prunes, dates, cranberries, bing cherries, figs, papaya spears, apple rings, pears, Turkish apricots, dried nectarines. Prices are extremely fair, and while much of what's here is pretty generic, such as bulk tortilla chips, you can stock up on a lot of goods with no loss of quality.

CHEESE

Chapter 3

Everyone adores cheese: for the variety of textures and tastes it offers and for its versatility. It is a foolproof nibble with cocktails; an essential ingredient in many favorite recipes; a meal on its own, with just some good country bread and a bottle of wine; or a separate, elegant course between entrée and dessert.

When we travel, cheese is our airplane food, smuggled on board to replace whatever hideous gruel will be served in flight. When we arrive on foreign shores, cheese is a destination treat. We search out cheese tastings at European shops, where you may find on each plate several different varieties of the same type of cheese. We'd love to see a comparable *degustation* available in Portland.

Cheese reflects its country of origin. French cheeses are complex and buttery, rich and fragrant. British cheeses tend to be wholesome, made from the fresh dairy products of which England is proud. Italian cheeses cover a broad spectrum from hard, sharp products to more creamy varieties. And American cheese? Luckily, like our best vision of ourselves, it has become more individualistic, for in recent years the handcrafting movement has taken hold and small producers are now delivering their own delicate goat cheeses and creamy Cheddars to regional markets.

The more recent availability of world-class cheeses in Portland is a reflection of the growing sophistication of the local palate. Not long ago, the cheese staples of most Portland kitchens consisted of plastic-wrapped American cheese bars, block slices of Muenster and Swiss, Tillamook Cheddar, and canisters of pregrated Parmesan. Now, decent cheese can be found in many groceries, and a few restaurants, including Paley's Place and The Heathman, offer a cheese course on their menus.

The Cheshire Cat

1403 N.E. Weidler Street (Irvington Market), phone: 284-5226. Open Monday through Friday, 9 a.m.-9 p.m.; Saturday, 9 a.m.–8 p.m.; Sunday, 9 a.m.–7 p.m.

This small vendor is a hybrid of wine shop, delicatessen, and cheese mart. The emphasis is perhaps more on the delicatessen, if only because that appears to be the area heaviest in demand.

The cheese case is a large one, though the cheese offerings don't quite fill it to capacity. The selection is a cut above that of most shops, with a strength in

I n the huge shed that's home to 450 goats (about 447 females and 3 very busy studs) at **Tall Talk Dairy**, the animals all seem content. The Sannen buck has a serene, glazed-over look, the babies are frisking, and most of the adult females have just finished giving their morning milk, lured to the milking machines by the promise of a good grain feed. Their milk is already on its way through the tubes, pasteurizers, and vats where, in a matter of days, it will become the yogurt, milk, and cheese of one of Oregon's very few and select goat dairies. Though there's no cottage cheese here—too short a shelf life—this is decidedly a cottage industry. Only nine workers staff the small operation, headed by **Harlen Peterson**, who for almost two decades has been on a quest to convince Oregonians of the virtues of goat cheese.

Some of the cheese is sold fresh, shipped out of cold storage within a week of being made, while some is aged for several months. If the crowds around the Tall Talk booths at the farmers' markets in the Portland area are any indication, Oregonians are snapping up the goat milk cheese and lapping up the goat milk itself. The taste is clean and slightly lemony, and all but the flavored varieties (jalapeño Jack, tomato, and basil feta) are gleaming white, lying in the cooler like slabs of frozen milk. They have a bracingly fresh aroma and make an ideal accompaniment to tangy olives and dark country bread. Peterson emphasizes the healthy nature of goat cheese. He claims that not only is it low in cholesterol, but because the human body metabolizes the fat in goat cheese as energy, rather than storing it in the arteries, it is less likely to contribute to heart problems. In addition, he says the cheese contains a third fewer calories than the typical cheese made from cow's milk.

Why have folks been reluctant to accept goat cheese? Peterson thinks that the cattle industry has such a propaganda machine that many people simply equate cheese with cows; beyond that some may think of goats as too smelly. Goat cheese does have a slightly pungent aroma, but it's as fresh as grass after a summer rain. The dairy makes *fromage blanc,* too, a kind of cream cheese that's sold in old-fashioned jars that look like antique milk bottles. One of their nicest products is *queso fresco*, a Mexican cheese similar to farmer's cheese that is good for grating and melting. Most popular of all is the feta, and Peterson especially recommends it for crumbling on pizzas or in salads.

Peterson has plans afoot for his dairy, which is out amongst the truck farms and hydroponic greenhouses in the Canby area. A goat mozzarella is in the pipeline, and he's thinking of raising ewes for sheep cheese, which would make him the only ovine dairy farmer in Oregon. He may also start using goats for a supply of meat, not raising them specifically for this purpose but using only those animals who turn out to be poor producers of milk: a powerful inducement for Tall Talk's goats to continue generating all that splendid dairy food.

A nother great handcrafted goat cheese, widely available in all the best groceries and delis in Portland, is from **Juniper Grove**, a five-acre farm and dairy outside Redmond, where ex-Portlander **Pierre Kolish** makes his cheese in the farmstead tradition of France. Kolish does it all: farming to provide forage for his goats, growing the herbs he infuses into several of his cheeses, engaging in animal husbandry, making the cheese, and marketing.

Though a city boy, he's always wanted to farm, and when he thought about a crop, nothing appealed to him so much as cheese. So off he went to the great cheese regions of France—Normandy and the Savoy (near the Alps)—to apprentice with a fellow who made Camembert. Eventually he entered a cheese-making school in a remote mountain area known as the Jura. By the early 1990s Kolish was ready to try his hand at it, so he built a cheese house in his beloved central Oregon. On a whim he chose goats as his milk source.

Kolish makes an aged pyramid-shaped cheese, a *crotin*, and herb-and-garlic *fromage blanc*, but most of his production comprises three soft, spreadable goat cheeses: one plain, another with toasted cumin and coriander, and a third with ash. Each has a satisfyingly tart flavor, smooth texture, and good body. When Corey Schreiber of Wildwood restaurant was invited to cook at the James Beard House in New York, he took along some Juniper Grove chèvre as an example of how Oregon purveyors are replicating many of the great products of France with excellent results. Kolish has plans for an aged sheep cheese made out of goat milk, and is always tinkering with new flavors for his soft *chèvre*, but for now he's content to perfect the cheese that has so pleased serious fanciers of *fromage*.

blue cheese (seven to eight varieties) and Brie (five to six varieties). Parmigiano reggiano and Romano can be grated to order, although the Cheshire Cat keeps jars of pregrated cheese for purchase by the pound. Fresh Polly-O mozzarella balls are perfect for mating with vegetables for a super sandwich or pairing with tomatoes and basil for a classic salad. (Creamy fresh Buffalo mozzarella—unavailable on the West Coast—is still the food lovers' cheese of choice, but it's so perishable that only Eastern seaboard cheese shops can carry it since the cheese can't survive the cross-country flight. We must make do with American-made fresh mozzarella.)

Elephants Delicatessen

See listing on page 8 for location and hours.

While the only cheeses at this tony delicatessen are prewrapped and weighed, we still like to come here for the one or two varieties that we can't find elsewhere.

Packages of cheese can be found in a cold reach-in at the back of the store. All the usual varieties are there, including Brie, Talegio, St. André, Gouda, Parmesan, and Asiago, along with six different blue cheeses. But we head straight for the Clawson cheese, a round of golden Cheddar swirled with a white cheese that looks like a child's pinwheel without the stick. We like the contrast between the rich, tangy Cheddar and the lighter, creamy filling. Another similar cheese that is good is the Leicester with herbs—a Cheddar disc with a green swirl. Both French and Bulgarian feta are found there, as is the handcrafted Juniper Grove goat cheese. You'll also find a few unusual sheep milk cheeses.

The cold case holds tubs of sinfully rich mascarpone, crème fraîche, and indulgent Devon (double) cream; plastic containers of grated Parmigiano reggiano and pecorino romano; and a selection of herbed and seasoned cream cheeses.

Pastaworks

See listing on page 12 for locations and hours.

No other store in Portland offers a cheese selection to compete with the one at Pastaworks. Whether we want a familiar cheese, something specific for a recipe, or something exotic or unfamiliar, this is our destination.

Cheese buyer Liz Werhli knows her curds and whey. More than 125 cheeses are regularly stocked at each of these food emporia. The display cases are crammed with blocks, wedges, and wheels of cheeses imported (directly in some cases) from Switzerland, Holland, Great Britain, Italy, France, and Spain. Local goat cheeses from Tall Talk Dairy and Juniper Grove are also available.

At Pastaworks, even types of cheese available elsewhere have a superior pedigree. Parmigiano reggiano—the champion of hard grating cheeses— needs twelve months of aging to earn its classification. Pastaworks only brings in wheels with an extra six months of aging.

Of course, we have favorites. We like to do traditional raclette, a simple Swiss molten cheese preparation made by heating raclette cheese under a special heater or broiler and scraping it off. It's eaten with boiled potatoes and pickled onions for a wonderful contrast of tastes and textures.

Among the Cheddars, the cheeses brought in from Neal's Yard—England's finest purveyor of its regional cheeses—are super. Try Appleby's Double Gloucester or Keen's Cheddar to taste the real flavor of farmhouse Cheddars. The precious Cougar Gold—the Cheddar made by Washington State University and parceled out to vendors in tins—is an all purpose, delicious cheese that stands up quite well to the British competition. Although Pastaworks only gets seventy-two wheels a year of this cheese, they are happy to sell it by the pound.

Italian cheeses naturally have a strong showing, as Pastaworks is first and foremost a purveyor of Italian foods. The range is amazing, and we discover new favorites each visit, including the soft Robiola, more buttery even than Talegio. Among the French cheeses, we admit a weakness for the rich and the creamy, and the selection here seems endless.

The selection of goat cheese is outstanding. Logs, rounds, wheels, and mounds of differently textured cheeses are arranged together. We love Le Chevrot, an aged, handcrafted cheese with a crumbly, flaky texture, much like Bucheron.

The staff will happily give you a taste of anything in the case. Always sample before you buy. They will also advise you on choices, offer helpful hints for serving, and suggest wines to drink with the cheeses you buy. We're still discovering new cheeses each time we walk into Pastaworks.

Strohecker's

2855 S.W. Patton Road, phone: 223-7391.
Open daily, 7:30 a.m.–9 p.m.

Though nobody else can really compete with the depth of the cheese selection at Pastaworks, two advantages of shopping for cheese at Strohecker's are the convenience of buying your groceries at the same store, and its good selection of cut-to-order cheese.

All the standards of up-market varieties are represented in the basement cheese department. You'll find two or three kinds of Brie, Explorateur, four or five blue varieties, good grating cheeses (both pregrated and ground to order), and lots of bright yellow or white cheese bricks for slicing and layering into sandwiches.

We've been impressed by the solid Gouda offerings, with seven types of the Dutch cheese usually available—different grades of smoked or aged wheels. As many Swiss cheeses are offered, and a reasonable choice can be made from among the Cheddars. Further down the display case, you'll find fresh mozzarella balls, two types of fetas, and sealed logs of goat cheese.

A cold reach-in case, separate from the main display case, holds crème fraîche, mascarpone, prepackaged imported cheeses, and tins of Cougar Gold Cheddar.

AND KEEP IN MIND...

International Food Bazaar

915 S.W. 9th Avenue, phone: 228-1960.
Open Monday through Saturday, 9:30 a.m.–7:30 p.m.; Sunday, 10 a.m.–6 p.m.

Many different kinds of feta.

Martinotti's Cafe & Delicatessen

404 S.W. 10th Avenue, phone: 224-9028.
Open Monday through Friday, 8:30 a.m.–7:30 p.m.; Saturday, 10 a.m.–6 p.m.

A good stop for the standards of an Italian cheese plate.

Nature's Fresh Northwest

See listing on page 11 for locations and hours.

A wonderful selection of imported cheeses, but all are prewrapped and weighed.

Trader Joe's

4715 S.E. 37th Avenue, phone: 771-1601; 11753 S.W. Beaverton-Hillsdale Highway (Beaverton Town Square), Beaverton, phone: 626-3794; 15391 S.W. Bangy Road, Lake Oswego, phone: 639-3238. All stores open daily, 9 a.m.–9 p.m.

Price is the driving theme here, with good, basic cheeses available in plain wrappers at lower

CHOCOLATE, CANDY, AND NUTS

L et the fat police scream, but the great eighteenth-century French food writer and cook Brillat-Savarin confidently proclaimed "chocolate is health." In fact, an early chocolate shop in Paris was begun by two idealists who trumpeted their product as a cure for obesity.

Sometime in the 1970s, designer truffles supplanted cherry liqueur chocolates as the epitome of the breed. Portland is lucky to have a great truffle-crafting chocolatier in Robert Hammond of Moonstruck Chocolates, several local shops that carry the excellent creations of Joseph Schmidt of San Francisco, and a Godiva boutique. Unfortunately, there's not much in Portland by the way of fresh chocolate from the great houses of Europe like Teuscher, Neuchatel, and Manon, probably because it does not have a long enough shelf life.

Chocolate is not just for nibbling, of course, so a word about cooking with chocolate is in order. Use as good a kind as you can and never settle for an inferior grade, just as you would not use commercial "cooking wine" instead of a decent varietal. Most of the time bittersweet chocolate will produce the best, not-too-sweet results.

As for nuts, they contain an enormous amount of oil (which makes them so good), so if you wish to use them sparingly, think about making a great cashew nut butter in your food processor, or toast macadamia nuts in butter and sprinkle kosher salt on them while they're still hot. Few foods have leapt into such prominence in recent years as pine nuts, not only essential in Genoese pesto, but wonderful atop many dishes, particularly Moroccan stews that might include dates and apricots. The great Oregon nut is the hazelnut or filbert. To see its many incarnations, go to the Made in Oregon store.

Chocolate, Etc.

5331 S.W. Macadam Avenue (The Water Tower at John's Landing), phone: 222-2068.
Open Monday through Thursday, 10 a.m.–7 p.m.; Friday, 10 a.m.–9 p.m.;
Saturday, 10 a.m.–6 p.m.; Sunday, 12 noon–5 p.m.

If it's Thanksgiving season, you'll likely find a chocolate turkey on the center table of this lovely shop; if it's near Valentine's Day, a dozen chocolate roses with red, yellow, and white chocolate blooms. There is very little "et cetera" in Chocolate, Etc., for this shop is strictly dedicated to lovers of the cocoa bean.

There's even a children's corner replete with chocolate Band-Aids (bonbons for boo-boos?), chocolate crayons, and little brown bugs and bees, all quite edible.

Annie Wall, the owner of the store, dreamed of creating a European chocolate shop with beautiful displays showing off the sweets she deems the perfect ceremonial treat. Everywhere there are lovely touches: chocolate champagne bottles that open to spill out truffles; Belgian chocolate ties hand-painted and boxed—the perfect edible spoof of the clichéd Father's Day gift; and sports truffles shaped like footballs, basketballs, and golf balls.

Wherever you look, there is temptation, from the chunks of bulk Belgian chocolate, meltable and used for dipping strawberries, to the chocolate oranges that come apart in segments, to the centerpiece swans of white chocolate that hold a pile of truffles.

The main focus is on glorious truffles. There are some decent ones from Fenton and Lee of Eugene, but they can't hold a candle to the pieces crafted by Joseph Schmidt of San Francisco. These stunning, large-domed candies resemble the fine chocolates of Brussels and Paris: the outer layer shatters in your teeth, while the smooth inner core is intense with a long-lasting taste. The Bailey's Irish Cream truffle and the white mushroom with a dark and light chocolate center are both memorably superb.

Godiva Chocolatier

700 S.W. 5th Avenue (Pioneer Place), phone: 226-4722. Open Monday through Friday, 9:30 a.m.–9 p.m.; Saturday, 9:30 a.m.–7 p.m.; Sunday, 11 a.m.–6 p.m.

It's ironic that the most elegant confectionery shop in town and the name that epitomizes choco-chic is owned by the Campbell Soup Company. Spot a connection between cream of mushroom and white chocolate mushroom creams? There's a corporate aspect to the operation: the chocolate is made in Reading, Pennsylvania, only sixty miles from Hershey (!), and the packaging is decided in New York for the chain's almost seventy boutiques.

The look of the shop is elegant, closer to a Parisian chocolate shop than you're likely to find in these parts. Godiva tailors chocolates to the season, so for summer you might find such gems as Key Lime (dark chocolate with a tart gooey interior), Lemon Chiffon, and Jasmine (a white mousse center wrapped in ivory chocolate), packaged in bright yellow St. Tropez ceramic bowls or azure-and-lime striped boxes that recall cabanas on the Riviera.

Godiva loves playful shapes, thus its collection of oceana: chocolate starfish, "oysters" consisting of an opened hinged dark chocolate shell revealing a hazelnut praline center, and marbleized seahorses. The old favorites are here as well: cordials oozing with liqueurs, large mints wrapped in gold foil, and dark chocolate demitasse mints. Some of the chocolate tastes a bit too sweet to us, but in general it's very good. Perhaps the best pieces in the shop are the flat 2-inch-square slabs of Belgian chocolate, pricier than the rest but with a more potent flavor.

A section of Godiva Chocolatier is dedicated to packages of all kinds: a set of chocolate golf balls, tins filled with raspberry buttercreams, and truffle assortments in many combinations. Or you can select your own pieces for the occasion. Godiva will also assemble wedding and party favors.

JaCiva's Chocolates and Pastries

4733 S.E. Hawthorne Boulevard, phone: 234-8115.
Open Monday through Saturday, 6:30 a.m.–6 p.m.

We're actually fonder of the chocolates at JaCiva's than the cakes. The kitchen blends American and European chocolate and does all the mixing and molding right on the premises. Molds imported from Belgium create marvelous shapes, including tulip and fluted dessert cups and chocolate beribboned gift boxes they fill with truffles. On Valentine's Day, you can liberally mound diamond and heart-shaped truffles into these cute edible containers. Americans are starting to eat more dark than milk chocolate, and this tendency shows up in the majority of darker items in the cases. White shows up as well, however, beautifully so in the roses that top wedding cakes.

You can have business cards made up in chocolate, and JaCiva's will turn out a company logo in chocolate when they cater a business event. For kids, there are chocolate dinosaurs and piggy banks with a slot for—what else?— chocolate coins. Roger once threw a birthday party for a violinist friend featuring a chocolate fiddle. If you want such an icon, JaCiva's is sure to comply with your wishes.

Made in Oregon

921 S.W. Morrison (The Galleria), phone: 241-3630 (plus five other outlets).
Open Monday through Friday, 9:30 a.m.–9 p.m.; Saturday, 9:30 a.m.–6 p.m.;
Sunday, 12 noon–5 p.m.

This is a touristy spot (you'll notice signs in Japanese), but one of the best places to stock up on Oregon's favorite nut: the filbert (named for St. Philibert, whose feast day on August 22 usually coincides with the time these nuts ripen). It's also called the hazelnut, the more common term these days. Over 98 percent of all hazelnuts in America are grown in Oregon, though that represents only a small percentage of the world crop. Oregon's soil produces large and intensely flavorful specimens. Local Native American legend claims that these nuts were one of five sacred nourishments given to humankind.

A number of product lines show up here, with everything from bags of the plain nuts to chocolate covered, salted, dry-roasted, and smoke-flavored types; there's even hazelnut toffee as well as hazelnut honey and hazelnut oil. (If you want hazelnut pancake and waffle mix and hazelnut syrup—both stunningly good—visit Bob's Red Mill; see page 17.)

Toutes Sweet

2108 N.W. Glisan Street, phone: 294-7097. Open Monday through Wednesday, 10:30 a.m.–6 p.m.; Thursday through Saturday, 10:30 a.m.–9 p.m.; Sunday, 11 a.m.–6 p.m.

Toutes Sweet is one of three shops in town that carry Moonstruck's extraordinary creations. They not only look special, but the quality of the chocolate is as fine as you can imagine. The other sumptuous line of chocolates here are from Joseph Schmidt, whose taste rivals that of Moonstruck. Pieces by Dilettante are quite good, but not up to the other two. There's some locally produced fudge in Oreo cookie and piña colada flavors as well as more commonplace varieties. Part of the store is occupied by jars of every imaginable candy, from coffee lentils to chocolate Jordan almonds to little milk chocolate baseballs. Bins of jelly beans offer a full choice. For those afflicted with nostalgia for childhood chocolates, there are almond clusters and buttercrunch. Lovers of licorice will be happy with the jars crammed full of black and red "buttons," "wheels," "thins," and even "cats."

Trader Joe's

See listing on page 26 for locations and hours.

Chunks of Ghirardelli milk chocolate bark are the last temptations before you check out at the register; if they don't get you, the chocolate raspberry and orange sticks will. Above the freezer is an impressive lineup of candies, at Trader Joe's usual low prices. The peanut brittle is crackly, and the peanut butter cups rival Reese's.

As for nuts, you'll be astonished at the range of choices. There are peanuts roasted, honey-roasted, salted, unsalted, raw, and in the shell. We love the

CHOCOLATE DREAMS

Robert Hammond has the sweetest job in the world: chocolate maker and head of **Moonstruck Chocolate**'s research and development. He has cut back from his own daily dose of 16 ounces of chocolate, but perhaps because he's developing a line of chocolate drinks, he recalls that Voltaire drank a dozen cups of chocolate a day and lived to eighty-four. Hammond presides over vats of satiny milk chocolate and silky dark chocolate. "I try to realize my childhood memories in chocolate," he says nostalgically, so he's producing an ice-cream line, including orange-flavored chocolate and a chocolate malted truffle that tastes of old-fashioned drugstore malts.

Moonstruck rivals the great chocolatiers of France for ingenuity of design, intensity of flavor, and sheer aesthetic appeal. There's a Cinnamon Roll Latte that looks for all the world like a miniature pastry; a Hot-Fudge Sundae of white chocolate, nuts, and marshmallow cream; and a Cappuccino shaped like a pyramid that conceals layers of coffee and chocolate froth. Hammond gleans his ideas from everywhere: he looks at a magazine illustration and sees bonbons. He puts amazing ingredients inside his creations: Sokol-Blosser Pinot Noir, Clear Creek pear brandy, even Stash tea.

Because Moonstruck's candies are 50 percent lower in sugar than most, their emphasis is on flavor rather than sheer sweetness. But it's the whimsy of the shapes and the craftsmanship that constitute Moonstruck's appeal— ice cream cones, tragedy/comedy masks, elegant little boxes, the addition of 14-karat edible gold. Hammond has caught up with the great Parisian chocolate houses with such creations as his candied version of lemon meringue and his dark bittersweet truffle laced with Cabernet. Moonstruck will soon open its first boutique in Raleigh Hills; until that glorious day, you can call them at (800) 557-6666 or find the little dark jewels at Wizers, Toutes Sweet, and the Nature's Fresh Northwest in Vancouver.

bags of deep green pistachio nut meat. Bags of Brazil nuts stand out, along with almonds of many varieties, cashews, macadamias, and the like. You can get such combos as cinnamon-glazed almonds and praline pecans. Hikers and other energy freaks will be ecstatic with the trail mixes: Thai blend with spicy peanuts; tropical blend heavy on dates, raisins, and papaya slices; and cranberry-nut mix. No one else in town, including the bulk food stores, sports such variety.

AND KEEP IN MIND. . .

Elephants Delicatessen

See listing on page 8 for location and hours.

Check out the dipped apricots and oranges, the fruit slightly glazed and peaking out behind their rich chocolate coating. There are wonderful Perugina kisses, boxes of dark chocolate and dried cherries, boxes of dried blueberry chocolates, and lots of packaged jelly beans in rainbows of colors.

Strohecker's

See listing on page 25 for location and hours.

A small but choice selection of chocolates at the end of the pastry case makes Stroh's one of the nice places to shop for candies. The prize Joseph Schmidt truffles are in place, including the classy flat disks of white and dark chocolate hand-painted with swirling and mottled patterns. The store stocks a good selection of nuts as well.

Wizers

330 First Street, Lake Oswego, phone 636-1414.
Open Monday through Saturday, 9 a.m.–9 p.m.; Sunday, 10 a.m.–7 p.m.
16331 Bryant Road, Lake Oswego, phone: 636–8457.
Open Monday through Saturday, 7 a.m.–10 p.m.; Sunday, 8 a.m.–9 p.m.

Locally made Moonstruck Chocolates are given their own display case for good reason: they deserve special attention.

The Food Lover's Companion to Portland

Chapter 5

COFFEE AND TEA

Remember when freeze-dried coffee was a marketing sensation or when Lipton's teabags were about all you could get in the markets? Things have changed dramatically, and in the process Portland is buzzing alongside Seattle as the twin coffee capitals of the country. These days coffee shops are the most prominent meeting places in town, and the coffee houses of N.W. 23rd Avenue have become our version of the bohemian Greenwich Village cafés of the 1950s.

Coffee drinkers are increasingly sophisticated in their selections; they speak with erudition about Arabian Mocha, aged Sumatra, and French roasts and know the difference between direct and indirect methods of decaffeination. Customers who several years ago would have been content with a generic instant now grind their own beans and understand the workings of a Neapolitan Flip-Drip.

Ironically, the coffee merchants around town all predict an interest in tea on a scale to rival the coffee boom. Tea drinkers discourse about Gyokuro and Pouchong, infusions and tisanes, flavored versus scented teas. A few years ago the hip tea drinker would only touch rose hip, now Chai is all the rage. Art galleries exhibit tea pots, and who would pass up the chance to drink green tea in a Yixing teapot from China?

Even the supermarkets sell first-rate beans and decent bulk teas. But the places to note are the specialty stores, some of whom do their own coffee roasting and all of whom rotate the leaves and the beans with frequency. Every serious purveyor will offer you sound advice on storing, brewing, and serving. If you want to read about these matters, take a look at local writer Sara Perry's two handsome books, *The Tea Book* and *The Complete Coffee Book*, both available at bookstores and some coffee or tea shops.

A number of these shops also carry fine spices and frequently turn them over to insure freshness.

Abruzzi Cafe

22 N.W. 23rd Avenue, phone: 241-6171. Open Monday through Friday, 6:30 a.m.–10 p.m.; Saturday, 7:30 a.m.–10 p.m.; Sunday, 8:30 a.m.–5 p.m.

You go into Crew House to buy a sweater or a T-shirt, and in the front left corner of the store a coffee tasting is in progress, including an erudite discussion of the distinctions between Zimbabwean and Kenyan beans. Mark Stell, a young roaster who leases a small section of the clothing store, wants Portlanders to appreciate the complexity of the world's great coffees. He believes that despite the coffee craze, most drinkers can't discriminate among styles from the same region or continent, and he'd like to help correct this deficiency.

Stell will custom roast beans for you, and you can experiment with the length of the roasting until you get just what you want in a particular blend; thereafter, he'll keep a card file on your preference. In addition to this service, he delivers coffees at no extra charge, within a five-mile radius of the store. Most of the roasting at Abruzzi is Italian style—full and intense but not too dark or bitter. Stell will also sell you green beans and teach you how to roast them at home, which sounds like good fun.

Bridgetown Coffee Company

1111 N.W. 16th Avenue, phone: 224-3330.
Open Monday through Friday, 7:30 a.m.–5 p.m.

Since the roasting machines in the back rooms at Bridgetown Coffee Company are working much of the day, coffee beans purchased here will likely still be warm, their oils (which deliver coffee's flavor) glistening on the beans.

Bridgetown makes some 180 blends, roasting 2,000 pounds of beans each day. The coffee goes out within hours of the roasting process, which keeps things spanking fresh. Most of the beans go to restaurants or retail stores. Only about 5 percent of sales are across the counter, but shoppers are welcomed to this pretty store, which prominently displays its monumental brass and copper Gaggia espresso machines, centerpiece attractions at the events that Bridgetown caters. What does a coffee-maker cater? Espresso nights, to encourage high school prom-goers to drink coffee instead of alcohol.

From the huge burlap sacks piled high in the back of the store come such blends as Hawaiian Kona and exotic, highly spiced coffees from Zambia, the Celebes, and Yemen. There's a good medium-dark roast called Portlandia and a very dark one called Ponte Citta—"bridge town"—from a bean that produces an intense, smoky flavor. You can have a coffee drink at the bar, then decide which blend to take home. If you're a home brewer of lattes, you can spruce your cup from a bottle of macadamia or coconut syrup from Dolce.

British Tea Garden

725 S.W. 10th Avenue, phone: 221-7817. Open Monday through Thursday, 10 a.m.–5 p.m.; Friday, 10 a.m.–6 p.m.; Saturday, 10 a.m.–5 p.m.; Sunday, 12 noon–4 p.m.

Sarah Bennett, whose mother owns Tea Traders, and Carmel Ross, who has such a Liverpudlian accent you'd think she were the fifth Beatle, run a tea house and retail shop that adheres strictly to British blends. There are no bulk teas here, only packaged varieties—both loose and in bags—and British Tea Garden is the only place in Portland where you can buy the fabled Murchies brand, which used to supply the tea to the British trenches in World War I.

The shelves are laden like a Victorian larder: tea cozies, jars of Wilshire lemon curd, and containers of Cole's plum pudding made with Tauton Blackthorn Cider. In addition to Murchies, there's Fortnum and Mason and all the other great English brands. This shop is just the place to stock up and honor the old days of the British Empire.

The Broadway Coffee Merchant

1637 N.E. Broadway, phone 284-9209. Open Monday through Thursday, 9 a.m.-7 p.m.; Friday, 9 a.m. -6 p.m.; Saturday and Sunday, 9 a.m.–5 p.m.

This was the first coffee store on Portland's eastside, and it remains one of the few places in town that sells fine coffees but has not a single table for coffee drinking. The coffee selection is impressive—some forty or fifty varieties, all roasted locally. Since many people request flavored coffees, like French Vanilla, Irish Cream, and Pecan, Broadway carries very good examples, as well as the usual run of East African, Indonesian, and Latin American blends. You can also find a half-dozen styles of green beans that await roasting at home.

The tea selection is, if anything, more impressive. Greens, blacks, and oolongs constitute the loose bulk leaves, and there are numerous decaffeinated varieties and herbals—fifty teas in all. British companies dominate the packaged teas, including the time-honored brands of Fortnum and Mason, and those long-standing rivals of the English tea table, Ty-Phoo and PG Tips.

On the upstairs level you'll find a large selection of mugs, French presses, roasters, filters, tea appurtenances, and espresso machines. The store stocks spare parts for all the paraphernalia it sells, a great help. Be sure to look at the beautiful line of coffee, tea, and demitasse cups from Lindt-Stymeist, which seem fit for Alice's tea party. See especially the huge latte cup, a bowl really, for hedonistic morning indulgence.

Caffé Luca

2337 W. Burnside Street (Thiele's Square), phone: 295-5822. Open Monday through Thursday, 6 a.m.–8 p.m.; Friday and Saturday, 6 a.m.–10 p.m.; Sunday, 8 a.m.–6 p.m. 3975 S.W. Kruse Way at Lower Boones Ferry Road (Mercantile Village), Lake Oswego, phone 699-5822. Open Monday through Saturday, 6 a.m.–6 p.m.; Sunday, 7 a.m.–2 p.m.

Even seventeenth-century London, with the introduction of coffee houses as social gathering places, could hardly match the caffeine-density that fills the trendy artery of N.W. 23rd Avenue. The most elegant shop along the street is Café Luca in the new Thiele's Square. With its slate floor, earth-tone sponged walls, marble café tables and Palacek wicker chairs, Café Luca has a hushed yet not overly formal ambiance. The display of the coffees in glass canisters, the gleaming bar, and the beautiful arrangements of the Faema machines complete the scene. It's a wonderful setting to enjoy superb coffee and a good place to buy coffee for home.

The espresso, made with the Gregorio dark roast, is rich, pungent, and deep. The Colombian coffee has a caramel taste, while the Leonardo provides a medium roast with a molasses flavor. The decaffeinated coffees are made with the Swiss water process, which gives a purer taste. Standing at the bar will transport you to the tonier establishments on Rome's Via Veneto.

John Dema, who worked at the Savoy and Claridges in London, carries extremely good beans from Royal Coffee in the San Francisco Bay Area. He also stocks his store with Le Sirop de Monin, a French syrup that's far superior to the ubiquitous Torani; the Swiss chocolate flavor is superb in a latte or a cappuccino. This brand recently won the World Championship of Syrup— there really is such an event!

On Friday evenings there's a showing of Italian films on video, and on Saturday evenings there's live jazz. Fellini and a latte sound like a high-wire act to us.

Casey Coffee and Spice

12480 S.W. Walker Road, Beaverton, phone: 646-7060. Open Monday through Friday, 7 a.m.–7 p.m.; Saturday, 8 a.m.–6 p.m., Sunday, 10 a.m.–5 p.m.

Lenka Casey has come a long way from the coffee houses of Prague, her hometown, to owning a pleasant shop in Beaverton that sells a wide range of spices, numerous loose teas, and a good selection of coffee beans. She carries six different ground chilies, ten types of pepper corns (including lemon, pink, and green air-dried varieties), and such unusual items as beet powder and apple pie spice. They're all packaged in special bags to ensure freshness. One of the nice touches at Casey's is that if you wish to sample several teas before deciding on a purchase, you can get a cup of anything in the store, from Gunpowder Green to Russian Caravan. Similarly with coffee: the store will French press a sample cup. Casey's also stocks espresso makers, a good selection of French presses, and a small section of books on coffee and tea.

Coffee People

533 N.W. 23rd Avenue (the flagship store; there are about a dozen
other locations), phone: 221-0235. Open Monday through Thursday, 6 a.m.–10 p.m.;
Friday and Saturday, 6 a.m.–11 p.m.; Sunday, 7 a.m.–10 p.m.

This high-ceilinged hangout hums day and night, populated by the young out for a good buzz. And if they seek a high-octane high, they turn to the Black Tiger blend, which contains 30 percent more caffeine than any of the company's other beans. The N.W. 23rd Avenue store alone sells some 400 milk shakes a day made with the fearsome Black Tiger brew. The lineup of Coffee People's blends is impressive, from a pricey hand-picked Salawesi Toraja to a Haitian Bleu harvested only once a year.

Coffee People tends to get a bit cute with their names: thus a James Joyce Blend and a Picasso Blend. The house blend is called Human Being Organic Coffee. But despite the fun and games, the beans, roasted in Portland by Coffee Bean International, are first rate. While most of the business seems to consist of cups consumed on the spot or taken to go, as well as seductive ice creams, many customers buy beans for home brewing. Just stay away from a late-night Black Tiger unless you work the graveyard shift.

The Hawthorne Coffee Merchant

3562 S.E. Hawthorne Boulevard, phone: 230-1222.
Open Monday through Sunday, 8 a.m.–6 p.m.

Doris Glasser runs one of the nicest neighborhood coffee shops around. She's been here over a decade, which makes her a pioneer of quality coffee in town. We're especially fond of the darkly rich Genoa blend, which was developed explicitly for the Genoa restaurant. Several blends of coffee are always brewing, so you can sample a variety of beans before you buy. The beans are roasted by Oregon Coffee Roasters expressly to the store's specifications.

The Hawthorne Coffee Merchant stocks numerous bulk teas and such packaged varieties as Jackson's of Piccadilly, a line of tasty instant ice teas from Davidson's, including sweet bing cherry, and the increasingly familiar TAZO teas. The store is loaded with latte bowls, thermos containers, deco-shaped Bodum water kettles, and other assorted implements for making good coffee or tea at home.

The Kobos Company

2355 N.W. Vaughn Street, phone: 222-2181. Open Monday through Friday, 6 a.m.–7 p.m.; Saturday, 8 a.m.–6 p.m.; Sunday, 12 noon–5 p.m. 5331 S.W. Macadam Avenue (The Water Tower at John's Landing), phone: 222-5226. Open Monday through Friday, 7 a.m.–9 p.m.; Saturday, 8 a.m.–9 p.m.; Sunday, 11 a.m.–6 p.m. 540 S.W. Broadway (coffee- and tea-related items only), phone: 228-4251. Open Monday through Friday, 6:30 a.m.–6 p.m.; Saturday, 8 a.m.–6 p.m.; Sunday, 12 noon–5 p.m. 200 S.W. Market Street (coffee- and tea-related items only), phone: 221-0418. Open Monday through Friday, 6 a.m.–6 p.m.; Saturday, 8 a.m.–12 noon 11655 S.W. Beaverton-Hillsdale Highway (Beaverton Town Square), Beaverton, phone: 646-1620. Open Monday through Friday, 8:30 a.m.–9 p.m.; Saturday, 9 a.m.–6 p.m.; Sunday, 11 a.m.–5 p.m. 1221 Lloyd Center, phone: 284-4831 Open Monday through Friday, 8 a.m.–9 p.m.; Saturday, 9 a.m.–9 p.m.; Sunday, 11 a.m.–6 p.m. 9673 S.W. Washington Square Road, Tigard, phone: 620-0775. Open Monday through Friday, 8:30 a.m.–9 p.m.; Saturday, 9 a.m.–9 p.m.; Sunday, 9:30 a.m.–6 p.m.

For years Kobos did much of its roasting at the John's Landing shop, but now you can watch the operation take place at Kobos's huge, new N.W. Vaughan Street flagship store, when one of the company's staff opens the burlap sacks and spills the beans into the giant Probat roasters and the Ethiopian Harrar pops like Mexican jumping beans. Roasting is a serious art, and one of the reasons Kobos's coffee has a large following is that their roasting process is conducted with great precision. Kobos's coffee beans never sit on the shelves for more than seven days; if the store hasn't moved them by that time, they're donated to a nonprofit organization. Another boast Kobos makes is that their flavored coffees—the Amaretto Chocolate, Cinnamon Nut Spice, Frangelica, Macadamia Nut Fudge, and Irish Cream—are all made with expensive, top-quality beans. These flavors make Kobos sound like an outpost of Baskin &

David Kobos, the first serious coffee roaster in Portland, remembers how it all started. Someone gave him a coffee grinder for a wedding present, and he was hooked. In those days, when Boyd's Red Wagon was the sole alternative to Maxwell House, the thrill of drinking coffee from fresh beans carried Kobos through a rigorous Masters of Arts in Teaching program at Reed. Soon he had an epiphany: he would open a store combining great coffee and teas and the finest cookware available.

In the early 1970s most coffee merchants came from a trader's background–they simply moved the beans. But Kobos was first a food lover, and for two decades **The Kobos Company** has been at the forefront of Portland's culinary revolution. It's amusing to learn that in the 1970s Kobos co-authored a volume on Portland food resources that stretched to all of twenty pages!

Kobos takes us into the warehouse and explains how one evaluates coffee beans. He shows us some very symmetrical green beans from Colombia, uniform in size, unblemished, and consistent in coloration. Then he opens a burlap bag of Sumatran beans, and the variations among them suggest a less careful harvesting. "These terrible looking beans were probably dried on someone's tin roof, picking up all sorts of impurities," he says, "but I know they are really very good." Before he purchases a lot he insists on a "cupping," or tasting. When Kobos was an undergraduate at Harvard and a member of a wine club, he developed his "taste memory," crucial for someone who must sample hundreds of coffees in a week. Like a good wine steward, he has learned to build a "taste profile" of a particular strain of coffee, sensing subtle differences among multiple examples of the same brew. He brings home every new coffee that comes into his store and drinks it for a week before he's satisfied. Few of us could distinguish between a Kenyan and a Zimbabwean coffee, but Kobos can sometimes discern the exact estate where it's grown.

Kobos loves the fact that Portlanders have become demanding about their coffee. A purist of sorts, he's opposed to "coffee that tastes like a milk shake," though he knows that if young people appreciate a café mocha, they might eventually be weaned to espresso. To further the process, several times a year he offers coffee classes, a two-hour dash through the roasting process from green bean to dark French roast, including a cupping of four different coffees.

Kobos runs his hands through a sack of Costa Rican beans the way a successful prospector might through a sack of gold nuggets. For Kobos and for Portland coffee lovers, everything's panning out just right.

Robbins, but these are strong and very good coffees. Kobos also uses excellent beans for its decaffeinated coffees, another uncommon practice.

While the store's dark roasts seem quite mellow, there's no diminution in taste. Kobos does not make a French roast; their Italian is the darkest blend. They offer more than fifteen nonflavored coffees and seven nonflavored decafs. The blends are standard ones, but extremely good examples of their kind.

Kobos also carries a goodly number of bulk teas, most of which are available in 5-ounce canisters. Try their Formosa Lapsang Souchong, whose flavor comes from smoking the leaves over pine wood fires. We're also fans of Dragonwell green tea, which has a delicate, clear liquor, and the very aromatic Gold-tipped Darjeeling.

The spices at Kobos are rotated frequently to guarantee freshness.

Sheridan Fruit Company

See listing on page 20 for location and hours.

Sheridan features a generous stock of Xanadu teas, many flavored with exotic fruits and spices, all heady and deeply aromatic, some bearing names that evoke the once-rare places of the earth. Xanadu teas are developed, blended, and packaged locally, and though this fine brand may also be found in bulk at Strohecker's and Tea Traders, Sheridan's stock is probably the largest in town.

Starbucks Coffee

More than twenty locations in the Portland area; hours vary by store

While a few coffee shops existed in the antediluvian days, the coming of Starbucks sparked the French (press) Revolution. It's hard to remember what things were like in Portland before it was easier to find a coffee house than a gas station, so inured are we to the Starbucks presence on practically every street corner. No other coffee enterprise publishes seasonal catalogues replete with gift packs, travel mugs, vacuum bottles, T-shirts, scone mixes, and even café tables and chairs. And, oh yes, coffee.

It's to Starbucks's credit that the expansiveness has not changed the quality of the brew. It continues to be very good; it's just that other places have caught up. We still like that slightly burnt, almost charred taste of the darker roasts, especially the espresso. And we're suckers for the beautiful stickers that identify the blends, each looking like a steam trunk label from the travel days of Evelyn

Waugh. Starbucks markets with panache: think of these stores as the United Coffees of Benneton.

Starbucks carries a wide range of coffees, perhaps the largest choice of fresh roasts in the Portland area (the roasting is done in the company's original home town of Seattle by a skillful staff). Starbucks labels its coffees very specifically, so you may know exactly where the beans originate, even to a specific small region of a country. The store also puts out free literature in all their shops: you can learn that beans from the Americas are generally light or medium-bodied, those from East Africa heavier and more floral, and those from Indonesia earthy and highly aromatic. At Starbucks you come for a cup of java and wind up with a B.A. in coffee studies. To appeal to your coffee conscience, Starbucks donates over 10 percent of all its receipts from the sale of its new Burundi blend to CARE's relief efforts in that Central African nation.

Tea Traders

515 S,W. Broadway, phone: 220-8533.
Open Monday through Friday, 9:30 a.m.–5:30 p.m.; Saturday, 11 a.m.–4 p.m.

It's somehow comforting to buy your tea from a Brit, who intuitively knows the mysteries and rituals of tea drinking that Americans never quite grasp. Judith Bennett, from Wales, presides over this shop in Morgan's Alley, and if you blink you might think you had stumbled into London's Burlington Arcade. Everything is handsomely and tastefully displayed. Her collection of teas is truly international—Russian, Chinese, African, Indian, Australian, and, of course, British.

If you have ever coveted Yixing teapots—made from one of the world's great clays taken near the Yangtze river town of the same name—you can order them from a catalogue displayed in the shop; the pots often have fantastic animals and whimsical fruits carved on them.

There's a variety of bulk teas, which Bennett will blend for you, and her advice is unerringly good. You may also choose from her extensive stock of packaged teas, including such venerable English brands as Fortnum and Mason, Harney and Son's, Jackson's of Piccadilly, and Mellrose—whose version of Earl Grey was Churchill's favorite. One of the best teas in the house is the Royal Gardens Darjeeling. At $80 a pound, it's a luxury, but you can start with the 1-ounce sampler, which goes a surprisingly long way. Tea Traders carries a version of chai, the heavy Indian tea that is the talk of tea drinkers these days. Their version was developed by Juanita Taylor, former co-owner of

Portland's Briggs and Crampton Catering. Her slightly peppery rendering of the drink comes in an herbal version blended with chamomile and in two regular versions blended with black tea leaves. People who like coffee are often fans of this beverage, which is usually mixed with milk.

Torrefazione Italia

838 N.W. 23rd Avenue, phone: 228-2528.
Open Monday through Thursday, 6:30 a.m.–10:30 p.m.; Friday, 6:30 a.m.–11:30 p.m.;
Saturday, 7:30 a.m.–11:30 p.m.; Sunday, 8 a.m.–10 p.m.
1409 N.E. Weidler Street (Irvington Market), phone: 288-1608.
Open Monday through Thursday, 6 a.m.–8 p.m.; Friday, 6 a.m.–10 p.m.; Saturday,
7 a.m.–10 p.m.; Sunday, 8 a.m.–8 p.m.

For our money, Torrefazione's coffee has the edge over every other one in town. It doesn't hurt that the shop itself is so attractive. Architect John Cava designed a stunning interior that's breezy and invitingly light, thanks to the barrel vault echoing Italian Romanesque structures, the European folding windows opening onto the street, and the terra-cotta hues that recall buildings in the Umbrian hills. Some respectable coffee houses serve perfectly good espresso in paper cups; Torrefazione serves its coffees in the famous Deruta ware, named after the Umbrian village that for centuries has made lively yellow and blue pottery with Raphael griffin designs. When you add this feature to the fact that much of the staff and numerous customers are Italian, you can feel as if you're in a Florentine café.

The coffee itself is roasted after a formula established by Umberto Bizzarri, Torrefazione's founder, at his family's company in Perugia. (Incidentally, *torrefazione* means "the place where roasting is done.") Pasquale Maddedu, the store manager, argues that their coffee's quality stems from the fact they make only six regular blends plus one decaffeinated, hence concentrating on a small number of coffees rather than trying to appeal to many different tastes. The blending is performed in a time-honored fashion, and, as Maddedu says proudly, "You'll find no raspberry or vanilla in our lattes." Some of Portland's best places carry their coffee: Zefiro, Jo Bar, Assaggio, and a few Marsee Baking locations.

We think the dark Palermo is the single best blend in the store—robust, thick, and heavy, bursting with strong taste. For a state-of-the-art granita, try the puckeringly tart *limone*; the coffee latte granita is satisfying as well, but the lemon is just right on a hot summer day.

I t is well known that with a different flip of the nineteenth-century coin, Portland would have been named "Boston," in which case the term "Boston Tea Party" might have implied a rather different revolution as the twentieth century draws to an end. Portland is beginning to hold its own tea party, and two new labels—**Xanadu** and **TAZO**—both created in town, are filling the cups.

"In Xanadu did Kubla Khan / A stately pleasure dome decree....[And] he on honey-dew hath fed, / And drunk the milk of Paradise." Samuel Taylor Coleridge's 1798 poem was the inspiration for the exotic Xanadu teas blended by **Coffee Bean International**, a Portland company that wanted its teas to evoke mystical locales of rare beauty. Working in an old industrial building, **Bruce Mullins** scanned ancient travel accounts and histories of medieval trade caravans for inspiration, then set out on an archival journey to the tea gardens near Lake Victoria in Kenya and the tropical tea stations of Java. His research led him not only to create new blends of classic teas dotted with flower petals giving sparkles of color and a floral dimension to the taste, but to conjure such lovely names as Garden of Sparrows Oolong, Star of Persia, and "Sencha Spiderleg" (made from leaves that fan out like the long legs of a spider).

This may seem like mere poetic marketing, but the teas themselves are splendid. Night Blooming Jasmine is a good example. Jasmine blooms at night in highly scented air and imparts a bouquet to tea leaves, the resultant quality determined by how long the leaves are exposed to the flower. Xanadu's crops are scented longer than most. The jasmine is layered among the leaves placed in chests, and at night the buds open up, dying the next day.

Xanadu has fifty items in its line, including exotic tisanes consisting of flower blossoms, natural herbs and spices, and flavored teas, such as Madagascar Vanilla, which contains pieces of vanilla bean scattered through the black leaves. It's fascinating to learn from the label on a Xanadu package that Temple of Heaven is the company's gentle title for the famous Pinhead Gunpowder Tea, so named because its tightly rolled cylinders of green leaves resembled the powder used in cannons on eighteenth-century British warships.

Mullins wants to express the allure of tea in the blends, the names and the packaging (Xanadu's tins resemble ancient Oriental tea chests), undercutting its association with sickrooms or stuffy Victorian parlors. In the Portland office, he spends much of his day evaluating the leaves that arrive at the plant, cupping the teas (he's spent twelve years as a professional taster), and mixing the leaves into Xanadu's unique blends. "I feel like a collector," he says. "I'm always on the lookout for the undiscovered Holy Grail of Tea."

*T*he tea guys over at **TAZO** are no less whimsical. You practically have to be a philologist and a mythographer to understand the meaning of the company's name as it appears on the box:

TAZO /taz-zo/ n. [It. *tazisto* modif. of Ba. *tazor*] (ca. 4786 B.C.)
1. a rejuvenating elixir made from teas, herbs and sometimes juices thought to have magical properties among the shamans of ancient Babylonia.   2. a toast to life popularized by Greek mystics in the third century B.C.

and on to

5. a salutation or greeting used by Druids and many 5th-century residents of Easter Island, usually accompanied by a wave of the hand.

Welcome to TAZO-land, where Captain Lipton meets Monty Python. Actually, this Portland company, staffed by the folks who brought you Stash Tea, makes quite wonderful tea, and you mustn't let their playful spirit distract you from its pleasures. Don't fret that each TAZO tea bag lists among the ingredients "the mumbled chantings of a certified tea shaman." Don't be disturbed when you're warned that drinking a particular tea will "spark feelings of love in the coldest heart," or that monks chanting and meditating in the Himalayas reach at their moment of their enlightenment for a tea like the one you're about to sip.

Steven Smith, TAZO's president, is a serious tea man, producing wonderful new blends with an intelligence born of twenty-five years' experience. His teas are served not only at Zefiro, but at New York's Guggenheim Museum. As for local shops, you can find TAZO teabags at Pastaworks, Nature's Fresh Northwest and Zupan's.

The most exciting product is a cold drink that blends Oregon fruit juice into liquid tea, an extraordinarily refreshing drink or, as TAZOspeak has it, a "rejuvenating elixir." The best examples of this beverage use marionberries and a combination of apples and pears, all microbrewed with herbal teas.

Smith reads his tea leaves and sees in Portland's future tea houses where people will consume the beverage for its own sake. "The Northwest is ideal ground for the tea revolution," he asserts. "We're open to experimentation here, and besides, in a damp climate, tea—make that TAZO tea—is the ideal drink."

ETHNIC FOOD STORES

Chapter 6

Asian

These days, even the most pedestrian supermarkets carry enough Asian foods to satisfy a neophyte at the wok, but when the urge for truly serious stir-frying hits, no ingredients will do but those sold by authentic Asian food purveyors. Throughout the Portland metropolitan area are treasure troves of the East, offering familiar foods and foods as precious as Ming dynasty vases.

With a large Southeast Asian population fully rooted in Portland, interesting groceries catering to this diverse community's needs spring up almost weekly. When you first enter these stores, the number of new and exotic foods can be a bit daunting. Of course you've probably had many of these ingredients in restaurant dishes, and cooking in these national styles is not as difficult as it might seem. Moreover, many of the ingredients work wonderfully in perfectly ordinary Western dishes. A bit of fresh lemongrass cut up in a chicken broth can transform that mundane dish into something heavenly. A few tablespoons of chili black bean paste stirred into a bowl of plain pasta is a great change from tomato sauce. The pleasures of exploration can lead you to the ingredients for an elegant Thai dinner or may induce you to stockpile such basics as a good fish sauce. There are imported items whose exotic packaging alone may induce you to try them, and there are amazing fish flown in from remote Pacific waters. After you've tried lotus root and winter melon, you can buy bamboo steamers, rice cookers, and jade chopsticks.

Spend a Saturday afternoon Asian market-hopping and you'll feel as if you've shipped out on the trade winds, and then returned with items you might obtain from the floating markets of Bangkok, the stalls of Singapore's Chinatown, or the food halls of the elegant department stores of Kyoto.

An Dong Oriental Food Company

5441 S.E. Powell Boulevard, phone: 774-6527 or 777-2463. Open daily, 9:30 a.m.–7 p.m.

One of the largest of Portland's Pan-Asian groceries, An Dong has an impressive array of everything the ambitious Asian chef could desire, and is especially good for fresh fish. The produce section is also bountiful, with a cornucopia of fresh fruits and Asian vegetables. There are taro and other roots so large they look like props from Woody Allen's *Sleeper*, fresh tamarind pods to pucker Thai fish dishes, and Chinese broccoli, which has large leaves and a much earthier taste than the Western kind—terrific with a bit of oyster sauce and sesame oil. Miniature quail eggs in 10-packs sit beside large incubated duck eggs from Washington state. The range of dried fungi is astonishing, from relatively inexpensive mushrooms in 10-pound sacks to a very pricey variety that look more like art objects.

Check out the variety of curry pastes, which are more pungent than powders; you can add pastes directly to the wok. The shelves are heaped with chili pastes, spicy, sour coconut paste, and jars of satay paste. The culinary equipment includes Japanese mortars and pestles, a dozen kinds of soup ladles, and cleavers of all sorts.

You can shop while sipping a ginseng bird's-nest drink or a refreshing can of coconut juice from the case.

Anzen Importers

736 N.E. Martin Luther King, Jr. Boulevard, phone: 233-5111.
Open Monday through Saturday, 9 a.m.–6:30 p.m.; Sunday, 12 noon–5 p.m.
4021 S.W. 117th Avenue, Beaverton, phone: 627-0913.
Open Monday through Saturday, 10 a.m.–6:30 p.m.; Sunday, 12 noon–5 p.m.

The flagship store of Anzen Importers on N.E. Martin Luther King, Jr., Boulevard, a home-away-from-home for Portland's Japanese community, boasts the most interesting stock of all the Asian markets in town. It is impressively strong in fresh seafood, and its fish cases are a pleasure to behold and a joy to plunder. Where else can you find both a tank of muscular geoducks bursting their shells *and* a case of the same giant bivalves cleaned and ready to stir-fry? Or numerous varieties of immaculate fresh tuna either for *sashimi* or for grilling? Anzen keeps only the freshest fish on hand, for they sell to the best sushi bars in the city; their marine menagerie could stock a respectable aquarium, and is always displayed with aesthetic appeal. The selection of frozen fish includes wonders: frozen flying fish eggs, teriyaki squid, and soft-shell crabs.

Anzan also has everything you could imagine for a pantry worthy of the Emperor's kitchen, from dozens of soy sauces to vinegar seaweed, which, when combined on a platter with pickled red daikon radish and tiny sugar-soy sardines, will dazzle the most jaded guest. Ask to see the range of wasabi, the green horseradishlike condiment that you mix with soy sauce for dipping raw fish. Contemplate the largest selection of saki in these parts, including outsized bottles of the finest extra dry distilled stuff for $34.

There are surprises galore at Anzen: green tea ice cream made from sweet rice, preserved lotus root, and dozens of Japanese shrimp snacks in a rainbow of hues. We haven't had the guts to try it, but there's an intriguing little jar of "salted fish guts." If you shell out close to $40, you can pick up a package of ten sea urchins. On the way to the food you will pass all manner of tempting products, many of which make thoughtful gifts: a saki warmer and cups, beautiful tea sets, lacquered rice bowls, flower-etched rice steamers and jade chopsticks. From hot and sour soup to beetle nuts, shopping here is a delight.

Asia Market—Beaverton

12350 S.W. Broadway, Beaverton, phone: 646-8118. Open daily, 10 a.m.–6 p.m.

This is a well-stocked market covering all the national bases—Chinese, Japanese, Thai, Korean, Vietnamese, Filipino—a central depot for suburbanites. The produce is especially handsome, and there is a plethora of herbs, including nine varieties of fresh mint. The shelves are bursting with jars of *sambal*, the inflammatory Indonesian chili paste; look for the richer version with onion. Panda brand *hoisin* sauces lend a dark sweetness to foods.

Examine the salted jellyfish, which, when combined with chopped Chinese cabbage, makes for an unusual crunchy and refreshing salad. There is an amazing range of bamboo shoots here: jars of the tender plants shredded, sliced, whole, and even sweet-pickled. Pick up a box of Thai coconut-ginger rice for something different.

Ben Thanh Market

5132 N.E. Sandy Boulevard, phone: 282-9795, Open Monday through Friday,
10 a.m.–8 p.m.; Saturday and Sunday, 9 a.m.–8 p.m.

Much of Portland's Vietnamese community lives in the neighborhoods bordering Sandy Boulevard, and one of the best Asian grocery stores serving this district is Ben Thanh Market, a family-owned operation that spreads out in an orderly procession of three rooms chock-full of everything you need to realize your woking dreams. The family and its assistants produce their own baguettes on site, glaze and barbecue the ducks and ribs that glisten on their hooks, and make up an array of Vietnamese takeout. If you're really not feeling up to snuff you can ask for assistance at the Chinese herb counter, where curiosities in jars are ground into powders for infusions. There's also a healthy-sized shelf of more recognizable teas, though even here exotica awaits: ginger drink and ginseng teas from Korea.

Ben Thanh is a bright, pleasant store, and everyone is eager to help you. You'll find a good selection of fresh produce, a nice meat section, and plenty of fresh and frozen fish. But be sure to indulge in the jarred goods: among them a dozen or more chili sauces from every country in southeast Asia. You'll find quail eggs looking like little speckled marbles in the refrigerated section. For sheer aesthetic delight, try a package of four large Singapore white fungi that resemble bleached flowery coral—pop them into a chicken-based soup and they'll expand and impart woody flavors.

Boo Han Market

1313 S.E. 82nd Avenue, phone: 254-8606. Open daily, 9 a.m.–9 p.m.

Here's another large market, with a decided Korean influence. There's a "salad bar" from Seoul—a collection of fresh Korean appetizers, mostly vegetables sautéed or pickled and chilled, all refreshingly delectable. Fill a plastic container with a mélange of these items, playing salt against sweet, or sweetened potato against oysters in a red pepper sauce. Incendiary *kimchee* appears in jars from a pint to a gallon. Hot but healthy are the chili pastes and the hot bean paste with beef—try some of the bean paste that comes in beautifully decorated ceramic pots. The frozen food case has packages of *mandoo*, vegetable and meat dumplings that make satisfying appetizers when browned and then steamed.

Fong Chong & Company

301 N.W. 4th Avenue, phone: 223-1777. Open daily, 10 a.m.–6 p.m.

When the line for Sunday morning dim sum at Fong Chong looks as if it might keep you away from those succulent shrimp dumplings longer than you can bear, spend the waiting minutes at the adjoining grocery. Fong Chong & Co. is noted for its window display of roast pork, crackly-skinned Peking duck, and slabs of barbecued spareribs, as tender and juicy as any you've had. Some of the best steamed and baked *bao* (puffy buns) are available at this shop. There are shelves of all the standard piquant sauces, from black bean and garlic to "Lingham's Chily Sauce." Some of the items, however, are more unusual: are you ready for pig tongue? Fong Chong also provides the chance to sample tofu very different from the garden variety: crisply fried with a very firm texture.

At Fong Chong, you can find preserved duck eggs, otherwise known as hundred-year-old eggs. Why the name? They've been artificially aged with a black coating of lime, salt, ashes, and tea, then cured for three months. Many people value their creamy texture and slightly cheesy taste. But there's nothing cheesy about the unbeatable fresh produce here. Sample the leafy Chinese broccoli, the various Chinese cabbages, and the baby bok choy from Shanghai, no more than 5 inches long, perfect for steaming and stir-frying.

Fou Lee Market

3811 S.E. Belmont Street, phone: 239-0215.
Open Monday through Saturday, 10 a.m.–7 p.m.; Sunday, 10 a.m.–6 p.m.

The produce section at Fou Lee is enormous and a visual treat, whether you're beholding stalks of lemongrass, the long green beans that are so good stir-fried, fresh water chestnuts, or Asian greens tantalizingly labeled "Misc." The store carries products from all of Asia, but it's mainly a Vietnamese market, and on a typical Saturday you'll see families with three generations of customers. In one section, there's a counter for homemade take-out dishes, in another, a case loaded with Vietnamese desserts, from pearly cups of coconut-flavored puddings to rainbow-hued ground mung beans. A sign of the French influence on Vietnam is the heap of baguette sandwiches laden with various meats, cilantro, shredded carrot and Daikon radish, and fresh chiles.

The meat market is large, and if your taste runs to the daring, you'll discover honeycomb tripe, pig feet, and even pork uterus. On a more mundane level, the fish case is terrific, with lots of beautiful whole fish for steaming or grilling.

Some of the best items to pick up include Pad Thai sauce, crab paste, and chili paste with basil leaves, the latter perfect for turning a humble packaged soup and fresh *choy sum* into a distinguished lunch. The noodle selection is outstanding—don't miss the shrimp-flavored variety or the slippery cellophane noodles, which marry well with spicy sauces. There are rice papers of all kinds—some as big as Frisbees—used to wrap meats and vegetables before dipping into various sweet and fiery sauces.

Hyundai Oriental Food and Gift

3482 S.W. Cedar Hills Boulevard, Beaverton, phone: 520-1777.
Open Monday through Saturday, 9 a.m.–9 p.m.; Sunday, 10 a.m.–9 p.m.

This emporium may be the largest Asian supermarket in the area, a treasure-trove of extraordinary finds, virtually a museum of Asian gastronomy. You can easily lose yourself for a few hours of serious browsing here, and it would be a shame if you did not fill your shopping basket to the brim. Hyundai is tucked into a mini-mall of Asian shops and is part Korean and part Japanese, which undoubtedly accounts for the immense display of packaged seaweed in every imaginable shape: shredded, leaves, long noodlelike threads, and multisized flat sheets. Amuse yourself with gingseng candy labeled "recommended for sportsmen, drivers and office workers"; check out the gallon jars of *kimchee* so potent you can feel the burn coming; and pick up a clear plastic jug of sesame oil. The frozen case contains marvels: blue crab, pollok roe, octopus tentacles, jack knife clams, and cutlass fish. One case holds tofu such as you've never experienced—quart containers of fresh bean curd so creamy-soft it looks like yogurt. There are 5-pound bags of sinister-looking red pepper powder for a lifetime of sizzling dining, dozens of varieties of dried anchovies, large jars of soybean paste, and on and on.

Manila Imports and Exports

12155 S.W. Canyon Road, Beaverton, phone: 641-4545.
Open Monday through Saturday, 10 a.m.–7 p.m.; Sunday, 10 a.m.–6 p.m.

Barreling down busy Canyon Road you could easily miss this small market, but then you'd never get to try Filipino ice cream in flavors that Baskin-Robbins has hardly dreamed of: Jack Fruit, Coconut and Lychees, and Purple Yam. More like custards, these low-fat desserts nonetheless are creamy and addictive. On Saturday, the aisles of Manila Imports are bustling with the most diverse group of shoppers around. The cuisine is a blend of Malaysian, Indonesian, Polynesian, and Spanish, and fellow shoppers will gladly help you out.

You'll chance upon banana leaves for wrapping sweet rice in pretty packages and vinegars blended with cane, onion, and garlic that are especially good for marinating and tenderizing the meats in the Filipino dish known as *adobo*. Coconut and guava are very popular: there's an impressive array of coconut in every form here, and you'll find packets of guava soup base which, fortified with a handful of rock shrimp and perhaps some peanuts, makes for a nice little lunch.

We discovered a number of Asian items not available in many markets, including a Thai fish powder with chili for perking up the blandest halibut, and frozen fruit bars made from durian—a fruit so obnoxiously smelly in its raw state that it's forbidden in every Asian hotel, though the taste is absolutely delicious.

Sandy Supermarket

6924 N.E. Sandy Boulevard, phone: 288-4741. Open Monday through Friday,
10 a.m.–8 p.m.; Saturday and Sunday, 9 a.m.–8 p.m.

In the thick of Portland's southeast Asian community, this market stocks mostly Vietnamese products, though Thai, Chinese, Filipino and Japanese items all make an appearance. The aisles are crowded, especially next to the long frozen fish compartment, where you'll discover 5-pound boxes of cuttle-fish, squid, shrimp, giant prawns, and clam meat. We hadn't seen frozen quail before, but Sandy Supermarket carries the little birds, as well as duck legs; if you want an even more intense flavoring for the latter, slather on some duck paste from a jar. Nor had we seen packets of fresh ground lemongrass for instant flavoring, particularly good on vegetable dishes.

Spring Market

3032 S.E. Hawthorne Boulevard, phone: 238-8828. Open Monday through Friday,
10 a.m.–8:30 p.m.; Saturday and Sunday, 10 a.m.–8 p.m.

Fairly new to town, Spring Market is one of the larger Asian groceries about. If you want noodles for soups or stir-frying you'll find rice sticks, *soba*, and *udon*; if you want something a bit more esoteric you'll find imitation shark fin and fresh octopus. Be sure to pick up a jar of Szechuan reddish brown peppercorns, which impart a heady aroma to many Oriental dishes. Next to the butcher shop, roast ducks and slabs of barbecued pork hang in all their shiny red glory. Along one wall, 50-pound bags of rice are stacked high, as if ready for any flood waters that may pour down Hawthorne Boulevard. Next to the jars of sauces are shelves of candles, joss sticks, ginseng soap bars, and a toothpick dispenser graced with a little parrot.

You'll get a hearty greeting from the owners; be sure to ask them about the many whole fish—such as yellowtail—for steaming with green onions and shaved fresh ginger. You'll find virtually everything you need for Asian cooking, and in amazing quantities.

Throughout the seductions of Asian markets are so palpable and the products often so unfamiliar that it's easy to be overwhelmed by the splendor and sheer variety of goods. Since each Asian cuisine naturally has its own special ingredients, who could possibly maintain the essentials to prepare spontaneous meals from Sri Lanka, Singapore, Burma, Cambodia, Vietnam, Korea, and the Philippines? But, if you like this kind of food, there are some fundamental items to consider for a well-stocked refrigerator and pantry, permitting you to move around several of the cuisines and be reasonably authentic without shopping for basics each time you crave a home-cooked Asian meal. In the name of simplicity, we'll concentrate on Thai, Vietnamese, Japanese, and Chinese ingredients, though there's inevitably some overlap.

FRESH ITEMS. Stalks of fresh lemongrass in the crisper are a treat, especially for cutting up in stir-fries and salads. Fresh ginger and green onions may be too common to mention, but it's useful to have limes on hand, as well as bean sprouts, fresh chilies, and such fresh herbs as basil, mint, and cilantro. Water chestnuts and bamboo shoots are available fresh and are superior in taste and texture to the canned variety. Bean curd marries well with many Asian spices, and some of the best is made locally by the Ota Tofu Company. You may enjoy searching out fresh *galangal*, an odd-looking yellow root with pink sprouts and knobs much like ginger.

HERBS AND FLAVORINGS. These items will get plenty of use: ground coriander, star anise, turmeric, cardamom pods, cloves, pungent Szechuan peppercorns, sesame seeds, and cumin. Japanese cooking uniquely calls for wasabi (powdered green horseradish). We keep several dry fungi on hand: cloud ears or wood ears, which expand into clusters of pungent brown petals, large bags of black Chinese mushrooms, and slivered mushrooms for stirring into soups.

NOODLES AND RICE. A stock of noodles is crucial. Try to have a range: Japanese wheat-flour *udon*, buckwheat *soba*, egg noodles, rice vermicelli, and cellophane noodles made from mung beans. Fresh rice noodles are also useful, especially for Japanese cooking, and they'll keep quite a while in the refrigerator. As for rice, consider a sack of the scented jasmine kind or some sticky rice to supplement the indispensable basmati.

OILS, VINEGARS, AND SAUCES. Most Chinese cooking begins with a good grade of peanut oil, but you'll also want pure black sesame oil for finishing dishes, some chili oil, and perhaps hot sesame oil. Rice vinegar and rice wine are needed for many stir-fries, as is, of course, soy sauce (you might want a low-sodium variety). You'll also want *Nam Pla*, a fish sauce that is the Thai counterpart to Chinese soy sauce and is the base of most Thai sauces. The Vietnamese foundation sauce is *nuoc mam*, usually prepared from fresh anchovies, garlic, chilies, sugar, and lime.

PASTES AND CONDIMENTS. Confusion and fun come with the flavoring pastes. You'll want several different versions. We keep on hand a fiery Indonesian sambal-badjak and a Hunan red chili sauce to perk up a variety of dishes. There are chili pastes with garlic and others with black beans for added saltiness and body. A great Szechuan specialty is a sweet paste of puréed red beans and sugar blended with crushed chilies. Experiment with different combinations.

A favorite flavoring of ours is Orient's Delight crab paste, an aromatic treat to slather on any fish. Lan Chi makes an interesting sesame seed paste that is good for rice dishes, and Yeo's peanut-based satay sauce is great for grilled meats. Another standard is worth mentioning: oyster sauce, which is wonderful mixed with steamed vegetables, especially Chinese broccoli or baby bok choy. It's good to have a few cans of coconut milk around, especially for hot and sweet Thai soups, as well as a jar of Vietnamese *pho*, which provides a strong soup base full of spiced, beefy flavors. You can fortify the soup with Mae Ploy brand curry pastes.

Neither of us would dare make sushi—sushi masters apprentice for a decade or more—but pink pickled ginger has uses other than as a sushi accompaniment, notably as a palate cleanser after something spicy.

German

We tend to think of Portland as a fairly homogenous town. It's rare to hear a foreign language while traveling on a bus or dining in a restaurant. Yet there are different cultures here, and strong ethnic identities spawn great ethnic food shops. Although Portland does not have a particularly large German community, one does quietly exist, as evidenced by two excellent specialty stores that hustle and bustle with activity and German conversation. Fresh German products and imports are featured at each shop, making both Fetzer's and Edelweiss interesting destinations on your food and grocery rounds, as well as tasty stops for a quick lunch.

Edelweiss Sausage Co. and Deli

3119 S.E. 12th Avenue, phone: 238-4411. Open Monday through Thursday, 9 a.m.–6 p.m.; Friday, 9 a.m.–7 p.m.; Saturday, 9 a.m.–6 p.m.

The deli case of this dark, very German emporium groans from the weight of its many sausages and meats. All the raw materials for an authentic German meal can be found in this crammed shop. You'll see hanging salamis of all sizes; round steak for rouladen; beautiful, lean ground beef labeled "tartar"; veal sirloin roasts; pork roasts; smoked pork chops; pork cutlets for schnitzel; and more hot dogs and sausages than all the vendors at Wrigley Field can sell on a hot August afternoon.

A bakery case displays cream-filled horns, tall tortes, and bars, all very pretty, but also a bit solid and hefty. Explore the deli case and discover tubs of fresh lard. We thought the fat police had banished all traces of lard in retail stores. While there is no longer the kind of demand for it that our grandparents' generation knew, it makes pie crusts toothsome and flaky and gives tamales their savory goodness. Too bad it has developed such a bad reputation. Out-of-sight but available goods include lutefisk, salt herring, and potato sausage. You can also request casings for home sausage making.

The shelves along the narrow aisles are jammed with jars of brightly colored fruits and vegetables, pretty boxes of cookies and biscuits, spices, soups, and sweets. Sometimes we come here simply for lunch—the ready-made hot sausage sandwiches are great—but we inevitably walk out with a sack of groceries.

2485 S.W. Cedar Hills Boulevard, phone: 641-6300.
Open Tuesday through Saturday, 9 a.m.–6 p.m. (except Friday, 9 a.m.–7 p.m.)

Upon walking into this suburban outpost of all things German, you're inclined to do a double-take when you realize the only chatter—between customers, between customers and staff, and among the staff—is in the mother tongue. When you're the only one ordering in English, you feel a bit like a carp out of the North Sea, although clerks speak English when you make your wants known. The small shop is stuffed chockablock with a dizzying display of German goods, from jars of pickles to *spaetzle* (noodle) mixes to chocolate. But the meat counter is the main focus.

The fresh meat selection properly reflects German cuisine: beef for sauerbraten; veal and pork cutlets for schnitzels; smoked pork chops; beef for rouladen; and *mautaschen*, a pocketed beef for stuffing. Among the large selection of cooked ready-to-heat sausages, you'll find *weisswurst* with parsley, bratwurst, and Polish smokies. Most of these can be ordered hot, grilled, and ready to eat, snug in a bun, for an instant lunch. Fetzer's has a grill stand at the Beaverton Farmer's Market where it sells sausage sandwiches, and there's always a long line.

The cooked meat loaves don't exactly look like Mom's—they come in a sauceless Bavarian style, the meat either smooth or coarse. Another precooked option is stuffed veal breast, which can be purchased by the piece. Standard deli fare is available as well—hams, head cheese, and air-dried meats—by the pound or made up into sandwiches while you wait. If you want to take home slices of this and that and make your own super sandwich, a good selection of cheeses and breads—all German-style, of course—is also available.

AND KEEP IN MIND...

Otto's Sausage Kitchen and Meat Market

4138 S.E. Woodstock Boulevard, phone: 771-6714.
Open Monday through Saturday, 9:30 a.m.–6 p.m.
A good selection of German-style sausages and meats.

Greek

When Roger was teaching American literature in Greece, he learned that upon his return to Portland he would be reviewing restaurants for the old *Oregon Magazine*. His Greek friends were puzzled: what could a reviewer possibly say? To them, all Greek cooking was essentially the same and all restaurants basically alike, with a minor variation here and there. One taverna might specialize in lamb, another in fish, but the only difference was a matter of atmosphere, they argued. There's some truth to this, but it's always struck us that Greek cuisine is a bit like ancient Greek architecture: just as there is an ideal model of the classical temple, and all individual examples seek the perfect form, so on a humbler level is the perfect stuffed grape leaf or the perfect lamb souvlaki, and all individual examples seek to emulate them.

You won't find a huge variation among the several Greek food stores in Portland. Greek indeed is Greek, and it's significant that the co-owner of one store listed here is the brother of the owner of another. Greek food has become firmly entrenched in Portland's culinary consciousness, and a Greek meal seldom brings real surprises, but rather the pleasure of returning to the familiar. The cuisine has a peasant heartiness and is full of strong, pungent flavors, never far from its roots in the land. One of the best ways for a Portland home cook to see what is possible is to attend the very popular festival at the Greek Orthodox Holy Trinity Church each fall, where a full panoply of homemade Greek cooking is on sale (see Food Fairs). The stores listed here will provide the ingredients you'll need to emulate the dolma-loving families of the Greek community, and to help you on your way, you can also purchase Alexis Greek foods in most of Portland's better markets and in Alexis's own store: prepared items like *tzatziki, melitzano,* or *spanakopitas,* and fine ingredients such as olives and their own brand of olive oil, all identical to what you'll find at Alexis Greek restaurant. As of this writing, Alexis Foods is about to open its own retail takeout shop at N.W. 14th Avenue and Everett Street (phone: 790-2572).

Foti's Greek Deli

1740 E. Burnside Street, phone: 232-0274. Open Monday through Thursday, 7:30 a.m.–8 p.m.; Friday, 7:30 a.m.–8:30 p.m.; Saturday, 9 a.m.–8 p.m.

This shop does a thriving lunch business; no wonder, since it turns out excellent souvlaki and calamari and a bracing Greek salad. Foti's Greek Deli is partly convenience store, partly Greek grocery and deli. Jars of grape leaves, cans of strong Greek olive oil, and a good selection of retsina are on the shelves, along with bunches of dried Greek oregano on long stalks, carrying the scent of Attic hillsides, and Greek fruit preserves, among them quince, fig, and rose petal. The deli case contains buckets of large black Kalamata olives and a nice selection of Greek cheeses, including the mild white *kasseri* (similar to provolone), which can be fried and flamed as the appetizer called *saganaki; manouri*, a soft cheese delicious eaten with honey; *mizithra*, used for grating when it's aged; and four different kinds of feta, including a Bulgarian variety that tends to be creamier and a bit more sour than the Greek. There are jars of the salty fish roe called *taramasalata*, which is great as a spread when mixed with yogurt or, more authentically, blended with mayonnaise and bread. Owner Foti Kosmas makes his own pastries, including a classic baklava. There's always a good supply of phyllo on hand.

One of the prizes in the store is the pistachio nuts, which come direct from orchards owned by the Kosmas family on the small island of Aegina, not far from Athens. They arrive green, and Kosmas roasts them with lime; this way they stay fresh and have a delicate and slightly tart flavor—very addictive.

The takeout is first-rate here, whether the delicious sandwich known as a gyro (sliced lamb on pita bread slathered with a garlicky *tzatziki*), the *pastitso* (ground beef and macaroni with cinnamon and oregano), or the homemade *tiropites* (cheese tarts) and *spanakopitas* (spinach tarts). If you want suggestions for Greek cooking, Kosmas will happily offer advice.

The Mad Greek Deli

18450 N.W. West Union Road, phone: 645-1650.
Open Monday through Saturday, 6 a.m.–9 p.m.; Sunday, 10 a.m.–7 p.m.

Tom Anastasias and George Athanasakis run a shop near Rock Creek that carries a good selection of Greek goods, both for take-out and for cooking with at home. The specialty here is the Mad Greek Sandwich, but it has nothing to do with Greece—it's just a good all-American Dagwood sandwich. If you want a more authentically Hellenic inspiration, ask either of the enthusiastic owners to show you the riches of the cooler: the creamy fetas, the containers of wonderful olives, the *taramasalata*. They'll give you a feta lesson, explaining that the Sicilian and Bulgarian versions come from sheep milk and the Greek from goat milk, the latter being lighter and easier to digest than milk from either sheep or cows (we detect a touch of understandable national pride here!). The shelves are bursting with retsinas, from the refined to the very rough and hearty. Try some *Mavrodaphne*, a sweet wine from Patras, wonderful with strong Greek coffee. The same excellent pistachios from Aegina are here as well, usually sold in 1-pound sacks.

The Mad Greek specializes in Greek desserts: there are platters of traditional baklava, made with amaretto, which fortifies it deliciously, and several less traditional kinds, including a version called Southern Queen, made with pecans, and another called Hawaiian Queen, containing macadamia nuts. We love their sticky sweet dessert known as *kataifi*, which resembles shredded coconut. You can buy boxes of *loukoumi*, better known as Turkish Delight, but since there's no love lost between Greeks and Turks, remember the Greek name. These square-shaped fruit jellies are studded with peanuts and covered with powdered sugar.

FROM THE PELOPONNISOS TO PORTLAND

T he legend would have it that **Alexis Bakouros** left his native Greek village of Filiatra twenty-six years ago to make his fortune, came to Portland as a struggling youth, ultimately forged a great success with his namesake restaurant, and never looked back. It's all true except the last part. Greeks are too devoted to family to ignore their roots, and furthermore part of Bakouros's success actually *entails* looking back. He has brought a superb line of Greek foods to many of the best stores in town, and much of what appears under the **Alexis** label comes direct from his native village and the surrounding region of the Peloponnisos. Because of Bakouros, many of the best foods of his homeland are flying straight as a Hellenic spear to Portland kitchens.

Every year some 168 tons of earthy olive oil derived from the ancient groves of the family farm arrive in Portland. A range of whole olives arrives as well, along with the best varieties of salty feta, soft white *manouri* cheese—often eaten with honey—firm, tangy *mizithria*, and suave, white *kasseri*.

But what customers at such stores as Nature's Fresh Northwest, Strohecker's, Wizer's, Elephants Delicatessen, Pastaworks, and Burlingame Grocery are most used to seeing are homemade foods to carry out, all stamped with the now-familiar blue square inscribed with a black "A" and a white maze. *Tzatziki* is the biggest seller: the yogurt and cucumber blend is so laden with garlic that if your dining partner doesn't join you, you're done for. We're great fans of the smoky

The souvlaki as well as the spinach and the cheese pies make splendid take-out fare. Another treat-to-go is an order of the sautéed potatoes—giant wedges that need nothing but a sprinkling of kosher salt and Greek oregano. The first-rate calamari doesn't travel quite so well—devour an order here while contemplating your cooking adventure.

AND KEEP IN MIND. . .

International Food Bazaar

See listing on page 26 for location and hours.
There's a full range of Greek products here, including a splendid selection of olives.

eggplant purée known as *melitzano*, great for slathering on Alexis bread. And *spanakopites*, little spinach-filled triangles of phyllo, and *tiropites*, crispy hot pastry tarts filled with feta, both make terrific snacks.

For full dinners, the kitchens of Alexis restaurant turn out containers of *moussaka*, and for dessert a wonderful baklava. A little-known fact is that Alexis Foods also imports sixteen kinds of Greek pasta, but labels them under the name "Angelina." Plans are afoot to bring in Greek sea salt and Greek rice.

When Bakouros returns to Greece, it's usually for a family vacation, but on a recent visit he did some business. Noticing that when his cousins packed the olive oil in the crate there was a bit of space on top, he immediately decided to fill it with herbs. So twenty pounds of fresh oregano now arrive squeezed atop every shipment of olive oil, and Portland can buy dried Greek oregano that's been perfuming the hillsides between Olympia and Sparta.

Bakouros and his family are great boosters of all things Greek, and if you spot any of them at the restaurant they'll delightedly tell you about the Greek specialties they've brought to Portland and those they prepare in their kitchen for retail sales. We're convinced that the local craze for squid sprang from Alexis's great *kalamaraki*, and so pervasive has the influence been of this restaurateur on Portland's palate that even supermarkets carry a portion of the Alexis line. Greece may be the cradle of democracy, but in Alexis Bakouros's eyes, it's also the cradle of dolmades.

Indian and Middle Eastern

Indian and Middle Eastern markets can make you feel like Marco Polo coming upon unknown riches of the East. These emporia may not be as romantic as souks with burlap sacks of spices, and you'll miss being overwhelmed by the pungency of cumin, cardamom, and mint, but there are scores of wonderful packaged spices such as *zatar*, sumac, and fenugreek; great selections of olives; and dried fruits of every imaginable kind. Unfortunately these stores do not usually have takeout. For spreads and dips, like baba ghannouj, or tabouli, you'll have to rely on restaurants or your own kitchen. But use this deficiency as a spur to adventurous cooking. We've found that someone in the shop will gladly suggest how to prepare an unfamiliar item, and you might find help from fellow shoppers, who seem to enjoy sharing recipes from their culture.

Golden Loaf Bakery and Deli

1334 S.E. Hawthorne Boulevard, phone: 231-9758.
Open Monday through Friday, 10 a.m.–7 p.m.; Saturday, 11 a.m.–6 p.m.

A tiny store that doubles as a café, Golden Loaf is owned by the Azar family who moved here from Syria, and stocks a small but interesting number of items for the Middle East pantry. The main product, aside from the pita bread baked on the premises, is the *tahini*, or sesame paste, sold in large jars and used to make hummus, delectable slathered over the pocket bread. You'll find *zahtar*, a blend of sumac, thyme, and marjoram that lends a tart flavor when sprinkled on kebabs and other grilled meats. From Israel, there are canned eggplants; from Syria, *qamaradin*, an Arabic sweetmeat made from apricot purée and sold in thin sheets for a sticky snack. If sweetness is what you're after, don't miss the huge mounds of *halvah* on the counter, in vanilla, pistachio, and marbled chocolate, or purchase an intriguing jar of pomegranate molasses.

India Emporium

10195 S.W. Beaverton-Hillsdale Highway, Beaverton, phone: 646-0592.
Open daily, 12 noon–8 p.m.

On a Saturday afternoon this attractive store hums with Indian and Pakistani families on a shopping spree for *ghee*. There's amazing bounty here, enough to keep devotees of sub-continental cooking sizzling with expectation, and lots of generous, knowing advice for those taking their first steps in this great cuisine. Indian music inspires your pilgrimage, and in this burgeoning shop you'll quickly forget all traces of the surrounding suburbia. If the curry leaves don't do it, or the 44-pound burlap sacks of basmati rice, then the line of chutneys—including coriander, date-tamarind, and mango—will. There are dals—lentils, dried peas, and beans—in all the hot colors of the spectrum, and spices that promise the fragrance of dreams—red sumac, mango and ginger powders, black coriander pods, asafetida. Colorful jars of lime pickles line the shelves, along with bottles of red hot mustard oil and a complete line of Patak spices and sauces, including spicy garlic pastes for what ails you. The breads here are wonderful: try the thick *tandoori nan*, a teardrop-shaped bread baked in an Indian clay oven, or the waferlike *papads* with cumin seeds. The frozen vegetables include *palal paneer* (cheese and spinach) and *undhiu* (a vegetable stew with coconut). You'll even find mango or saffron-pistachio ice cream to go with your cardamom tea.

India Emporium is a pleasure-house of rare treats, seductive aromas, and sheer adventure. And don't forget to pick up a Bombay broom for the final sweep of authenticity.

International Food Bazaar

See listing on page 26 for location and hours.

Here's a remarkable shop with many stamps in its passport. The well-named emporium stocks provisions from dozens of countries and regions, most prominently Greece, Russia, India, the Middle East, and North Africa. This is ethnic cuisine heaven, and no other food shop in town can match its breadth of imported exotica.

Since several émigré Russians have joined the store, the deli case now contains smoked fish and caviar from the Caspian Sea, as well as *bastourma*, sun-dried beef seasoned with garlic, cumin, and paprika (you'll recognize its distant kinship to pastrami). Try it in pita bread with *lebne* (a thick yogurt-based cheese) and mild Italian pickled peppers, a sandwich known as Armenian Delight.

On one shelf you'll see a dozen or more styles of basmati rice. There's a full range of Indian breads, and in the bulk section numerous bins of *dal* (the Hindi name for grains, legumes, and seeds), including chickpeas, lentils, and beans, available in a variety of colors.

Greece chimes in with phyllo dough, grape leaves, and *tarama* (fish roe) in jars, and the Middle East is liberally represented with an assortment of mint waters, Medjoul dates, and Turkish apricots. The best brand of pomegranate syrup can be found here, according to Paula Wolfert, author of *The Cooking of the Eastern Mediterranean*, who searched Portland for her favorite. The depth of the store is evident when you spot feta cheese from Greece, Turkey, Bulgaria, and France; four different kinds of Kalamata olives; and its extensive spice selection.

This shop is infinitely browseable, and you're sure to succumb to its many temptations. All that's missing are the aromas of a souk in Damascus. And perhaps a camel tethered to a parking meter out front.

International Food Market

12070 S.W. Allen Boulevard (Belaire Shopping Center), Beaverton, phone: 520-1850. Open Monday through Saturday, 9 a.m.–9 p.m.; Sunday, 10 a.m.–5:30 p.m.

When Mourir Achour arrived from Beirut not many years ago, he opened a Middle Eastern market because there was no store around entirely devoted to the food of his homeland. This small shop is fully stocked with foodstuffs from Syria, Egypt, Lebanon, Turkey, and Morocco. Achour will make recommendations, as he did when encouraging us to concoct sandwiches from pieces of the immense, flat bread Tonir *lavash* and wrap it around *hallourni*, a salty cheese from Cyprus, along with green onions, roasted pepper, tomatoes, and greens.

International Food Market carries some frozen Hallal meat, the Arabic version of the Jewish koshering process, as well as many spices in bulk and bins of addictive munchies: salted chickpeas, black watermelon seeds, and shelled pistachios. Pine nuts scooped from the barrel are cheaper than you'd pay elsewhere. You'll find giant Armenian bread sticks topped with sesame seeds and a display of lovely Middle Eastern sweets made on site, including *baqlawa* (the Arabic spelling of the Greek dessert) and *mamour*, a Lebanese date pastry. Don't miss the *lebni*, a cheese paste made from whole-milk yogurt—it's slightly sour, has the consistency of cream cheese, and is eaten with dates or fresh figs.

Srider's India Imports

11945 S.W. Pacific Highway (Tigard Plaza), Tigard, phone: 620-8665. Open Monday through Friday, 11 a.m.–8 p.m.; Saturday, 10 a.m.–8 p.m.; Sunday, 12 noon–7 p.m.

There are saris, costume jewelry, and videotapes in Srider's, but you're here for different game. If you've eaten the table-sized crepes from Madras at Swagat restaurant in Beaverton and have a yen to concoct your own, pick up a package of *dosa* mix. When you've made the *dosa,* you might wish to dip them lightly into a wicked *sambal,* an inflammatory condiment made from onions, various chilies, and an intriguing ingredient called Maldive chips. All your favorite Indian condiments are on hand. Srider's, like most such shops, carries the Patak line, which is made in Lancastershire, England. There are also three or four brands made in India, each tailored to a different region of the subcontinent. The Empire strikes back with jars of powerful pickle relishes such as *amla,* made from a fruit much like gooseberry and fortified with tangy tamarind, garlic, lime juice, and chiles. A little goes a long way if you mix it into plain rice.

Indians love to snack all day, and on the streets of every city *chat* vendors are as popular as espresso carts in Portland. You won't find sesame seed and beetle nut sellers on S.W. Pacific Highway, but Srider's will satisfy every esoteric snack impulse imaginable; we like the Hot Bombay Mix, an addictive combination of rice flakes, split chickpeas and mung beans.

Many Indian restaurants offer a palate cleanser near the door on your way out, a sort of indigenous version of mints; try one of several versions here, known as *mukway* and *supari,* containing such ingredients as fennel seed, melon seed, sugar balls, and beetle nuts.

Italian

A common lament in Portland concerns the absence of a sizable Italian community to nourish and sustain the Italian food haunts familiar to anyone who has lived in places with communities known as Little Italy. You can't imagine *The Godfather* being filmed in Portland, nor can you imagine clams on the half-shell shucked in front of Italian fish markets, fully dressed rabbits hanging in a store window, or balls of waxy provolone suspended from the ceilings of local shops. Like a hedonistic Diogenes, we're still looking for an honest cannoli.

Nevertheless there are a few stores here to satisfy one's longings for Italian cuisine–stores where you'll find a wealth of products from the Old Country and numerous Italian-inspired fresh goods made with expert attention. One of Portland's best cooks, Amelia Hard, formerly of the extraordinary Northern Italian restaurant Genoa, gives Italian cooking classes in several venues around town (see Chapter 22); she once cooked for Pavarotti and knows it's possible to find good Italian ingredients in Portland. Portland may not have rollicking Italian street fairs, but almost everything you'll need to turn your home into a temporary trattoria is here.

Martinotti's

See listing on page 26 for location and hours.

This pleasantly crammed store has been in the Martinotti family (of Liguria and the Piedmont) for nearly two decades. You can have lunch on one of the small marble tables scattered amidst shelves bulging with imported pastas and tables crammed with imported sweets. The kitchen turns out interesting dishes, like garlic-sautéed fresh boletus mushrooms, as well as the more traditional spicy salami sandwiches. But Martinotti's is best known for its fine cold cuts, wines, pastas, and Italian cookies. Those used to Italian delicatessens in San Francisco and New York will bemoan the absence of cured Parma hams hanging from the ceiling, but Oregon health regulations being what they are, you'll just have to be content with the deli case. There you'll find Parma pro-

BRINGING HOME THE PROSCIUTTO

Joe Guth learned about food the hard way—washing lettuce and serving as a busboy at Chez Panisse in the 1980s (having decided he'd get a better culinary education in Alice Waters's legendary Berkeley kitchen than at any standard cooking school). While doing a stint on the line, he began to order ingredients for the restaurant, and when he moved to Portland in the early 1990s, working in one of the best restaurants in his adopted city, he helped convince Zefiro's chef to search out unusual olive oils and stunning new pastas.

Eventually he ventured out on his own, and his company, **Provvista**, has become the city's premier Italian food distributor. No one but Guth would hold a cornichon tasting before loosing gherkins on the city's pâté platters. He encourages restaurants to put the names of certain products on the menu, so customers can search out in the stores something they particularly like. Thus a restaurant might inform diners that its salad is finished with Argrumato olive oil pressed with lemons, a product available in the better markets.

sciutto, Molinari salami, pancetta, mortedella spiked with pistachios, fresh mozzarella, aged provolone, Parmigiano reggiano, and lots more. The visual stimuli include a pyramid of tins containing Amaretti de Saronno—anise cookies light as Tiepolo clouds and wrapped in pastel tissue paper—and a mound of chocolate-covered almond biscotti in artful giftboxes.

Dixie Martinotti and her son Frank speak glowingly about the line of dry pastas from Il Trullo; the extruded pastas are shaped by pressing with the thumb or by wrapping the dough around pencil-thin cylinders, and they have a superlative taste, making the extra price worth it.

The stars of the store are its confections. Tables are heaped with Italian packaged pastries, beautifully boxed for gift-giving. The next time you're a dinner guest, offer your host Panforte di Siena—a kind of dense, nougatlike cake, or little chocolate eggs from Perugia. For everyday binging, there are bars of Torrone nougat.

Crammed into the back corner is a wonderful wine section—not just a good choice of Italian bottlings but a superb display of old French vintages and a remarkable case of ports from the 1950s and 1960s.

Guth is passionate about his unpasteurized *picholine* olives with their firm texture and intense taste, and waxes ecstatic about a new item, New York-made sausages known as *sopressata*. In the cold locker, Guth shows us a gorgeous *prosciutto di Parma*, sold with the bone in to lend it greater sweetness, since the cure penetrates best when the center of the ham is not compromised; his awareness of this difference is what makes him special.

He brings out two rounds of cheese: a pecorino romano from the Roman countryside, where the cheese is stronger and creamier in texture than its Sardinian counterpart, and a dried Jack from Sonoma, smooth and mild but with a country-rough, crumbly texture, its rind coated with cocoa to impart sweetness and to offer natural protection against drying out.

When Guth visits his thirty restaurant kitchens every week, the chefs perk up, for he's like an ambassador from another world, bringing tidings of what's newly wonderful. And buyers in the markets pay similar attention, for if Guth gets a scent of a terrific new balsamic vinegar, you can be sure it will be on the shelves long before you toss too many salads.

Pastaworks

See listing on page 12 for locations and hours.

Pastaworks is one of the great food emporia in town, and food-loving owners Peter de Garmo and Don Oman deserve immense credit for raising the gastronomic consciousness of the city. The Hawthorne Boulevard flagship store has expanded impressively from its simple beginnings in 1983 as just a seller of pasta, and now both it and the City Market locations provide a wealth of goods—homemade and imported from Italy—to satisfy the most discriminating Italian gastronome.

Since the Hawthorne store adjoins Powell's Books for Cooks, you can scan or purchase one of the hundreds of Italian cookbooks next door and then come over to shop. Both Pastaworks shops still sell their own fresh pasta, made at Hawthorne and cut into shapes at each location. Each shop carries a wealth of sauces: pesto, *puttanesca*, sage butter, and *marinara*, to name but a few; more modishly, there's even mango salsa. Even though Pastaworks makes delicious fresh pasta, you shouldn't overlook the splendid dried varieties, especially the crunchy and full-flavored *Rustichella D'Abruzzo*.

It's hard not to rave about virtually all the departments at Pastaworks. The cheese selection is as large as it gets in Portland. The kitchen turns out stunning Italian desserts (a recent visit revealed a rich *cassata*, *cornetti*—small puff pastry horns filled with mascarpone—lemon tortes, and chocolate almond macaroons). There are fine take-out dishes: focaccia sandwiches for lunch or picnics, a terrine of eggplant and roasted red pepper, and greatlooking salads. Down the line are twenty bowls filled to the brims with olives from Spain, Greece, Italy, France, Israel, and California.

The wine selection is astonishing in its depth of and special finds among the Barbarescos, Barolos, and Chianti Classicos. Both Oman and de Garmo give very expert advise—they have shopped the vineyards of all the major Italian wine-producing regions, and have drunk the drinks.

There are some fifty different brands of olive oils, in shades from Renaissance gold to chartreuse. If you ask, someone will gladly offer you tastes of several oils with some bread for sopping. The rest of the condiment section is fabulous: scores of balsamic vinegars, nine varieties of capers alone, a halfdozen brands each of olive pastes, roasted peppers, and sun-dried tomatoes.

Everywhere you look, there are surprises: Dean and Delucca risotto, round tins of imported *acciughe* (so much better than supermarket anchovies), and in the freezer a very useful supply of homemade stocks—beef, chicken, turkey, tomato vegetable, and a fish fumet. Pastaworks is the only place in town that stocks homemade veal *demi-glace*, the mother of all brown sauces that's been reduced after hours of cooking; a tablespoon adds real depth and dimension to sauces and will transform any amateur cook into an instant pro. Serious bakers will seek out Plus Gras, one of the best butters you can buy, containing less water and more fat for very rich baking.

The meat and salumeria sections are outstanding (the latter is especially strong in its terrines, mousses, sausages, and cold meats). In the Hawthorne store, Kruger's has taken over the superb produce (at the City Market location Kruger's has had the produce concession from the outset).

Pastaworks publishes an informative newsletter, "*La Lummaca*," which will tell you about new products, the latest wine releases, and suggestions for particular wines to accompany seasonal dishes, with a recipe or two thrown in. And there are cooking classes galore in the Hawthorne store; each summer features sessions of Mediterranean regional foods. Pastaworks is an invaluable resource, and if there's one food shop in Portland to show to visitors, this is it. An expedition might even inspire out-of-towners to make a move.

Jewish

Ask anyone from the East Coast to describe a delicatessen, and it will be virtually synonymous with a Jewish deli, the adjective all but redundant. Ask a Portlander with local roots to do the same thing, and it could be anything from a grocery store with a few pasta salads to a gourmet shop selling fancy mustards. What we consider a *real* deli, that is, a New York deli, is a specialized affair, focused on smoked sable, sturgeon, and whitefish; corned beef, pastrami, and tongue. It is frenetic, noisy, and so steamy your glasses fog up within twenty yards of the brisket. The countermen, who have been at their spots for decades, discourse with Talmudic intensity about the relative merits of barley versus noodle kugel.

Okay, okay. We know Portland isn't on the East Coast. Most ethnic communities here are very assimilated, and Jewish delis cater largely to a non-Jewish community. A good bagel didn't hit the Portland scene until the early 1980s. Smoked fish—not the thick chunks of salmon long favored here, but silken whitefish, sable, and Nova Scotia sliced so thin you can see through it— arrived around the same time with Gary Suttenberg (a Kornblatt's partner) via his uncle in the Brooklyn fish business. As more and more New Yorkers moved out to Portland, a nostalgic longing for real deli foods followed.

The delis here still wouldn't gain respect in New York, but decent matzo ball soup, knishes, corned beef, brisket, and kosher hot dogs are easy to find.

And at holiday times (Jewish New Year, Hanukkah, Passover), two grocery stores make an effort to stock a wide range of appropriate and freshly prepared foods.

Kornblatt's Delicatessen & Bagel Bakery

See listing on page 10 for location and hours.

Kornblatt's is one of two offspring of Josh Kornblatt's Portland Bagel Baking empire. Here, as at Murray's downtown (see page 70), a luncheonette and a takeout counter share space. Most customers opt for the bagels and combinations or sandwiches, stuffed with Portland's rendition of hot corned beef or pastrami that comes closest to The Real Thing. Breads are all house-baked, from the wonderful onion-studded rolls to the too-thickly sliced rye bread.

All the proper accoutrements are lined up in the deli case: sides of rosy Nova Scotia, the less salty loxlike salmon that is hand-sliced into thin shred; smoked whitefish, in a salad or as whole small fish called chubs; smoked sturgeon, the king of fish, sliced into moist chunks for a royal ransom; rustic chopped liver; and bowls of flavored cream cheeses, from cinnamon raisin to vegetable to chive. Noodle kugels, studded with raisins, line up next to such homey childhood desserts as creamy rice pudding and a smooth chocolate pudding.

But traditional dinner options should not be overlooked. The blintzes are arguably the area's best: fat crepelike tubes stuffed with the grandmotherly mixture of creamed cheese and cottage cheese. If this were New York, the cottage cheese would be supplanted by the proper farmer's (or pot) cheese, but, hey, this ain't The City. Potato latkes (pancakes) are crisp, and the matzo balls, if not the perfect floaters of our memories, are a pretty good second best.

At Passover, Kornblatt's offers matzo kugels, farfel, gefilte fish, and other Jewish holiday foods. For Jewish New Year's it makes the special sweet, round challah, that signifies the richness and continuity of life.

Mavens

3535 S.W. Multnomah Boulevard, phone: 977-0000. Open Monday through Thursday, 6 a.m. – 8 p.m.; Friday 6 a.m.–9 p.m.; Saturday, 7:30 a.m.–9 p.m.; Sunday, 7:30 a.m.–8 p.m.

Marsee Baking co-owner Vivian Osserteil took advantage of the closing of Gelfand's Deli last year to convert it to her own shop, a combination deli and Marsee outlet called Mavens. The stellar Marsee products are the main focus, but at this location—inside a small greengrocer and convenience store in

Multnomah—a dozen or so tables and stools at two counters give the bakery a more friendly café feeling. Decor is typical of Marsee's style, with dark mahogany woods and brass trim—not exactly your true deli atmosphere.

But the non-bread and pastry options help to define the place. The menu includes about a dozen regular sandwiches—made on house baked rye or brioche slices—and eight special combos, two soups including matzo ball, and a case full of salads such as black bean and cucumber. Sandwich fillings include pastrami, corned beef, kosher salami, chopped liver, and turkey pastrami. Hebrew National hot dogs are also on hand.

While we wish that Mavens offered more menu items and a few more authentic options, the sandwiches are generous, tasty, and well-crafted, and we're delighted to have a Marsee outlet in this neighborhood.

Ron's Center Deli

6651 S.W. Capitol Highway (inside the Mittleman Jewish Community Center), phone: 244-0664. Open Monday through Thursday, 7 a.m.–9 p.m.; Friday and Sunday, 7 a.m.–5 p.m.; closed Saturday.

We liked the former name of this glorified hot dog stand—Dragoon's—better than its current one, Ron's Center Deli, but the great hot dogs and sandwiches are exactly the same. The new name actually better describes this little café inside the Community Center. No sign alerts or beckons you. You have to know that this tiny hot dog emporium is buried inside Mittleman, past the main information desk and beyond the spartan seating area.

It's important to know where Ron's is, because this spot serves little else than terrific Hebrew National hot dogs. These all-beef franks have an almost crispy exterior—a skin than resists tooth pressure and gives back a bite as savory juices explode in your mouth. Slathered with mustard and relish, these beat any other variety hands down. And at $1.85 a link, they're a bargain.

Ron's sells a few other deli items, including corned beef or tongue sandwiches, salads, and a credible potato knish: a lumpy "box" of mashed potatoes encased in a chewy, thin dough. It's served warm and meant to be eaten out of hand, sort of like a Jewish calzone. At $1.50, it's another cheap snack or light lunch.

Ambience isn't Ron's strong point. You gotta love hot dogs to make this spot a regular on your rounds. For hot dog fans like us who swear by Hebrew National, Ron's also sells them uncooked by the pound so you can prepare them at home. Since its store motto is "Catering to the Kosher Community" you can rest assured that the shop brings in the best meat, fish, and poultry from New York.

Albertson's

5415 S.W. Beaverton-Hillsdale Highway, phone: 246-1713.
Open daily, 6 a.m.–12 midnight.

At Passover time each spring, this branch of the supermarket chain stocks the most comprehensive selection of *Pesach-dicher* foods in Portland. You'll find all the national brands and a wide selection of goods year-round as well.

Kienow's

7300 S.W. Beaverton Hillsdale Highway, phone: 297-5787.
Open Monday through Saturday, 8 a.m.–9 p.m.; Sunday, 8 a.m.–8 p.m.

The manager of the deli section keeps the competition lively with Albertson's at Passover: she makes and sells a number of Passover dishes, including gefilte fish, matzo kugels, *haroseth*, fruit compotes, and vegetable dishes.

Murray's

1000 S.W. Broadway, phone: 242-2435. Open Monday through Thursday, 6 a.m.–8 p.m.;
Friday, 6 a.m.–10 p.m.; Saturday, 7 a.m.–10 p.m.; Sunday, 7 a.m.–8 p.m.

This downtown cousin to Kornblatt's offers bagels, and a full line of sandwiches and hot and cold deli foods.

Challah: See Marsee Baking, page 10; Pastaworks, page 12; and Ron Paul, page 16. *Bagels*: see Bagel Basket, page 6; Bagel Sphere, page 7; and Marsee Baking, page 10.

Spanish and Mexican

We both come from New Jersey, and often on going back to The Garden State we make visits to a section of Newark that contains more than thirty Spanish and Portuguese restaurants, not to mention scores of Iberian groceries. It takes a strong ethnic community to support such a wealth of food enterprises, which is one reason Portland has never had a strong Spanish (as distinct from Catalan) restaurant. And there are few really authentic Mexican restaurants in town—the most genuine places are out-of-the-way taquerias such as La Sirenita and Mi Ranchito, little holes in the wall where everything has a home-cooked taste. This is why it's especially important to know about good Spanish and Mexican groceries, for adventurous Spanish and Mexican cooking may just have to emerge out of your own kitchen.

There are only a handful of such shops, and they tend to be small, but you'll find many of the spices and herbs as well as the major ingredients you'll need for authentic Mexican fare, especially the dried chilies, corn husks, plantains, tortillas, chorizo, and cactus. Diana Kennedy's classic *The Cuisines of Mexico* and the lively and useful *The Taste of Mexico* by Patricia Quintana will start you on your way, and if you liked the film *Like Water for Chocolate*, you should buy the novel on which it was based to consult the passion-inducing recipes.

Spanish ingredients can occasionally be found in the Hispanic stores, though the emphasis tends to be on Latin American cuisines. Be sure you have on hand saffron, pimientos, Spanish paprika, and a range of very good sherries. For Spanish recipes, we like Penelope Casas's *The Foods and Wines of Spain*, which contains a list of mail-order sources throughout the United States.

Becerra's Spanish Groceries

3022 N.E. Glisan Street, phone: 234-7785.
Open Monday through Saturday, 8:30 a.m.–8 p.m.; Sunday, 10 a.m.–8 p.m.

Richard Cruanas, of Cuban birth, runs the best Hispanic grocery store in town. This is where you come if you're seeking *menudo* mix, jars of brown or green mólé to slather on chicken or turkey, corn husks for tamales, or jars of mango jam for exotic breakfasts. From the sacks of rice on the floor to the *piñatas* hanging from the ceiling to votive candles on the back wall, it's a crammed place. But there's room for racks of dried spices, containing pasilla chilies, *mulata* pods, and scorching habaneros. Huge freezers hold frozen okra; a Caribbean fruit called *mamey*, good for blending into delectable shakes; corn fritters; and *loroco*, a Guatemalan vegetable that can be sautéed and mixed with rice. Cruanas will gladly explain how Cubans eat *queso fresco*, a mild, white cheese, along with slices of guava paste as a dessert, and he'll describe the taste of jerk seasoning, island spices that bring chicken or beef to life over the grill.

Becerra's also carries a line of Jamaican products and items from Africa, including the intoxicating palm wine. You'll find all the chilies you could possibly need, and if you've purchased one of the numerous recent cookbooks emphasizing "hot" cooking, you'll want to stock a range of the incendiary pods. You won't easily shake the aromas of cinnamon and chocolate that waft about this entertaining store.

El Caballito

3024 N.E. Alberta Street, phone: 282-0775. Open daily, 9 a.m.–9 p.m.

After a burrito at La Sirenita or Mi Ranchito down the street, head over to "the little horse," a neighborly Mexican grocery, and pick up some flank steak marinated in red sauce, or a jar of molé for your next turkey. You'll discover numerous inviting food in jars, including cactus—a good appetizer— *menudo* (tripe soup), and *albondigas* (a hearty meatball soup). The mixes for several heavenly drinks may be found here, including *horchata*, a luscious sweet "milk" made from almonds and rice, and *tamarindo*, a tart and slightly sour concoction. Check out the several fresh cheeses, packages of corn posole, and several tasty Mexican sweetbreads. If you get hungry while you shop, the kind woman at the meat counter will sell you a taco or two, liberally doused with homemade salsa.

La Tienda de Guadalupe

847 E. Powell Boulevard, Gresham, phone: 669-4119. Open Monday through Thursday, 9:30 a.m.–8:30 p.m.; Friday through Sunday, 9:30 a.m.–9 p.m.

This small grocery is part of a Hispanic food triumvirate in a small Gresham shopping center—the others are La Esperanza, a Mexican bakery, and Mariscos 7 Mares, a new, authentic Mexican seafood restaurant. La Tienda de Guadalupe is smaller than Becerra's, but what distinguishes the store is the fresh produce—such items as cactus leaves, tomatillos, pasilla chilies, and mangoes— and the meat department. On a recent visit we were jolted by the presence in the meat case of two immense cow heads, their eyes bulging like ping-pong balls. The owner told us, "When a family buys one of these heads, you know someone's getting married." The cow heads are boiled to make a wedding soup into which everyone dips a taco as a gesture of good luck. On the *somewhat* more prosaic side, the case also holds tripe for *menudo*, pigs' feet (a common appetizer in Mexico, often served in a vinaigrette), and fresh tongue. And on a positively mundane note, there's fresh chorizo and skirt steaks marinated in a lethal-looking salsa. The shop is one of the few in the area where you can dependably find sweetbreads. Fresh fish and shrimp are beautifully displayed on ice and covered with slices of lime, onion, and bunches of fresh cilantro, bringing to mind ceviche and hot days in Mazatlán.

Near the cash register is a case of popular sweet items, including *camote* (candied sweet potato), sugar-coated tamarind, and a sort of almond fudge. If you are a serious Mexican cook, you'll find *masa*, the dough used for tortillas and tamales; otherwise look for stacks of freshly made tortillas. And of course all the chilies imaginable are here, many of them in bulk.

Miscellaneous Ethnic Markets

Ethnic markets both come from and are maintained by a substantial ethnic population. That may sound like a truism, but it's one of the reasons that Portland doesn't have a real Jewish deli or a Portuguese restaurant. So it was with great pleasure that we discovered a few unusual markets, catering to small ethnic populations, places where unusual accents can be heard and even more unusual products can be found. You might not be itching to make stews with Ethiopian *injera* at home, but the ready-made spongy pancakes are available for you if you do. Sometimes we get a craving for Indonesian food, and the restaurant options for that cuisine are quite limited. Luckily we found a Dutch market that stocks many necessary ingredients (the Dutch occupied Indonesia for many years and adopted parts of that exotic cuisine into their own). And there is a small shop that offers Scottish and English goods for stocking an Anglophile's larder.

Dutch American Market

12125 S.W. Canyon Road, Beaverton, phone: 646-1518.
Open Monday through Saturday, 10 a.m.–6 p.m.

All things Dutch are crammed into this bright store. Blue and white Delft porcelain decorates the narrow space: tiles, plates, shoes, and bowls occupy every surface. Candies from Holland take up a lot of shelf space: bins of licorice in dots, buttons, bits, blocks, and ropes fill much of it; boxes of little chocolate shoes line up next to Droste chocolate bars; and bags of mysterious sweets tumble onto each other. The shelves are lined with cans of prepared soups, stews, vegetables, pickles, and salad dressings, all from the mother country. Spices and condiments reflect the Dutch presence in the Spice Islands, the place where the Dutch explorers learned to make exotic dishes for the rice table (*rijstaffel*), a multidish Indonesian feast.

Square logs of rye and pumpernickel bread in the refrigerated case are shoulder-to-shoulder with odd containers of something called *bumbu*, consisting of fat, onions, and spices. You'll see plump red balls of Dutch cheese, jars and jars of herring preparations, Dutch sandwich meats including tongue *worst*, *leverworst*, smoked beef, and Black Forest ham. The market also makes sandwiches to order, and it does a brisk mail-order business; a catalog of the store's inventory is available for reference.

Queen of Sheba

2413 N.E. Martin Luther King Boulevard, phone: 287-6302.
Open Monday through Saturday, 9 a.m.–9 p.m.; Sunday, 11 a.m.–9 p.m.

There's nothing fancy about this tiny shop and restaurant. Very few grocery items fill the space: only two or three display racks hold everything from everyday goods (soap and paper towels) to Ethiopian spices. Jars of chili paste, legume powders, spices, and herbs share shelves with ready-made *injeras*. For those seeking to make the spongy, breadlike pancakes at home, there's teff flour, an Ethiopian grain essential to authentic preparation.

Owner Alem Gebrehiwot operates both the shop and the small Ethiopian restaurant at the back. He also teaches Ethiopian cooking classes at Portland Community College. (See Cooking Classes.)

Scottish Country Store

3568 S.E. Powell Boulevard, phone: 238-2528. Open Monday through Friday,
10 a.m.–6:30 p.m.; Saturday, 10 a.m.–5 p.m.; Sunday, 12 noon–4 p.m.

Although this is more a general store than a food shop, stocking brick-a-brac, clothing, jewelry, and music tapes from the British Isles, food products receive a decent exposure as well. Bottles of lemon barley water, tins of golden syrup, jars of HP sauce, ginger beer, and the veddy English Marmite (we think you need to have grown up with the stuff to appreciate it) are all tightly packed into a narrow case. Baxter soups–lobster bisque, Scottish leek, cream of asparagus–share space with English candies, and another rack holds crackers, biscuits, oat cakes, preserves, pickle relish, and tea. A form lets you order frozen items such as steak and kidney pie, beef pasties, bangers, haggis (you really have to develop a taste for this Scottish national dish), kippers, Irish bacon, and Belfast ham.

The Food Lover's Companion to Portland

FISH MARKETS

The fish markets of Portland boast impressive catches not only from local lakes and rivers but from the farthest reaches of the Pacific Rim. It's
the perennial favorites that always impress: whole chinook and coho
salmon, or, during their brief three-week spring run, lean Copper River
salmon with their deep, rich red flesh; iridescent black mussels from Oregon's
Winchester Bay; pricey but delectable razor clams; smelts during the spring
and summer runs; oysters from the breeding beds of pure coastal estuaries;
and Dungeness crab. But more exotic items abound: thresher, Mexico Bay
scallops, Chilean swordfish, marlin, flying fish eggs, even mudfish.

But despite the abundance of fish in the Northwest, Portland has never had
a comparable abundance of fish *markets*. On single city blocks in central
Paris, there are more fish stores than we have in the whole town. This lack
may be due to the fact that Portlanders often do not look beyond salmon,
shrimp, and halibut when they think of a seafood dinner. Perhaps because we
are inland from the ocean, we have never enjoyed the great fish stalls that
bless Seattle's Pike Place Market. And yet Portland's oldest restaurant—
Jake's—is an esteemed fish house, the Northwest salmon is among the best in
the world, and recent southeast Asian immigrants as well as the more-estab-
lished Japanese and Chinese communities have introduced many species of
seafood to our menus, including octopus, mahi-mahi, tombo tuna, and ono.
Go to any Asian market on a Saturday afternoon in Portland and see the buying frenzy at the fish case. We sometimes don't realize just how good we have
it: food writer Calvin Trillin has often lamented being a "Dungeness-
deprived New Yorker."

Newman's Fish Company

1200 N.E. Broadway, phone: 284-4537; 6141 S.W. Macadam Avenue,
phone: 244-5954; 735 N.W. 21st Avenue (City Market), phone: 227-2700;
3771 S.E. Hawthorne Boulevard (in Pastaworks), phone: 232-1010;
1409 N.E. Weidler Street, phone: 284-4537.
Open Monday through Saturday, 10 a.m.–7 p.m.; Sunday, 10 am–6 pm

Newman's boasts the widest selection of fish in the city. Though you won't
find them bedded upon mounds of ice, they glisten spanking-fresh in their
stainless trays, and they'll look at you with a bright, clear gleam in their eye.

Newman's sports an advantage over other firms: it has its own wholesaler and is thus free to cut deals direct with suppliers in Florida, Boston, or Hawaii, managing quick delivery from far-flung waters. Newman's will sell only fish it deems in perfect condition. The variety on any given day is impressive: scampi, spot prawns, steamers, razor clams, clam steaks, boned ruby trout, swordfish, mahi-mahi, blue marlin, sturgeon, yellowfin and tombo tunas, and, of course, salmon. You'll find shad roe and smelts as soon as their runs begin. Newman's stocks a range of smoked products, including chinook they brine themselves, mussels, albacore, and halibut. You'll find herrings in wine and in cream, and a mild seafood sausage.

Newman's will gladly handle special orders, whether for tiny Olympic oysters, skate wings, river eel, or, at Passover time, gefilte fish. You'll also find items virtually impossible to obtain at other markets. Frequent appearances of monkfish will gladden the hearts of Francofishophiles; known as *lotte* in

THE MUSSEL LADY

I t's a long way from Winchester Bay at the mouth of the Umpqua River to the Waldorf Astoria in New York City, but **Cindy Sardina's** mussels occasionally make the trip. Not all of her bivalves take so long a journey—some wind up in the cases of Newman's fish stores and Zupan's. These mussels begin a privileged life in a calm-water triangle formed by two jetties and a beach, where, in the cleanest mussel-breeding beds on the West Coast, they're protected from the buffeting of the ocean and develop to their plumpest capacity.

Sardina, along with her former husband, began **Umpqua Aquaculture** after having picked mussels from Haystack Rock at Cannon Beach like numerous other foragers. The idea of developing a breed of mussels not susceptible to pollution-born diseases carried by the red tide, as wild ocean-washed mussels inevitably are, encouraged the Sardinas to cultivate their own.

Umpqua mussels have a slightly salty, clean taste, in part because there's no industry on the banks of the river. The shells are glossy with a blue-black sheen, and the meat is either bright orange (the females) or shiny ivory (the males). One of the reasons Umpqua mussels are prized is because Sardina sells them with the beard (the gathering of vegetation on the shell) still attached. It means more work for the restaurant or home cook, but it makes for a heartier species and guarantees longer freshness. "I want to ship mussels that aren't practically on their deathbed," she asserts. Another factor in making them so fresh is that they come to market direct from the mussel farm, without any wholesaler intervening.

France, this meaty item is always a prize on Parisian menus and lends itself to a wide range of preparations. Don't overlook Newman's salmon pâté, especially the variety spiked with horseradish for extra zip.

Pacific Seafood Company

3380 S.E. Powell Boulevard, phone: 233-4891. Open Monday through Friday, 7 a.m.–6 p.m.

If you pull into the parking lot of this small retail store before noon, you'll see the only oyster conveyor belts this side of the Coastal Range. Tons of oysters are dumped every day from trucks into scoopers that take the bivalves to the rear shucking rooms, where the oysters are opened on heavy metal plates, cleaned, and sized from "large" to "yearling." Another belt carries the empties back up for a recycling trip to the oyster beds, where the shells are reseeded.

Umpqua mussels were originally from California, but they've long since become adapted to Oregon waters. Out in Winchester Bay, long strings of buoys with ropes running down the sides suspend the mussels on fifteen-foot lines, the shells hanging like so many beads on a curtain. On the lines, the Umpqua mussels weather the elements and grow to a much fuller size than most other varieties, including the Penn Cove of Whidbey Island, a more fragile species though certainly a delectable one.

The Umpquas are the foundation of wonderful dishes in Portland: the Steamed Mussels with White Wine and Herbs at L'Auberge, the Wood-Oven Roasted Mussels with saffron, garlic, and tomato at Wildwood, and the Mussel Chowder chock full of peppers and potatoes and served with saffron cream at Café des Amis Because mussels attach themselves to the hulls of ships, they often thumbed a ride and propagated in distant climes. Some locals still see them as odd interlopers and shun them, but Northwesterners are beginning to make the shellfish a significant part of their diet, and Umpqua mussels have been playing no small role in this development. When Sardina watches the daily tidal exchange that allows her mussels and oysters to become sweet and plump, and when she goes out to check on how well they are fastening to their lines, she's engaging in a process that brings about a lot of happy eating. "At the end of the day when I watch the sun fade over Winchester Bay and sit there drinking wine and sopping up the juice of mussels with good bread, what could be better?

Pacific Seafood is a minifactory as well as a store, and if business is slow they might let you peek into the oyster-processing rooms or the kitchen, where prawns are boiled and jarred in a bath of heady spices.

Oysters are the star attraction, and the cases are filled with bottles of the succulent creatures taken from Willapa Bay or lower Puget Sound. There's also a lobster tank, temporary home to dozens of former Maine residents. Razor clams harvested by the Quinault tribe and shad roe make their appearance when in season, as does an occasional small octopus, more often than not a victim inadvertently trapped in someone's fishing net. Since Pacific Seafood's operation is mainly wholesale, the back lockers are filled with fish not seen up front; you should definitely ask what's available, and the friendly help at this fifty-year-old, family-owned business will be happy to tell you about marvels not in view. If you want to make fish stock, there's usually an abundant supply of halibut heads and tails, not often available at Portland's fish markets.

S & S Seafood Company

13650 N.E. Whitaker Way, phone: 252-8889.
Open to the public for retail sales only on Saturday, 10 a.m.–4 p.m.

There is no other place quite like this in Portland. If you arrive for the 10 a.m. opening on Saturday, you'll find several hundred other fish lovers scrambling to get into this piscatory warehouse. S&S Seafood is largely a wholesaler, except on this day. It is strictly a no-frills operation: you'll shop next to forklifts hoisting boxes of fish to be shipped all over the country, and you may get a tad sloshed from the water splashing over the concrete floor. Fish guys heave 100-pound halibuts into bins laden with ice, and you sense the frenzy as serious eaters pick their way through another bin of "miscut" fillets for 99 cents a pound. S&S Seafood provides throwaway gloves if you wish to plunge into the bins and select your whole perch or Dungeness crab, or scoop out exactly the mussels you wish.

There is a table laden with prawns and fillets, but the fun lies in the bins; there are no other places where you can buy so many whole fish (great for steaming Asian-style with ginger, green onions, and some sesame oil). If the rush has subsided, the guys will clean and gut your fish for you, and at all times you can have them filleted. The seafood is so fresh because S&S purchases it directly from the fishing boats. In fact, in the back of the cavernous space, you can see where fish come in within hours of the catch and are prepared on the spot. Prices are rock-bottom, and that's not just for bottom fish.

There are lots of choices not shown out front: don't hesitate to ask for lobsters you can pick right from the holding tanks. Loyal consumers come from all over: there's a contingent of Old Believers from Woodburn who will snap up 1,000 pounds of snapper for a Russian Orthodox feast, and there's a woman who comes in every week from The Dalles in her Jaguar to seize the great bargains. Shopping here is fun, and you're sure to take home a prize in an ice-filled plastic sack.

Victor's European Meat Market

13500 S.W. Pacific Highway #30, Tigard, phone: 684-2580.
Open Monday through Saturday, 10 a.m.–7 p.m.; Sunday, 10 a.m.–5 p.m.

Jakub Lunkiewicz presides over this wonderful shop in a Tigard mall, bringing his Old World expertise as a smoker and curer of sausages, hams, and fish. All the smoking and filleting is done on the premises, and the products are rich, moist, and redolent with woody aroma. On any day, the case may be stocked with smoked sea bass, sturgeon, mackerel, halibut, or herring, all prepared with the skills of a man who understands the taste of the Baltic. He also puts up his own caviar, whether the delicate black eggs of Caspian Sea sturgeon or the much larger, palate-popping red roe of salmon, a bargain at $20 a pound.

AND KEEP IN MIND...

Anzen Importers

See listing on page 46 for location and hours.
Anzen is especially good for imported fish, both fresh and frozen, much of it exotic, from Japan, Taiwan, Korea, and other waters of the Pacific Rim. You know you're getting the most pristine fish available, because many of the city's sushi bars buy their supplies here.

Kornblatt's

See listing on page 10 for location and hours.
This is one of the best places in Portland to buy a range of smoked fish, including good chubbs and handcut lox.

Murray's Bagels

See listing on page 70 for location and hours.
Montrose whitefish and other smoked delicacies abound in the deli case.

Nature's Fresh Northwest

See listing on page 11 for locations and hours.

The case always gleams with great tuna, fish sausages, and a strong selection of shellfish. You can trust the quality down the line, from the extremely rich salmon sausage patties to the ahi kabobs. Calamari tubes are great for those unwilling to clean their own squid, and the spot prawns and oysters are as fresh as they come. The farm-raised salmon, the black trout, and occasional special treats like Fiji albacore are absolutely reliable, and you'll always get informed service.

Talarico's Market

8502 S.W. Terwilliger Boulevard (Burlingame Grocery),
phone: 246-0711 or 246-7619. Open daily, 6:30 a.m.–10 p.m.
8605 S.W. Beaverton-Hillsdale Highway (The Market Place), phone: 203-1668.
Open Monday through Saturday, 7 a.m.–8 p.m.; Sunday, 9 a.m.–7 p.m.

The salmon is especially noteworthy here. They also stock hard-to-find items, such as shad roe in season.

Good Queen Bess regarded it as such a regal fish that her favorite courtier, Sir Francis Drake, felt right at home when he saw it while exploring the mouth of the Columbia River in the sixteenth century. Northwest Native Americans have long revered it, James Beard extolled it, and we never get enough of it. Salmon is our regional treasure.

Debates rage: some think the tail section is the more delectable because it contains the most oil, others love the head section for its sheer meatiness. Some believe that farm-raised salmon is not only more ecologically sound—given diminishing supplies from overfishing, poaching, river pollution, and the barrier dams—but is simply tastier. Others swear that troll-caught salmon have more flavor because line-caught fish are handled individually by the fishermen (usually gutted and iced on board) and treated more carefully by processors, lending a cleaner taste and a higher price. Some experts claim that farm-raised fish is the best for grilling, because they have a high fat content and cannot easily be overcooked and dried.

There are five kinds of Pacific salmon, and you'll see them all in the markets. Within each type, salmon are distinguished by their ties to specific watersheds and natal streams, differing in size, color of the flesh, and even taste to predators:

CHINOOK, OR KING SALMON. The majority for this area comes from the Columbia River. It is the largest species (averaging 10 to 20 pounds) and is most in demand; look for it as the spring runs begin in April. Chinook have the greatest amount of fat and thus the most intense flavor. They carry so much fat because they spawn farther upstream than other species (the Columbia is 1,200 miles of ladders, waterfalls, and rapids), and therefore need fat for the arduous journey. The Grand Coulee Dam made the headwaters of the Columbia inaccessible, so huge 40-pounders no longer ply the Columbia. For the really huge Chinook, you have to look to Alaska's Yukon River, whose salmon need that extra fat for the punishing 1,800 mile trip upriver. If they're caught near the river mouth before they fight their way upstream, they're at the peak of flavor. The best version of Chinook, and nearly twice the price of others, is from Alaska's Copper River, a swift and icy stream that gives them a lot of muscle, a hefty amount of oil, and deep red flesh. They appear for just four weeks, in late May and early June.

SOCKEYE SALMON. Prized almost as much as the chinook, the sockeye appear in early summer, have about the same fat content, and are extremely succulent and sweet. Because the flesh is a brighter red-orange, many prefer this kind for smoking, and sockeye are the principal source for lox. Their diet of minuscule crustaceans and shrimplike plankton give them their exquisite flavor. The best of them hail from Bristol Bay in Alaska and from the Fraser and Thompson Rivers in British Columbia (and they are at their best when caught in Georgia Strait just as they head for fresh water). In general, the best-tasting salmon are caught in sea water near river mouths, just before they begin to lose muscle tone and flavor on their extended voyage to the spawning beds.

COHO OR SILVER SALMON. This fish has a rosier, paler flesh and about half the fat of the sockeye or chinook. (If you are keeping tabs on your fat intake, you should know some doctors believe fish fat actually *lowers* cholesterol.) Baby cohos that are farm-grown on the West Coast taste a bit like trout.

CHUM. A fall salmon, this is less flavorful because it is low in fat, and it tends to wind up in cans or in smokehouses, though the small fish do make it fresh to market at very reasonable prices.

PINK SALMON. These are smaller and far less rich, usually canned.

Salmon spend most of their lives in the open sea or in large bodies of salt water like Puget Sound, returning inland after traveling as much as 2,000 miles to the very stream where they were born. After the females spawn and die, the emergent fingerlings gradually migrate back to the open sea to perpetuate the cycle. The upriver runs, during which time the salmon cease feeding and live on accumulated fat, take place in the spring and fall. Spring salmon are the tastiest because they're the oiliest, the result of a winter in cold waters. The Pacific Northwest runs, including the Alaskan, occur between April and November; salmon do appear in the markets from December to March, but these are usually farm-raised fish out of Alaska or Washington.

GENERAL FOOD STORES

These stores carry a large range and variety of food and as such differ from specialty stores, though some of them have special departments. We do not include the local supermarkets because they are so well-known and so much alike they don't need elucidation from us. We're pleased that even the giants are awakening to the times: some Fred Meyer stores boast fine wine sections with their own wine stewards; other supermarkets have expanded their produce sections to include wild mushrooms, cactus leaves, and Asian pears, items unimaginable only a few years ago.

The stores in this chapter have very distinctive feels, reflecting the tastes of their clientele and the points of view of their owners. These values are reflected in the foodstuffs, the displays, even the attitudes of the staffs. Strohecker's, nestled amidst the homes of Portland Heights, carries an aura of confidence born of long service to established families; there's an understated elegance about the place. Nature's Fresh Northwest rode the natural-food wave of the 1960s and early 1970s and in the past dozen years has diversified to become an emporium of both upscale health food products and free-range beef, the latter an unthinkable option during the days when Bill Walton scooped granola out of its bins. Nature's feels very "Oregon," while Trader Joe's trails its California pedigree. Burlingame Grocery has grown from a convenience store into a remarkable source of condiments, one of the largest purveyors of wines in the city, and a great center for fresh produce. Sheridan took over the bulk kingdom from its erstwhile rival and neighbor when the immensely popular Corno's went out of business and it now hosts the town's best cooking classes. We've included the Made in Oregon store here because it offers such a vast array of all-Oregon products.

Burlingame Grocery

8502 S.W. Terwilliger Boulevard, phone: 246-0711. Open daily, 6:30 a.m.–10 p.m.

Burlingame Grocery was once a nondescript convenience store, but in the last few years it has blossomed into a major resource. It leases two spaces to Gary Talarico, who handles meat, fish, and produce. Burlingame Grocery is not very large and is definitely not the place to go for commonplace items—prices too high, selection too small—but for great produce and meats, spectacular oils and condiments, and one of the largest wine selections in the city, it's a magnet.

Talarico's produce is impeccable, because his staff picks out each particular piece for display. He buys many items direct from farmers' trucks, and in the summer almost all his fruits and vegetables are grown in the region. There are a dozen varieties of lettuce, peppers in hues of chocolate and green-black, and vine-ripened cherry tomatoes so juicy you have to eat them with caution.

The fish section is small but choice. The salmon, including the short run of Cooper River chinook, is gorgeous. The store will gladly order whatever you don't see: one of us recently requested shad roe, hard to find in local markets, and it was in the next day. The meat section is more extensive. Don't miss the sinfully rich rounds of beef stuffed with blue cheese and pine nuts, the herbed rack of lamb, or the lemon chicken, as well as hard-to-find New York strips and a dozen varieties of chicken sausage.

Burlingame Grocery doesn't make any of its own baked goods, but buys from the better bakers in town, including Marsee's, Joseph's, and Beaverton Bakery. We especially like Joseph's intense lime tart and blackberry and lime mousse cake. Stock your Sunday brunch needs at the baker's shelves, provisioned with muffins of all persuasions.

Burlingame Grocery excels in its selection of bottled salsas, hot sauces, relishes, and the like. It tends to carry and display generous amounts of a line, so you'll find a number of Silver Palate jars, including their spectacular chocolate sauces, and Mark Miller's Coyote Cocina line of salsas and taco sauces. Many of these items make wonderful dinner party or house gifts. Look for the Peloponnese brand of wild herbs with garlic and olive oil, their grape leaf and walnut pesto, and their classic Kalamata olive spread. Burlingame also has a stunning display of oils. Check out the International Collection, small bottles that look as if they contain rare perfumes or body lotions, but in fact hold grape seed oil, sweet almond oil, and pistachio oil. Try a fruity olive oil called Landemio, made by no less a personage than the Marchese de Frescobaldi.

Richard Elden, the impressively knowledgeable wine steward at Burlingame, presides over an inventory of some 2,000 labels, dispensing advice with unpretentious expertise and wit. Caches of more labels rest in the cellar. The selection is especially strong in French and West Coast labels; there's even a fine representation from Australia. If you're buying a white and need it cold pronto, you can use the wine chiller. As for beer, this selection may be the best in town. More than 350 different brands comprise a veritable U.N. of beers, including Hue Beer from Vietnam, Farson's Shandy from Ireland, Sheaf Stout from New Zealand, or White of Bruge from Belgium.

Food Front Cooperative Grocery

See listing on page 19 for location and hours.

Food Front is a co-op, with almost 1,000 members who have a large say in what comes into the store. There are monthly meetings, newsletters, and many of the perks of ownership. Customers use a question and request board near the entrance to convey their wishes, and the store's information center provides updates on products and the organic food industry. More than Nature's, to which it's often compared, Food Front retains its health-store image: no red meat.

The single best feature is the produce. Everything is extraordinarily fresh and is nicely displayed. In the early spring, you'll discover melons not seen elsewhere: orange honeydews and galias. Food Front does very well with baby vegetables, and there are lots of unusual items, including mizuma mustard, dandelion greens, Thai eggplants, and lemongrass—most everything organically grown. The fresh herb section is outstanding.

Food Front's bulk section shines, with a whole wall and four tiers of bins. It's the range of choices that impresses, with fourteen different kinds of rice, including white sushi rice for budding masters of the California roll. Several mueslis, kasha, the grain sensations amaranth and Peruvian quinoa, and even dried chestnuts all make an appearance.

If there's a motif to the deli section, it's "fusion food": a "Chinese burrito," vegetarian pot stickers, and knishes. The meat case contains a good selection of turkey and chicken sausages, and some free-range chickens, but the fish selection is skimpy and unpredictable. The prepared items include the usual suspects: meatless sausages, vegetarian pepperoni, veggie chili dogs, King Harvest products, and of course several kinds of miso and tofu burgers. Even prepared tofu has gone exotic: see the Szechuan garlic and peanut ginger varieties.

Made in Oregon

See listing on page 29 for location and hours.

We've put the Made in Oregon stores into this chapter not because they are even vaguely like the other stores in this category, but because they carry such a range of Oregon foods. Of course, many nonfood products find a home here—Pendleton shirts, blankets, and crafted jewelry—but the items that most intrigue visitors and most interest us are those "caught or grown in Oregon," as the poster has it.

Nothing's fresh at Made in Oregon, but the local bounty is in evidence. This is a fine one-stop resource if you plan to visit relatives in Nebraska and want to impress them with what they're missing; it's also an ideal venue if your friends from Texas need a last-minute culinary keepsake. You can make up your own gift packs or purchase prepacked boxes, some made of crated wood. You can focus exclusively on Oregon berry jams, smoked salmons, Oregon Pinot Noirs and Chardonnays, or scone and bread mixes together with various pancake syrups and chocolate toppings.

If salmon is the centerpiece of a gift, you have a choice among alder-smoked salmon fillets, smoked salmon jerky, and smoked chinook. Displays of preserves made from Oregon marionberries, strawberries, and local blueberries dominate the shelves. The Trailblazer dessert sauces created from berries are popular, as are their toppings and fillings used in shakes, cobblers, and as a poultry glaze. There are regionally produced vinaigrettes from Dundee Hills Farm, jams from Wall Berry Farm, and blueberry syrups from Oregon Hill. Hazelnuts appear in various forms: plain, smoked, dipped in chocolate, made into toffee, and roasted.

Nature's Fresh Northwest

See listing on page 11 for locations and hours.

People actually look healthier and happier at Nature's than at most shopping venues, whether because they follow saner food regimes or they feel cheered to be here, we're not sure. We always enjoy shopping at Nature's: the clerks are helpful and knowledgeable about their merchandise and seem genuinely to enjoy their work. In this entry we've focused on the Division Avenue flagship store, though the new Vancouver operation is by far the largest and contains some unique features: a body and facial salon, an on-site bakery, a cooking school, a flower shop, a pizza shop, and a commons area where you may eat and listen to music.

Nature's began on Corbett Avenue (that store retains its original counter-cultural atmosphere); the grains and organic sprouts have mushroomed into big business, but Nature's has never lost its charm. Though it attracts patrons who wouldn't welcome a wheat germ any more than a cold germ, it still relies on a solid foundation of folks who care about healthy eating combined with good taste. Nature's is a monument to culinary democracy, where a New York strip can cohabit with a strip of kelp.

Produce is very reliable. There's a lack of variety compared to Kruger's (though occasionally exotic greens pop up), but in general Nature's fruits and vegetables are splendid and displays picture-perfect. Little signs inform you where crops were raised, so you know if an item is local or from California. And the guys who work the produce are honest—if the tomatoes are not sufficiently juicy, they'll tell you. However, since not all produce appears in both organic and non-organic modes, it can sometimes be annoying to pay "organic" prices if it's not important to have the pure variety.

As for prepared foods, Nature's makes its own smoky version of hummus and several salsas with a clean, bright taste; the black bean dips are also quite good. He never thought he'd admit it, but Roger's grown to like Toby's jalapeño tofu pâté. All new products welcomed into Nature's have been scrupulously tested by the staff, for both nutritional value and taste. In the bulk section, the rices, beans, granolas, pastas, dried fruits, and nuts are the categories that have more bench strength than the Phoenix Suns. Nature's carries the very highly regarded Allegro Café among its packaged coffee beans.

Although all the cheeses are packaged, this department scores quite high. Most of the expected varieties are on hand, but there are surprises as well. Spanish *manchego*, a sharp cheese that goes well with sherry, is a find, as are goat-milk gouda and goat-milk Brie—both earthier than their bovine counterparts. Not long ago, Nature's snared some hand-crafted cheeses from England.

The delicatessen abuts the juice bar, so it's always a lively corner of the store. There are comfort foods such as Baked Beans, Squash Enchiladas, and creamy Black Bean Polentas. Nature's generally does best by its Tex-Mex items—try the Santa Fe Tortellini with olives, corn, and chilies.

The fish department may be the best in the store. From the extremely rich salmon sausage patties to the ahi kabobs, everything is wonderful. In the splendid meat section the chicken is all free-range, and Nature's butchers were among the first in town to produce chicken sausage.

Nature's also shows some casual dinnerware, notably white bistro and Mexican blue glasses, and some useful cookware items. One of us bought a Champion juicer here years ago, a kitchen favorite ever since.

Sheridan Fruit Company

See listing on page 20 for location and hours.

While Sheridan has evolved from a fruit store to a full-service grocery store including a demonstration kitchen used for cooking classes, the emphasis here is on value rather than elegant presentation. The space feels a little tired, with dingy floors, low lighting, and very narrow aisles. The produce is arranged in bins, giving the store the honest look of a farmers' market.

Everything is fresh and seasonable, but not too fancy. You're convinced that the goods just came in from the farm.

Packaged items are a little more limited at Sheridan than at other grocery stores. Breads come from most of the area's better bakeries, and whole-grained loaves get good exposure. Bagels and muffins are sold by the piece. Olive oils and vinegars are strong suits, bolstered perhaps by the needs and influence of Gayle Jolley, who runs In Good Taste cooking classes.

The meat counter has a supermarket-standard selection of chicken, beef, pork, lamb, and the lot, but the advantage here is that you may choose what you want from the case rather than from prewrapped packages. Service is pleasant and accommodating.

The most fun at Sheridan is exploring the wonderful bulk food selection. We sometimes come here just for that. Around the corner from produce, a

Stan Amy and Nature's Nurture

Stan Amy calls himself a "pragmatic idealist" and a "low-level entry capitalist," seemingly quite a change from his 1960s activism as a student leader at Portland State University. But perhaps not so, for the president of Nature's Fresh Northwest has always advocated consumer power. As consumer tastes—even those of Nature's earliest followers—changed in subtle ways, Amy shepherded the growth of a of a tiny macrobiotic food co-op with "a clinical, guilt-based, Puritanical orientation" into an empire of healthy, tasty, and surprisingly various foods that would amaze and maybe dismay the original founders, who scorned nonorganic radishes, let alone red meat. Nature's stores celebrate what Amy calls "the democratization of quality," meaning that they make readily available food that is produced and gathered while respecting the environment. There is a "large minority" who has learned to demand and enjoy healthful eating that is every bit as flavorful as mainstream tastes. Portland has been the ideal venue for this development, for it's a town that combines old-fashioned innocence and up-to-the-minute sophistication. Amy wants shopping to be a social and educational experience, and he envisions his stores as centers where people can gather and define themselves as a community of sensible, responsible hedonists.

The stages of Nature's evolution are instructive. In 1978, Nature's decided to incorporate nonorganic produce, which soon came to represent less than half the total fruit and vegetable sales. In 1983, it introduced coffee and wine, seek-

narrow alleyway is lined with barrels of all kinds of things: dried fruits, grains, cereals, pastas, seeds, and nuts. Spices and honey are also available in bulk.

Strohecker's

See listing on page 25 for location and hours.

When running all over town to find the items on our grocery list—like a culinary scavenger hunt—takes too much time, Strohecker's is the one place where we can meet all of our shopping needs. No other grocer in town stocks goods of a comparable range and quality, from aluminum foil to Vietnamese *nuoc man* sauce. Where else in Portland can you find fifteen kinds of caviar at Christmastime? Each department of this longtime family-owned Portland Heights market tries to carry the best ingredients of its kind.

ing to define itself more by what it *did* carry than by what it refused to carry. Of course, the coffee was organically grown—no DDT on those beans! In 1986, Nature's scandalized its vegetarian hardcore by bringing in fish and red meat. But most of its salmon is farm-raised so as not to contribute to the depletion of ocean resources, and its oysters are from a Willapa Bay breeder, who gets rid of pesky river grasses in the estuary by hand-cutting them, thereby avoiding toxins. The new Vancouver store is almost in the enlightened mainstream, its stock including rather conventional brand names so long as they square with the company's philosophy.

The ordinary supermarket consolidates its buying, using some 50 vendors; Nature's diversifies its buying and uses more than 500. Many come from tiny manufactures and no product comes into the store unless it meets rigorous ecological, nutritional, and taste standards. There's a social mission, to be sure, and a drive to make the clientele aware of the origins and quality of all Nature's products, but Amy is also interested in "making everyday living gracious." He sees the acceptance of pleasure as part of the Europeanization of America, an end to the puritanism that the 1960s ironically produced. Walk into a Nature's store and you'll witness the aestheticization of culinary health. The pioneers might be appalled by a case full of sausages and rabbits, but the purity of nature is still at the center of things.

Strohecker's stocks all the familiar packaged products that any reputable store would. But it manages to one-up the competition. The pasta selection, for example, is tremendous. Standard American brands share shelf space with De Cecco fine dried pasta and three other upscale imports, including Rustichella d'Abruzzo, a pricey Italian import packaged in a simple brown wrapper, the Lamborghini of dried noodles. The selection of sauces for the pasta is no less comprehensive. Canned jars and tins of toppings, refrigerated sauces, and frozen options are available: you just have to roam from section to section to realize the depth of the choices. Barbecue sauces are equally well represented. Mass-produced products share shelf space with handcrafted gems, including our current favorite, Mr. Brown's Lemon Pepper Sauce.

The produce is lovely. Beautiful specimens of all things fresh and seasonal are laid out in pretty rows. Strohecker's buys from the same places that Kruger's does; Kruger's may have a bit more depth in selection than Strohecker's, but not much.

The baked goods section is an outlet for the town's premier bakeries, wholesale and retail. Strohecker's carries the legendary fluffy Hillvilla pies in lemon, strawberry and chocolate flavors: these are cloudlike confections wrapped in a meringue crust. If you've seen a bakery product elsewhere and want Strohecker's to stock it, they'll try.

Ethnic grocery products are also represented. We've had long lists of Asian ingredients, like black sesame seeds, won ton wrappers, and toasted sesame oil, and been surprised at Strohecker's ability to fill our needs. The same is true for Hispanic products. Strohecker's spice selection is amazing as well. Big and little bottles line a wall, not unlike a pharmacy. Jars of multicolored peppercorns line up next to different grades of salt. This is the place to find four different varieties of chili powders for your next Mexican sauce or stew.

The meat department is a first-class operation and among the best butcher shops in town. Beverages make up another remarkable section: soda in flavors we'd never seen! Colored bottles call out from the refrigerated case, suggesting a Pantone palate. The beer selection is one of the most impressive in the city, with bottles from far-flung countries lined up next to the hometown competition. The range really can't be beat.

Downstairs, more options abound, with deli, cheese, and takeout cases and a remarkable wine department. This is where small cooking utensils, cookbooks, and glassware reside—all a credible selection.

Prices at Strohecker's are mixed: sometimes, you pay a bit more to find such a staggering array of sophisticated choices, but often, the prices are no greater that what you'd pay elsewhere in town.

See listing on page 26 for locations and hours.

The famed trader from California has finally come to town. The store carries very little that is fresh or perishable, save some packaged cheese and a few takeout items. Its modus operandi is to buy huge lots of goods direct from producers, thus bypassing brokers and getting things cheaply. Trader Joe's is a monument to packaging, a store that puts all its goods into cans, boxes, packages, and the freezer.

Shopping here is always quirky and fun. One might call the experience of Trader Joe's impulse buying, but not at the high end. Prices are astonishingly reasonable, and since you don't exactly come here for basics, you never know what might strike your eye or indeed what will be in the store once but never again. The store keeps up with ethnic food trends, so the freezer compartment contains such interesting items as Gyoza potstickers, Biryani curried rice, a *Nasi Goreng* Indonesian rice dish, and chicken and duck sausage meat with cilantro.

Among the best items in the store are the bottled juices, many of which are unavailable elsewhere (we like the Pippin Apple Cider, Dixie Peach, Blueberry Spring, and Apricot Blossom); the dried fruits (especially the cranberries and papaya); and the vast array of nuts (pistachio nut meat is a dynamite snack). There are endless varieties of crackers and tortilla chips.

The deli case holds a few prepared goods, such as Eggplant Parmesan, Couscous Salad, Tabouli, and Tofu Enchiladas. You'll find chicken liver mousse and several pâtés, Montrachet cheese marinated in olive oil, and other cheeses ranging from fat-free Cheddar to a triple cream Brie with 70 percent fat. Nevertheless, Trader Joe's tries to meet consumers' desires for low-fat goods, and it puts out a sheet listing 99 percent fat-free products. As for wines, most are California vintages and almost no bottle is over $8.99.

See listing on page 32 for locations and hours.

The original, downtown Lake Oswego Wizer's has an old-time feel that takes you back to the 1950s. You're almost surprised to see women in modern dress and certainly startled by someone using a cellular phone. (The Bryant Road outpost looks pretty modern, as it was opened only a year or so ago.)

We like the original store better than the newfangled place. The crowded space, narrow aisles, soft lighting, and old-fashioned produce lanes evoke fond memories of the grocery stores of our childhood. The major difference between Wizer's and the corner grocery of earlier times is its range of unusual and gourmet products sprinkled among the more standard supermarket fare.

The small bakery counter stocks a remarkable array of goods, given its size. Lacy Florentine cookies (that we haven't seen anywhere else) are a great find: big, buttery discs filled with white chocolate that crumble when you bite them. And a whole display case is devoted to Moonstruck chocolates (see page 31).

The produce selection is supermarket-standard, with few exotic choices and only single varieties of each item. But nice touches abound, like orange juice that's squeezed fresh daily. Meats are mostly prewrapped in a display cooler, but the selection is better than average. Free-range chickens roost in the fresh meat display case, where you'll also find lamb chops, tenderloin steak, and a selection of fresh fish that's serviceable, but doesn't make us want to swallow the lure.

Like other groceries in this hustle-bustle age, Wizer's offers a selection of salads and other ready-to-eat items. Cheeses are all prewrapped and weighed. But crème fraîche and mascarpone are always available for those who indulge. The cold case houses ready-made sandwiches on both croissants and plain bread, Alexis Greek spreads and dips, sauces, and fresh pasta, from both Pazzo and Pastaworks.

It's fun to wander the aisles and discover little coves of ethnic authenticity: an array of dried chilies including New Mexican, pasilla, California, chile de Arbol, and chipotle; dried seaweed, bottled Asian sauces, and Thai seasonings.

An impressive selection of Bob's Red Mill flours and grains takes up a big section of an aisle. And one of our favorite snack foods gets special attention, crisps from a California company called Just off Melrose.

Wizer's also has an adequate wine selection offering competitive prices on a very good showing of Oregon and California wines. European wines get less shelf exposure than the West Coast varieties. The cellar holds a cache of older wines, and they, too, have a West Coast orientation. You won't find great deals, but there's enough choice to make Wizer's a good stop for dinner or gift wine.

2340 W. Burnside Street, phone: 497-1088. Open daily, 24 hours

Zupan's is a fine store for the busy cook and homemaker—or for those who work nonstandard hours. The largest space in the brightly lit store is the center island filled with prepared foods. Here you'll find a dozen or so fresh salads and a good selection of hot items such as lasagna, macaroni and cheese, chicken, and spare ribs. Deli meats are available in slices by the pound. And a large rotisserie is in constant motion, spinning and turning chickens until they reach a deep nut brown.

Pastries come from many of the city's best-known bakeries, and the reach-in case beyond the baked goods offers individually wrapped portions of lasagna, salads, soups, dips, and sandwiches. A display stand holds the Grand Central lineup along with Alfredo-label breads. All cheeses are preweighed and packaged, very convenient if you want speed and the amount that's already been cut.

Across the aisle from the center station, through the decent wine selection, the meat case displays more ready-to-heat dinner options. Some meat cuts—like free-range whole chickens and parts, veal chops, and Porterhouse steaks—are available at the counter, while others are packaged and arranged in a neighboring case.

The frozen cases contain a few real finds. Right between TV dinners and Wolfgang Puck pizzas, you can find a veritable duck farm. Packets of Grimaud farms Muscovy (the meatiest and best flavored) duck breast sit next to tubs of veal and duck *demi-glace* from D'Artagnan, the very French New Jersey purveyor of all things duck. (We use *demi-glace* as a sauce and soup enhancer: a little bit intensifies flavors and adds a rich dimension.)

Packaged goods vary, with little selection on some items and a goldmine of others. The particularly strong pasta selection includes DeCecco, Delverde, and Guissepi Coco along with fresh pastas from Pastaworks. The beer selection is good, with bottles from local microbreweries and distant shores.

Everything at Zupan's is attractively displayed and nicely laid out, especially the outstanding produce where you'll find many inviting surprises. Service here is truly accommodating. Staff people smile and are eager to help you find something or to special order a request.

Chapter 9

ICE CREAM

Ice cream isn't only a summer food. The sensation of something cool and creamy that melts in your mouth is a refreshing and indulgent treat any time of year. Maybe we retreat to childhood pleasures when we lick around an ice cream cone, going back to dog-day afternoons and simpler times. Ice cream does have a magical, childlike quality. And sometimes ice cream straight from the carton is a satisfying pleasure.

Ice cream is also a useful element in more elaborate desserts such as Peach Melba, Pears Helene and baked Alaska. Sundaes topped with homemade caramel and fudge sauces are delicious, and nothing completes an elegant, rich dinner as cleanly and simply as a pretty glass filled with sorbet. At least one sorbet tops the dessert menus at a number of Portland's better dining spots, including Zefiro, Wildwood, and The Heathman.

Like all good food obsessives, occasionally we each make our own ice cream and sorbet. But with the terrific products being churned out by local purveyors, we just as often head to Zero, SDK's, or Bravo for immediate gratification or a pint to go. Even most of the local grocery stores carry great brands including Häagen-Dazs, Ben & Jerry's, and the herb-infused Out of a Flower.

Bravo Italia

4110 N.E. Fremont Street, phone: 282-2118.
Open Monday through Saturday, 7 a.m.–10 p.m.; Sunday, 7 a.m.–2 p.m.

This coffee shop-cum-ice cream parlor in the Beaumont neighborhood makes the only version of Italian gelato we've found in Portland, and while the texture isn't as transcendent as the stuff we've had abroad, we still gravitate toward this dense confection: it's chewier due to less air beaten in, so the flavor seems richer and more intense. The counter case holds a good selection of ice cream for takeout or enjoyment on the spot at one of the many café tables. Pick from flavors such as Hazelnut, Banana, Vanilla Bean, and Chocolate or sorbet varieties including Mango, Lime, and Marionberry. Flavors change regularly.

Coffee People

See listing on page 37 for locations and hours.

At these shops where coffee reigns supreme, Black Tiger ice cream is an equally popular draw: chewy coffee ice cream is studded with so much ground espresso that you get a serious buzz from a mere scoop. Other flavors include seasonal fruits, Mocha Chip, and a dynamite Peppermint that's the color of cotton candy but not nearly as sweet.

Milk shakes are another big draw, and Black Tiger makes a wicked warm-weather sweet beverage. With so many Coffee People scattered all over town, it's easy to indulge an impulsive desire even for a late treat, when you feel a witching-hour craving.

Roberto's Homemade Ice Cream

921 S.W. Morrison Street (in the Galleria), phone: 224-4234. Open Monday through Friday, 11 a.m.–7 p.m.; Saturday, 11 a.m.–6 p.m.; Sunday, 12 noon–5 p.m.

Brothers Bob and Steve Naito—scions of real estate baron and Galleria developer Bill Naito—were inspired to make ice cream after visiting the famous Steve's Ice Cream near Boston. They talked their father into retail space and started to make creamy, flavorful ice cream, offering bowls of candy and nuts to mix in. Flavor choices include a favorite, simple Cream, allegedly created by accident when someone forgot to add vanilla to the base. Oreo Cookie is another popular choice. Oversized crisp waffle cones in chocolate or plain sugar—more like cookie cornucopia—are made on the premises; sometimes you can watch the batter being poured onto the small hot presses. (Traditional cones are also available.) Sundaes of all kinds can be assembled, incorporating sauces (butterscotch, berry, or flavored hot fudge), nuts, brownies, sprinkles, candy, and of course, whipped cream.

Rose's

4444 N.E. Fremont Street, phone: 282-4615.
Open Monday through Saturday, 11 a.m.–9 p.m.; Sunday, 12 noon–9 p.m.

Here you'll find an old-fashioned ice cream parlor that has been a neighborhood fixture since 1951. Waffle cookie cones are now offered along with cake and sugar cones, and sundaes come with a variety of toppings. Ancient

Hamilton Beach blenders line up on the back counter, ready to mix milk shakes, sodas, and freezes.

The ice cream made here contains only 14 percent butterfat, a figure lower than most other versions, whether commercial or hand cranked. The creaminess is still intact and at least twenty-four flavors are always available, including such unusual varieties as Licorice, Tutti-Fruity, Butterscotch, Cantaloupe, and Cinnamon. Hand-packed quarts are available in the freezer case and 3-gallon tubs can be filled with your flavor of choice for a big gathering. (Quarts of Rose's ice cream can also be purchased in the frozen food sections of area markets, including Burlingame Grocery, Zupan's, and Sheridan's.)

SDK's

344 S.W. 2nd Avenue, no phone. Open Tuesday and Wednesday, 12 noon–5:30 p.m.; Thursday through Saturday, 12 noon–9 p.m.

This downtown shop is rather austere, a sharp contrast to the frozen custard they make and sell. Frozen custard is similar to ice cream, but it's smoother and creamier, with an elasticity you'd never get in traditional ice cream. Think of a cross between the textures of ice cream and frozen yogurt. Then think of the sweet creaminess of the richest ice cream. The egginess of frozen custard also helps to set it apart.

Only two flavors are made daily—Cascade Cream (vanilla) and Cocoa Cream (chocolate). Multnomah Mint makes an appearance the third Thursday of each month, replacing Cocoa Cream for the day. Cones, cups, and hand packed pints are available, as well as sundaes made with chocolate, marionberry, or raspberry sauces. Hazelnuts are optional.

Owner Steve Keeler answers questions about his old-fashioned products indirectly, pointing you to one of many framed letters and promotional displays. Are the berries fresh? Read the letter from the fresh-frozen berry supplier. Is frozen custard a new product? Read the custard history on the wall. But make sure you read with a cone in your hand.

Zero

See listing on page 15 for location and hours.

More a son of Zefiro than an independent retailer, this quirky shop sells Zefiro's fabulous ice cream, long one of the best desserts in town. The silky smooth sorbets and ice creams are never too sweet, due to dessert queen Michelle Dennis's technique of infusing flavor for a more subtle taste.

Expect a dozen or more changing flavors, from the old-fashioned (Raspberry Sherbet, Vanilla) to the modern (Espresso Chip, Caramel, Mexican Chocolate) to the quintessential 1990s (Lemongrass, Crème Fraîche). The "50-50" is a grown-up creamsicle variation: a swirl of sorbet and ice cream with knock-out flavor combinations such as Ginger ice cream and Peach sorbet or White Chocolate ice cream and Boysenberry sorbet.

You can get a scoop in a cup—add some of the terrific caramel sauce—brownie sundaes, cones, or hand packed pints. Root beer floats are another nostalgic option.

AND KEEP IN MIND. . .

Baskin Robbins

Locations all over town. Hours vary
The best thing about these shops—where the colors of the ice cream can assume day-glo proportions—is the decorated ice cream cakes in a myriad of sizes, a sure hit at kids' birthday parties.

Häagen-Dazs

526 N.W. 23rd Avenue, phone: 225-9488; and
other locations around Portland. Hours vary
Sure, you can buy pints of this boutique ice cream in almost every food store. But Häagen-Dazs retail shops always stock a few flavors not available in your grocer's freezer.

Nature's Fresh Northwest

See listing on page 11 for locations and hours.
Nature's carries more than the standard supermarket selection of ice creams and sorbets, including a good range of low-fat options.

Pastaworks

See listing on page 12 for locations and hours.
Pastaworks is the best source for those lovely Out of a Flower designer ice creams, in seasonal flavors including Lavender Honey, Plum and Armagnac, and Orange Mint.

Tillamook Ice Creamery

12890 N.W. Cornell Road, phone: 641-8013; 37 A Avenue, Lake Oswego,
phone: 636-4933; 11485 S.W. Scholls Ferry Road, Beaverton, phone: 579-4292.
Open Monday through Thursday, 6 a.m.–10 p.m.; Friday and Saturday,
6 a.m.–11p.m.; Sunday, 7 a.m.–10 p.m.

The same folks who make Oregon's ubiquitous Cheddar cheese bring you ice cream that's better than many commercial national brands, but not as rich as Ben & Jerry's or Häagen-Dazs.

MEAT AND POULTRY

E ven in an era when meat consumption is on the decline, meat markets seem to be thriving. Beef may not be consumed in every household every day, but beef, veal, and lamb are still at least special occasion meals in most homes. The National Restaurant Association periodically releases numbers showing that beef is still the number one entrée in U.S. restaurants. At Paley's Place, one of our favorite spots in Portland, the Steak with Garlic Mashed Potatoes out-sells every other entreé when it's offered, and the signature dish at Café des Amis is a Filet with Port Garlic Sauce. The appeal of steaks at The Ringside has never flagged.

The supermarkets of the 1950s, 1960s, and 1970s have been out-flanked by smaller, European-style grocers and purveyors. As a result, boutique butchers are making a comeback. Good quality precut and wrapped meats and birds are available in almost every grocery store. But to get exactly what you need or to find unusual cuts or varieties of meat, a specialty butcher is your best bet. (It needn't be a free-standing meat market, for excellent meat cutters operate out of the several major food stores.) There, you'll find marinated or stuffed entreés ready for the grill or oven, such as spice-rubbed baby back ribs, kabobs of every denomination, boneless stuffed chicken breasts, and herbed boneless roasts.

It used to be that the best-quality meats and poultry went to hotels and restaurants. While those places still command high quality, local meat markets now offer prime meats, organic beef, free-range chickens, and game not commonly found in the chain grocery stores.

Galluzzo's Choice Meats

1200 N.E. Broadway (Holladays Market), phone: 282-0223.
Open Monday through Saturday, 9 a.m.–7 p.m.; Sunday, 10 a.m.–6 p.m.

The head butcher here is eager to please and will order anything you can't find in his case. Ready-to-cook marinated or stuffed meats help to set this small shop—really just a meat counter—apart. Thick boneless pork chops have either a moist bread stuffing or a spiced marinade. Skewers of kabobs, threaded with pork, beef, or chicken, line up next to oven-ready chicken breasts that are stuffed with a variety of fillings, including a tasty combination of roasted garlic, roasted red peppers and four cheeses. Marinated ribs are ready for the grill: the "Maui" style is unusual, not for its teriyaki sauce but rather for the thin slices of beef ribs, more like the Jewish cut of flanken. Game hens—backbones removed and birds flattened—are herb-marinated and ready for grilling. The two-dimensional bird ensures even cooking. Meats from Harris Ranch (which breeds a lean beef) are available both prime and choice, and nationally known high-quality Provini veal makes a regular appearance.

Gartner's Country Meat Market

7450 N.E. Killingsworth Street, phone: 252-7801.
Open Tuesday through Saturday, 9 a.m.–6 p.m.

Out in the vaguely desolate, charmless industrial flats looms an old-fashioned meat market, a huge box filled with hanging sausages and slabs of meat suspended on hooks from the ceiling. Welcome to Gartner's, a friendly, long-established market where the butchers know every customer by name and usually their preferences as well. The meats are somewhat old-fashioned, too. Hams chockablock in the case greet you at the door. Slabs of bacon are snugly aligned: lean, peppered, Canadian. And slices of bacon overlap each other like accordion pleats.

Ground beef blocks line up next to all the usual cuts of beef. Thick slices of beef liver are stacked in a long row, next to the beef shanks. Sausages get center stage: wieners and rings of every style and flavor, including chorizo, bratwurst, smokies, and all-beef red hots and cheese knockwurst. Homemade chipped beef sells well, we're told.

Chitterlings are available frozen, and even dogs and cats are provided for with a selection of offal (beef kidneys) at 25 cents a pound. Posted signs announce that Gartner's will cut up deer, elk, and moose for hunters. In addition, the market can cure, smoke, grind, or store whatever you bring home from the hunting season.

Nature's Fresh Northwest

See listing on page 11 for locations and hours.

Nature's stores boast some of the most amazing meat sections we've encountered. With an orientation consistent with the rest of the operation, they offer mostly poultry-based products, along with a generous selection of red meat, all organically grown and hormone-free. But that's not the amazing part.

What's staggering is the range of ready-to-cook products. The marinated and skewered selection is creative, and the most remarkable sausage assortment imaginable is lined up, two trays deep, across two large display cases. Where to begin the remarkable sausage inventory?! It's hard work to focus on more than a few links at a time. There is Turkey Romano; Thai Chicken; Blue Cheese, Walnut, and Turkey—about twenty-five different poultry varieties in all. The several pork fillings are laced with garlic or a combination of Mediterranean spices, pesto, and olives, and there are a few lamb-based versions as well. Bulk sausage includes four or five basic varieties (chorizo, basil, Italian); and there are smoked links, too.

The butchers are more than happy to tell you exactly what each link contains, and to discuss the merits of, say, the Chicken Chorizo versus the Kung Pao Chicken. While we were waiting our turn, studying the plump sausages lined up on tray after tray, we overheard a spirited discussion with a customer who needed to buy a chicken sausage for an ill friend who couldn't eat any spices. The staff went through an inventory of types and ingredients, but nothing sounded just right. The butcher suggested that the customer call and have a special sausage made for her. That's service.

Nicky USA, Incorporated

233 S.E. 3rd Avenue, phone: 234-4263. Open by arrangement

Home cooks can now buy game birds and meats directly from the distributor, just as restaurants do, albeit with a $50 minimum order. Geoff Latham, the owner of Nicky USA, offers an impressive assortment of familiar and exotic meats. He has no display space all you'll find on a visit is a bleak, cluttered office and a meat locker, both located within the large Organic Grocery Coop warehouse.

If you're armed with the four-page inventory of his exotica, Latham will arrange a delivery date and agree to meet you. This is not like going to the supermarket and eyeballing the goods; you'll have to order in advance, after which Latham will hand you an unlabeled bag or box, just as restaurants receive. Latham supplies most of the hot spots in town, like The Heathman, Higgins, Esparza's and L'Etoile.

Here's the only place in Portland to buy fresh foie gras, direct from major U.S. producer Hudson Valley Foie Gras. The duck liver comes wrapped in its natural twin-lobed state. Each package weighs in at about a pound, enough for six to eight diners, or more if appetizer portions are used. Expensive— about $28 per pound—but there is simply nothing better than fresh foie gras.

Other finds include fresh boneless quail, poussin, whole ducks, duck breasts, and a plethora of wild game. Keep in mind that Latham is not a butcher: he simply distributes these delightful products as prepackaged goods. There's no hand-cutting or trimming to order. When you buy from Latham, expect to trim and prepare the meats and birds with more care than if you had bought them from a butcher. Remember, this is where restaurant chefs purchase their special ingredients.

Otto's Sausage Kitchen

See listing on page 55 for location and hours.

Although Otto's Sausage Kitchen carries fresh meat, this longtime meat market and deli makes sausage the main focus. Ground beef, kabobs, stuffed pork chops, and a few varieties of stuffed chicken breasts share part of one display case. The remaining three cases are devoted to sausage, with varieties that include Danish Medisterpolse, German bratwurst, Swedish potato sausage, and chunky Tex-Mex chorizo. Bacon lines up with ham hocks, pepperoni, and hams—all house-cured. The sausages sport little name tags, listing ingredients and the origin of each type.

For home sausage grinders, both sheep and hog casings are for sale. Game processing is a serious fall enterprise, when hunters bring in bounty for grinding and sausage making. Otto's also smokes fish in their house smoker, which has been on site for seventy years.

Pastaworks

See listing on page 12 for locations and hours.

Is there nothing this Italian grocery doesn't do well? A meat department exists only at the southeast store, since Salumeria di Carlo's (see below) shares space at the westside location. Carlo's sausages are sold here, too, along with traditional Italian meats such as pancetta, cured hams and salamis. Fresh meats include free-range poultry, locally grown rabbit, and certified Angus beef. Wonderful Mediterranean-style stuffed pork roasts and lamb roasts share display space with terrines and pâtés. Luckily for eastside shoppers, the offerings are very similar indeed to the delicious Salumeria products across town.

Phil's Uptown Meat Market

17 N.W. 23rd Place (Uptown Shopping Center), phone: 224-9541.
Open Tuesday through Friday, 10 a.m.–6 p.m.; Saturday, 10 a.m.–5:30 p.m.

This little butcher's shop is squeezed into the Uptown shopping center next to Elephants Delicatessen. Besides its proximity to the treats next door, we like shopping at Phil's because the selection of meats is strong and the prices saner than elsewhere. Veal chops are a dollar or two cheaper per pound; beef tenderloin is similarly lower in price than the competition's.

Phil is a large man who wields a sharp knife. He'll cut and trim anything to order and loves to chat about recipes and preparation, offering his ideas about what sounds good. (He looks like he should know!)

In front of this shop is one of the city's best teriyaki stands. The $3 skewers (beef and chicken) are prepared by Phil and grilled by his team of *bento* guys.

Strohecker's

See listing on page 25 for location and hours.

Almost any department of this longtime Portland Heights grocery could qualify as a distinct food boutique, whether dry goods, cheeses, deli, wines, produce, or meats. In the meat department, nothing is prewrapped and packaged: all goods are attractively displayed in a long glass case. Boneless chicken breasts are only available with skin on, and you have to ask to have a whole breast split into halves.

Strohecker's tries to ease dinner preparation by marinating or stuffing meats to pop in the oven, and selling chicken by the part, not just whole. Rabbit hindquarters are regularly available, and fresh poussin are usually lined up in the case like ducks in a shooting gallery. You can order fresh quail, squab, and duck. Most of the selection is exactly what you'd expect to find in a fine butcher shop: beautiful steaks, nicely marbled and trimmed of fat; thin, pounded veal for scallopini; beef rib roasts, either on the bone or off; and boned-to-order legs of lamb. If you don't see what you want, inquire. The staff is happy to order what you want. Veal chops, roasts, and skirt steaks can be ready with a day's notice. Bacon is sold by the strip and available either pepper-edged or plain. Sausages come from Zenner meats and Fred Carlo, and the case offers a good if not unusual selection.

At holiday time, Strohecker's really shines. Smithfield hams arrive from Virginia, and custom meat cutting and preparation fills the butchers' days:

they do a great job with crown roasts of lamb or pork, dressed turkeys, and perfectly trimmed beef roasts, fresh goose, duck, and pheasant.

From time to time, recipes are taped to the display case. The butchers love to talk about preparation, and long conversations with customers are often punctuated by helpful suggestions from anyone within earshot. When *The Oregonian* printed a story with a recipe for rib roast of beef cooked in a salt crust, every butcher shop in town had a rush on the roasts, but at Strohecker's that article also engendered a running disagreement among butchers and customers about the accuracy of the recipe. For weeks after the story ran, variations on the original recipe appeared on the meat counter.

Talarico's

See listing on page 80 for locations and hours.

While the Talarico family runs meat shops in two fine grocery stores (Burlingame Grocery, see page 83, and The Market Place), these full-service, customer-oriented counters could just as easily survive as free-standing shops.

Competition is strong in the meat world. With perfectly acceptable meats available in all of the bigger grocery chains, small purveyors have to find a niche to lure customers to their smaller shops. Talarico's succeeds because their customer service, high quality, and unusual variety sets them apart from most other vendors.

Choices among the offerings are exciting. If you're tired of the same old thing, try one of the London broil rolls—thin pieces of flank steak rolled around a choice of cheesy, herbed fillings, looking like red-and-white pinwheels. Boneless chicken breasts come stuffed with a variety of fillings. Game hens are split and marinated, perfect for individual servings. A dozen or so sausages (pork or chicken) are made fresh on site, and if you desire a particular combination or seasoning, Talarico's will happily make some to order.

Almost any cut of meat can be ordered or prepared. Gary Talarico loves to talk about how you'll use his meats and what recipes you like. When Lisa ordered a skirt steak, Talarico perked up, excited that someone wanted to use a cut of meat not normally found in local butcher shops (even though skirt steak is what is traditionally used for *fajitas*). That engendered a long discussion about how and why certain cuts of meat are popular in some areas of the country and not in others.

735 N.W. 21st Avenue, phone: 221-3012.

Open Monday through Saturday, 9:30 a.m.–7 p.m.; Sunday, 10 a.m.–6 p.m.

On weekends, the first thing that greets you at this tiny meat market is a whole roasted pig, stuffed with sausage, fully cooked, and ready for slicing. The pig's face is at eye level, and the eye contact is your eerie welcome to Portland's most amazing meat emporium. Beyond the pig are two small display cases, organized to hold a dazzling array of pork, lamb, veal, beef, and poultry.

Viande is unlike any other butcher shop in Portland. Fred Carlo spent a few years living in Europe before returning to Portland to start a custom sausage-making operation. His handcrafted links soon became the hottest dogs in town. The choices are amazing—we once took home one of each for a grilled feast and had a helluva time choosing a favorite. Each tray of goods sports a tag labeling the ingredients.

But Viande is much more than a sausage shop. It is especially strong on heavenly pâtés, including one of silky duck foie gras. The range of options is so large and seductive, you could shop here daily for months and not repeat a selection. The marinades for chicken breasts, pork and lamb tenderloins, pork chops, veal chops, duck breasts, and quail change with the seasons and the moods of the staff. You might find duck breasts in cassis, thyme, and balsamic vinegar; or boneless quail bathed in blood oranges, basil, and honey. Chicken halves are coated in adobo chili and spices, ready for the barbecue, as are spice-rubbed baby back ribs.

Carlo only stocks free-range Rocky chickens; if you wish free-range turkeys for Thanksgiving or Christmas you need to order them at least two weeks ahead. Other poultry includes quail (unstuffed or filled with seasoned polenta or basmati rice) duck, poussin, squab, and an occasional pheasant.

Venison loins are usually available, as are racks (or chops) of local milk-fed veal. Lamb is local, from Ellensberg, Washington. Carlo also routinely stocks both high-end Angus beef and dry aged beef, a supreme indulgence. The emphasis is on the pricier cuts of meat, including rib roasts, strip steaks (or whole loin), porterhouse steaks, and tenderloins. Pork is another specialty.

Carlo plans to move back to Europe in the summer of 1996 and hopes to turn over his business to one of his longtime employees. Customers will probably not notice the new ownership for no changes are anticipated.

Victor's European Meat Market

See listing on page 79 for location and hours.

Old Europe still exists at Victor's European Meat Market in Tigard. The Lunkiewicz family, from Poland, operates the small, tidy shop and specializes in smoked meats and sausages—both hot smoked and cold smoked. They proudly make their products in the different styles of many countries: Lithuania, Poland, Rumania, Hungary, Russia, the Czech Republic, and Germany. You'll find sausages in mild, medium, and hot strengths. Some of the hams are studded with large pieces of garlic, making the roasts look more like mortadella than the traditional smoked hams that are also in the case. Wood, never liquid smoke, is used to flavor the meats. Victor and family will create any type or flavor of sausage requested—just ask. And if you bring in freshly killed game, sausages can be made up to order.

Tasty dishes from the Old Country are available, such as tender pierogi (dumplings) filled with pot cheese, potatoes and cheese, ground beef, or lamb. *Bigos*, the national dish of Poland—a hunter's stew of mixed meats and vegetables—is also offered. The family members will chat endlessly with you, describing the different sausages, giving you tastes, and inviting your comments. Also worth checking out are the varied canned and packaged goods from eastern Europe, such as jars of brightly colored roasted peppers, flavored syrups, and hard candies.

OILS, VINEGARS, AND CONDIMENTS

Chapter 11

F or anyone who has spent time in Mediterranean countries, good olive oil casts a spell; its flavor, texture, and color lending the mind an almost Proustian ability to recapture the hill towns of Tuscany and the plains full of silver-gray olive trees, or the sun-streaked Aegean islands with grilled lamb turning on spits. We keep several very good olive oils for special uses and an inexpensive one for daily cooking, along with toasted sesame oil to impart an Eastern taste, peanut oil for Asian cooking, and walnut oil to scent and flavor certain dishes.

The last minute drizzle of a really fine extra-virgin olive oil can make an enormous difference in the flavor of, say, a risotto, a soup, or a pasta sauce, and will transform a piece of crusty peasant bread into a first-rate appetizer, especially when it's smeared with fresh summer tomato and basil. Portland is full-to-bursting with great olive oils, as well as fine hazelnut and walnut oils, wonderful for splashing on soft goat cheese or cold sliced duck, as well as on tender greens. Our Asian stores carry a variety of sesame oils, some backed with hot chilies, which can be terrific on Chinese salads of raw bok choy and pea pods.

Oils now come from an astonishing range of sources: pistachios, grape seed, and pumpkin seed, to mention only a few. These days, oils are frequently infused with herbs and spices, but *infused* oils are nothing in intensity compared to *concentrated* oils. As many as 400 pieces of fruit might go into a 5-ounce bottle of pure lime oil, and mere drops can add great flavor to grilled fish or broiled chicken. Such intense oils are never used for sautéeing or frying, only for last-minute flavoring.

Vinegars have come into their own of late. They are always distinguished by the wine that contributed to their making: good wines make for good vinegars. Many of the better vinegars are used not just as acidifiers: sherry vinegars are excellent for deglazing pans with a sweet pungency, and some fruit-flavored vinegars are splendid in cream sauces.

Of course the balsamic vinegars are the prizes: they're usually made from Trebbiano grapes reduced and thickened before fermentation in oak or chestnut barrels, where the liquid concentrates to a thick ambrosia. Balsamics tend to be more aged than commonplace vinegars, and their price goes up with their age. The range of fine oils and vinegars available in Portland shops is astonishing, but no more so than the willingness of some customers to pay $35 for a liter of oil and much more for a few ounces of long-aged, sweet, and highly concentrated *balsamico*.

Portland stores are also crowded with sauces and salsas of all kinds. With the advent of hot foods from the world over, we've become addicted to incendiary Indian sauces, Moroccan *harissa*, American Southwest chili pastes, Cajun blackening spices, Jamaican barbecue rubs, and Thai *massaman* paste. A careful scanning of the stores can provide a vivid culinary introduction to both tropical and Mediterranean lands.

Burlingame Grocery

See listing on page 83 for location and hours.

The olive oils take up a goodly amount of shelf space, and some of the best of Italy's production are here. You'll also find oils infused with lemon and orange, good for perking up meats after grilling. The vinegar selection is impressive—be sure to see Mike and Diane's hand-painted bottles. Mazetti balsamic vinegar is a heady $36 for 8 ounces.

Burlingame really shines with its condiments, especially the more incendiary sauces. There's a fiery number called D. L. Jardine's Jail House Caviar, and a marinating sauce from North Carolina with the moniker Bone Sucking Sauce. More than twenty-five barbecue and hot sauces are here, with names like Desert Fire, Stubb's Legendary Moppin' Sauce, and Dave's Insanity Salsa. There are "grownup" catsups, fruit salsas, and something we haven't dared to try called Carolina Pine Tar.

Elephants Delicatessen

See listing on page 8 for location and hours.

Elephants Delicatessen has a number of items from the very worthy Silver Palate line, including its barbecue sauce, numerous chutneys (try the blueberry), and tomato Alfredo pasta sauce. The store's selection of mustards is phenomenal and should satisfy any palate: tarragon, orange-ginger, champagne, and jalapeño are some of the best ones, all from Willamette Valley Mustards. You'll even find a tamarind sauce here, as well as a strong selection of salsas from Saguaro of Tucson.

Standing before the overwhelming selection of olive oils at Pastaworks you might be as confused as a neophyte at a computer store. Help is at hand, however. Behind the deli counter there's a cache of twenty-odd bottles of olive oil, all opened, and if you ask for a tasting of different grades, the store will be happy to oblige you. There's no reason why you shouldn't sample these gorgeous oils just as you might expect to try the cheeses. If there's a lull in business, ask Peter De Garmo, Don Oman, or Liz Wehrli for a minilecture on oils. They've been to the Tuscan estates, know their olive orchards, and love talking about what they've learned.

The Ligurian oils tend to be full, coating the mouth thickly, "golden green, satiny, and sweetly fruity," as Marcella Hazen describes them, while the Tuscan oils have a richer, more buttery taste. Spanish oils are lighter, those from Catalonia more peppery, the French ones (from Provence) nutty, the Greek oils very assertive and with less finesse than the others, and the California oils heavily fruited. One of our favorites is the Umbrian Mancianti label from the hill town of San Feliciano: De Garmo tells of going to that estate and seeing the aged patriarch carefully skimming the best of the oil off the top of the tubs, much the way one might skim cream from a bottle of nonhomogenized milk. This oil has a much-prized peppery aftertaste. It is made like a fine wine, in hand-numbered, vintage-dated bottles, and only 35,000 liters are sold in a year, the olives gathered from 150-year-old trees. Oils like this are never used for cooking, but for brushing on grilled *bruschetta* or meats, or for flavoring soups and sauces.

There are many balsamic vinegars at Pastaworks, in a range of prices. You might think that paying $20 or more for vinegar is sinful, but wait until you see the exquisite little bottles of aged, or "traditional," balsamics kept under lock in the case, looking like fine perfumes and priced in that league: $175 for 3 ounces! These extraordinary vinegars have been aged thirty years in wooden casks; they are not the kind of vinegar to put on iceberg lettuce, or any salad for that matter. Rather, a couple of drops are used to finish a sauce, or on a piece of reggiano cheese for dessert, or even on fresh strawberries. De Garmo once saw a barrel that still held a small pool of *balsamico* dating from the seventeenth century; the maker mixed a few of its precious drops with a more contemporary batch, producing what De Garmo calls "the best single liquid I've ever tasted."

The condiments at Pastaworks are mostly Italian and Spanish, though the store expects to handle Latin American and Southwestern items in greater profusion. The sheer quantity of certain items always astounds us: many brands and styles of anchovies, capers, tapenades, sun-dried tomatoes, and the like. There are garlic pestos galore, and several kinds of saffron. Many of the sauces and olive pastes are fine mixed into the store's pastas.

Strohecker's

See listing on page 25 for location and hours.

Strohecker's carries a good selection of olive oils—many Italian varieties but more from California than the Continent. Its vinegar section is outstanding: an immense selection of *balsamico* from Modena dominates the condiment shelves, and there are such fruit-flavored vinegars as peach and mango. While there are plenty of new brands of salsas, such as Bob-A-Loo's Rompin' Raspberry, the majority of the condiments are familiar to traditional tastes: piccalillis, mustards in great profusion, and lots of marinades and barbecue sauces. Downstairs, near the deli case, you'll find an amazing choice of chutneys. For those who think the genre begins and ends with Major Grey's, you'll be surprised that the venerable colonist has taken a back seat to Carol's, Gloria's, and Neera's and that most of these are the fusion-hyphenated kind: ginger-pineapple, apricot-curry, pear-cardamom.

AND KEEP IN MIND...

India Emporium

See listing on page 60 for location and hours.
Look for a great range of every imaginable jarred condiment from the Subcontinent.

International Food Bazaar

See listing on page 62 for location and hours.
Condiments from all quarters of the globe are here, especially from the Aegean, the Middle East, and India, including one of the city's largest selection of hot pickles, biryani pastes, vindaloos, and curry pastes.

The Food Lover's Companion to Portland

6141 S.W. Macadam Avenue, phone: 246-0650.

Open Monday through Friday, 7:30 a.m.–9 p.m.;

Saturday, 7:30 a.m.–8 p.m.; Sunday, 7:30 a.m.–7 p.m.

735 N.W. 21st Avenue (City Market), phone: 221-3004.

Open Monday through Friday, 9:30 a.m.–8 p.m.;

Saturday, 9:30 a.m.–7 p.m.; Sunday, 10 a.m.–6 p.m.

1409 N.E. Weidler Street (Irvington Market), phone: 288-4236.

Open Monday through Friday, 7 a.m.–9 p.m.;

Saturday, 7 a.m.–8 p.m.; Sunday, 8 a.m.–6 p.m.

3731 S.E. Hawthorne Blvd. (at Pastaworks), phone: 232-1010.

Open Monday through Saturday, 9 a.m.–7 p.m.; Sunday, 10 a.m.–6 p.m.

Kruger's stocks a very wide range of salsas, mustards, rubs, and chutneys. This is a good place to find several varieties of olive paste, which we like to spread on crusty bread for a simple but tangy warmup to an informal meal.

Chapter 12

PASTA

Twenty years ago, if Portlanders ate pasta at home it was inevitably boxed macaroni or spaghetti from a can. Who even used the word "pasta" in those dark days? Now Portlanders dine on Ravioli Filled with Roasted Eggplant and Sun-Dried Tomato, or even with Sweet Potato and Pumpkin. We are all cognoscenti of flat pasta shapes—*tagliatelle, linguine, fettucine,* and we recognize butterfly-shaped *farfalle,* ring-shaped *anellini,* and twisted *fusilli.* We hardly blanch when someone produces a chestnut-flavored pasta. As for sauces, we not only devour *puttanesca,* we know it's the robust and spicy sauce named after prostitutes. Pesto is almost passé; we turn to sauces with wild mushrooms, walnuts, even lamb ragout. We've become semolina-savvy. Of course, some shapes still baffle us: who can identify *gemelli, bumbola,* or *creste de galli?*

Americans have taken to pasta for many reasons: it is relatively inexpensive, easy and quick to prepare, healthy (if fat-laden sauces are kept away), colorful, and extremely tasty; it joins us to a great cuisine and its powerful traditions. We're happy to report that the pasta salad craze—something unknown in Italy—seems to have run its course. What seems new these days is the interest in fine dry pastas, the firm, dense-textured, sometimes hand-made kinds that produce a nutty flavor and crunchy texture; some aficionados and pasta-makers far prefer it to fresh pasta. Many stores in Portland now carry the extraordinary Rustichella d'Abruzzo pasta, sold in a brown bag with a little window allowing you to peer in at the particular shape. But in this section we focus on places where the pasta is made on-site and where you can even glimpse the process.

Antonia's Homemade Pasta

12580 S.W. Broadway, Beaverton, phone: 644-5941. Open Monday through Friday, 10 a.m.–5 p.m.; Saturday, 10 a.m.–3 p.m. Also available from May through October at Beaverton Farmers' Market on Saturday (see page 144).

All the packages of pasta sold in this shop bear the picture of Antonia, mother of pasta-maker Theresa Sirianni and her culinary muse, who brought recipes for homemade noodles to this country from her village outside Rome. Theresa Sirianni duplicates those recipes and turns out a variety of excellent pastas, all dried, for she believes that "fresh-dried" pasta has a firmness the overly chewy fresh kind cannot match.

She does a dark mushroom fettucini, a very spicy Cajun pasta, and other shapes in lemon thyme, peppercorn, and plain egg, but she's proudest of her garlic-parsley spaghetti. One of the nice features of her lasagna noodles is that you needn't boil them before layering them in the dish: they cook properly from their dry mode.

Justa Pasta

1336 N.W. 19th Avenue, phone: 229-0646.
Open Tuesday through Saturday, 2 p.m.–7 p.m.; Sunday, 12 noon–5 p.m.

Dave Mamuska and Roland Carfagno established such a reputation for pasta that Atwater's, Pazzo's, and Ron Paul imported the stuff all the way from Justa Pasta's Hood River kitchen. Now Justa Pasta operates out of a tiny shop in the northwest part of Portland. The freezing compartment under the front counter contains some of the best ravioli around. It's quick-frozen immediately after being made, thus keeping better while sacrificing none of the flavor.

The pasta is made from top-grade 100 percent semolina, farm-fresh eggs, and superior ingredients for fillings. The shop has some ribbon pasta for sale, but the greatest part of the business is ravioli. A blackboard lists nearly twenty fillings, including a spectacular lamb, spinach, and feta combination. We love their very sharp walnut-and-garlic filling, as well as the wild mushroom and brie filling—dark, nutty, and redolent of autumn woods. You'll even find fillings of sweet potato and pumpkin, and black bean, cilantro, and jalapeño. Justa Pasta does carry a few sauces, but they'd prefer you make your own simple sauce (say butter and olive oil with fresh herbs) than sell you marinara and have you risk masking the delicate flavors of their ravioli.

Pasta à la Carte

2309 N.W. Kearney Street, phone: 222-4879.
Open Tuesday through Saturday, 10 a.m.–7 p.m.

Molly Dolan, the proprietor of this shop in Northwest Portland, helped begin this town's fresh pasta renaissance fifteen years ago. The cases are filled with pretty baskets of *fusilli* in flavors of tomato, basil, and spinach. Her raviolis are first-rate; they change almost daily, and she stocks only one or two since she likes to keep them very fresh. Stuffings of porcini and green onion, lamb and fig, and lox and mustard greens are all excellent. Like other local purveyors, Dolan encourages simple sauces that complement rather than dominate the ravioli fillings: "What's the point of using a delicate center of fresh spinach and herbs only to overpower it with a heavy cream sauce?"

Wicker and twig baskets hang above the counter; a few exquisite bottles of olive oil, including *agrumato* extra-virgin pressed with lemons, appear on the shelves; and a number of glazed terra-cotta pasta bowls, plates, and pitchers are scattered about. The shiny black glazes are perfect for showing off any color of pasta and its sauce, from fiery tomato reds to deep lemon golds to celadon greens.

Pasta Pazzo

229 N. Main Street, Gresham, phone: 667-5617. Open Monday,
8:30 a.m.–5 p.m.; Tuesday through Saturday, 8:30 a.m.–5:30 p.m.

David Dedrickson, resident pasta-maker, has figured out a way to "laminate" two distinct flavors on one sheet of rolled dough and is turning out several wonderful combinations of noodles at this Gresham store. There's a cilantro-*chipotle* fettucine, as well as a basil-chestnut style, the latter smoky and sweet at once. Still in the experimental stage is a squid ink and egg combo, which Dedrickson hopes to hand-mold into ravioli wrapped around smoked salmon. His ravioli are handcut and are often filled with a sublimely smooth ricotta. He does a version with a spicy-tomato envelop and another with sun-dried tomato. He suggests that instead of immersing them in boiling water you sauté them for a couple of minutes on each side in a thin film of good olive oil. The result: Slightly crunchy skins playing against a creamy interior.

The homemade sauces are fine, too, and include a fat-free Neapolitan and an artichoke-studded Raphael sauce. If you can't trek out to Gresham, you can purchase these at Zupan's, Strohecker's, and Wizer's.

Pastaworks

See listing on page 12 for location and hours.

In 1983, Peter de Garmo and Don Oman produced the first fresh pasta in the city, after de Garmo saw it done in Boston's North End Italian district and thought it looked pretty inviting. The two men purchased a pasta sheet-rolling machine and another for extruding dough, and the Portland Pasta Revolution was underway.

There's hardly a grocery in town where Pastaworks' products cannot be found. The quality has never flagged—if cooked properly, their pasta has a good chewy texture and just the right amount of spring and bite. You get intensity with Pastaworks' flavored varieties, such as sun-dried tomato, garlic and parsley, and spinach. During the holidays there's a chocolate pasta, and occasionally you'll discover a stunning chestnut pasta— terrific with pesto. On Friday, gnocchi make an appearance.

The cutting machine by the counter slices sheets into a range of ribbons. At the Hawthorne store, in the area just behind the display case, the extruders pop out the little shells and tubes, while separate machines turn out the filled raviolis and tortellinis. In all, ten tons of pasta leave the Hawthorne store each month.

The reach-in case contains a range of sauces, in all some fifteen classic Italian kinds. Besides pesto, *puttanesca*, and marinara, you'll find *romesco*, a Catalan red pepper and tomato sauce with pulverized nuts that isn't really intended for pasta but tastes spectacularly good when blended into a seafood stew. The store's interest in things Catalan also shows up in a pasta known as *fideus*, a short, thin noodle imported to Barcelona by the Moors; you don't put *fideus* in boiling water like an Italian pasta, but rather in a hot sauce, which it sops up and absorbs.

You may think we're joking, but Pastaworks has the perfect gift for your gourmand pet: dog food pasta! Now you can please your pup with Fido's *Fideus* or Rover's *Radiatore*. Both varieties—totally fit for human consumption, by the way—consist of pieces of the pasta ribbon normally discarded. As of this writing there's no canine sauce.

AND KEEP IN MIND...

Burlingame Grocery

See listing on page 83 for location and hours.
This is one of the best places in Portland to buy dried pasta, with a dozen imported brands to choose from. Be sure to try the Rustichella d'Abruzzo and Martelli brands.

Elephants Delicatessen

See listing on page 8 for location and hours.
You'll find a superb selection of fresh pastas and homemade sauces, some Elephants' own, some from Pastaworks.

Martinotti's

See listing on page 26 for location and hours.
Colorful packages of dried pasta from Italy scattered throughout the store make for a worthwhile treasure hunt.

Chapter 13

PASTRIES AND DESSERTS

*T*here was a time, not that long ago, when a discussion of baked goods centered around layer cakes with fluffy frostings, bear claw pastries, local fruit-filled pies, circular coffee cakes veined with jam, and humble cookies, thick with oatmeal and raisins or studded with chocolate chips. Mighty good, but nothing fancy. If you wanted a glistening fresh fruit tart that shimmered like a jeweler's case, or perhaps an elegant mousse cake, rich with cream and butter, the home kitchen was the only option.

But in the last few years, the sophistication of Portland's sweet-toothed shoppers has been gaining momentum, so that the most dazzling and picture-book creations are now available. They're delicate, creative, and, in an odd sense, honest. Shortening is no longer de rigeur: butter is the choice. Real vanilla, fresh fruit, local nuts, and designer chocolate flavor the most sought-after pastries.

Whether you seek a kid's birthday cake, elegant dinner party fare, special holiday favorites, picnic sweets, a morning wake-up treat, or just sinful indulgence, there are pastry emporia galore, and as the expectations of Portland dessert fanciers increase and the level of sophistication climbs higher than a Dobos torte, enterprising and creative bakers arrive on the scene to satisfy these passionate cravings.

Though nobody is going to confuse Portland with Paris or Vienna, a large number of establishments offer one or more spectacular items. And if a shop has something great to offer, we've included it here. We also identify the home-based dessert wizards who bake to order.

Beaverton Bakery

12375 S.W. Broadway, Beaverton, phone: 646-7136.
Open Monday through Saturday, 6 a.m.–6 p.m.

Once the only place in the Portland area to consider for special-occasion cakes, fancy rolls, and breads, this reliable bakery still creates the favorite treats many remember from long-ago childhoods. The coffee cakes and crumb cakes are good, and the Parker House rolls, cheese sticks, and puffy Fugasa bread with Cheddar and onions still appear on many dinner tables.

Large picture books show off fancy cake decorations and wedding cake designs. The repertoire is a bit old-fashioned and homey. Although the cookies look more fragile than they taste, everything in the long display cases is likely to have been the same forty years ago, but there is something to be said for consistency, and this trip down memory lane can be fun.

Helen Bernhard Bakery

1717 N.E. Broadway, phone: 287-1251.
Open Monday through Saturday, 6 a.m.–6 p.m.; Sunday, 8 a.m.–3 p.m.

Like the Beaverton Bakery, Helen Bernhard's is an old family friend to many Portlanders, having provided cookies, tarts, rolls, and birthday cakes for generations. Even the setting is quaintly old-fashioned: a small red brick and white cottage along Northeast Broadway, left to stand among the commercial development—very approachable and friendly.

Generally, the baked goods are a little on the sweet side. Cookies are a good bet and can be purchased loose, by the pound, or already weighed and bagged. The nut crisps are a favorite. Filled and decorated layer cakes are close to the kind Mom used to make—nothing too fancy, but familiar and good with gooey shortening frostings. The bakery will happily make sheet cakes and special-occasion decorations.

JaCiva's Chocolates & Pastries

See listing on page 29 for location and hours.

Of the basic types of European pastries, the rich but delicate French treatment of dough and fillings is most to our taste. JaCiva's pastry loyalties lean toward Mittel-Europa. Most of the baked goods at this shop are on the heavy side, Viennese-style. The cakes and pastries look beautiful, with their careful decorations and flourishes. The chocolate frostings are thick; the glazes dense. Even the pastry creams and mousses have a weightiness to them.

Of all the cakes, the Grand Marnier Mousse Cake is one of the most eye-catching and flavorful. A dome of pretty, decorated hard chocolate surrounds a thin shell of chocolate cake; beneath is lots of Grand Marnier chocolate mousse. Flavors are good and strong, a chocoholic's delight. The chocolate flowerpots deserve a medal for creativity. What look to be ordinary terracotta pots filled with fake flowers turn out to be entirely edible. From the chocolate "dirt" to the molded, sugary flowers, the presentation is witty and well executed.

Joseph's Dessert Company

3436 S.E. Milwaukie Boulevard, phone: 231-0989. Open by appointment

Joseph Vasquez's first Portland area stint at creating spectacular cakes was the dearly departed Custom Chocolates. Luckily for local confectionery buffs, he has been on his own for the last few years, whipping up baked goods for area restaurants, specialty retail shops, and individual sweets shoppers who know how to find him.

His current operation does not have a retail storefront. He loves to bake for the public, though, and happily accepts phone orders. His basic line of cakes includes fruit tarts, layer cakes, several varieties of cheesecake, and luscious fruit mousse cakes. About four times a year he adds and subtracts from his repertoire, taking advantage of seasonal fruits.

Vasquez also does a brisk business in wedding cakes. He favors the traditional white, tiered type but also likes to create custom designs with nontraditional flavors and fresh flowers for decoration.

Marsee Baking

See listing on page 10 for locations and hours.

It's easy to understand why Marsee Baking has been jammed ever since its first shop opened three years ago. Marsee has it all: quality, variety, and creativity. As a result, a first encounter can result in visual overload. Display cases are jam-packed with tasty treats. Besides the changing roster of top-notch breads, Marsee's pastry is remarkable. There is a grand array of morning goods, including muffins, croissants in a range of flavors, great sticky buns, and filled Danish. Fabulous cookies are a strong point: the chocolate crinkles, Italian almond, and chocolate chip each has a loyal following for good reason.

The homier choices are great everyday treats, but don't overlook the elegant desserts, for Marsee's European-style sweets have no real competition in Portland. Opera tortes, mousse cakes, Napoleons, and double-decker cream puffs known as *religieuse* regularly glitter in the display case. Head baker Joann Vazquez knows her trade, having worked with the best in the business in the San Francisco Bay area: Jim Dodge (when he was winning accolades at The Stanford Court Hotel) and Grace Baking. Her real claim to fame is a stint in Italy as Carole Field's assistant. (Field is *the* name in Italian baked goods and has published the definitive books on the subject.)

Papa Haydn

5829 S. E. Milwaukie Avenue, phone: 232-9440. 701 N.W. 23rd Avenue, phone: 228-7317. Open Tuesday through Thursday, 11:30 a.m.–11 p.m.; Friday and Saturday, 11:30 a.m.–12 midnight; Sunday, 10 a.m.–3 p.m.

If you ask Portlanders who has the most spectacular desserts, most would respond, "Papa Haydn." Long known for their array of tortes, tarts, cookies, and ice cream bombes, these two sister establishments draw big crowds for their flavorful lunches and dinners, but their desserts are the most popular magnets.

The outstanding Autumn Meringue—a classic Parisian cake made famous by Gaston Lenôtre, a dean of French baking—is composed of alternating layers of crisp meringue and soft chocolate cream. The Boccone Dolce, an Italian towering mass of meringue, whipped cream, and seasonal berries, tends to get smashed down into a creamy, crunchy mess when your fork dives in. And the Marjolaine—an oblong affair of meringue layers and buttercream—is one of the standbys. Seasonal fruit tarts and ice creams are also available.

Pastaworks

See listing on page 12 for locations and hours.

That Portland's premier outpost of all things Italian should turn out terrific baked goods is no surprise. Only a small display case at each store is devoted to desserts, but the baking team changes the offerings frequently, sometimes to take advantage of the seasonal bounty, or to prepare typical Italian holiday fare. Whatever is available is top-notch.

The strength of these desserts is in the great flavors, which are not overly sweet. Jars of crunchy biscotti sit side by side with jars of oversized cookies—the kind to nibble slowly and savor. Other, more delicate cookies lurk in the case. Fruit turnovers are a summer mainstay, filled with the ripest flavor of the moment. Cassata cake—a loaf of many thin layers of pound cake filled with ricotta and candied fruit cream and frosted in chocolate—is rich and flavorful and surprisingly light. Cups of custard and fruit or chocolate mousses are lined up next to individual plastic boxes containing squares of creamy-rich *tiramisu*, the classic indulgent layering of mascarpone, lady fingers, liqueur, and espresso.

If you're lucky, you'll find freshly made cannoli shells on display, filled only by request so the creamy ricotta cheese filling doesn't sit too long in the ultra crisp and fragile shells and render them a soggy mess. These delicious logs of crunch and cream—a classic Sicilian confection—should be consumed immediately, just the way they are served and eaten in many Italian neighborhoods. The staff will sell you empty shells and a container of ricotta cream for home filling, if you ask.

The selection of sweets here may not be as vast and grand as other spots around town, but the integrity and quality of the products are remarkable. If you're planning an Italian dinner and need a ready-made dessert to impress your guests, Pastaworks is your source. Their offerings are a nice contrast to the sweeter and more French-influenced pastries available elsewhere.

Ron Paul Charcuterie

See listing on page 16 for locations and hours.

Even though knife-and-fork meals bring in the crowds, the baked goods at Ron Paul Charcuterie have a very loyal following. When Ron Paul first opened, the baked goods were the highlight of his shop, and they still draw crowds on their own.

The attractive displays make selection difficult—your eyes wander from item to item—but it's wise to hone in on the dessert selection. Fruit tarts twinkle, cups of mousses and creams are seductively lined up in a row, and oversized cookies are arranged on platters along the top of the cases, luring weak-willed souls like sirens calling to chocolate-starved mariners.

Ron Paul's signature Black Angus cookies are legendary in Portland. These huge, dark, evil rounds of chewy, bitter chocolate are like rich brownies on hormones. Your teeth sink into the cookie, occasionally hitting a piece of nutmeat. Good stuff. Also worth noting are the unusual rugulach. These long, rolled horn cookies—cream cheese dough filled with nuts, raisins, cinnamon and sugar—are more than twice the size of traditional versions, and twice as good.

Three Lions' Bakery

See listing on page 14 for locations and hours.

Three Lions' was one of the first upscale bakeries in the area, providing delicate, refined baked goods to grateful people who were hungry for them. The company has grown over the last few years and now operates a wholesale business with three retail outlets.

Credible morning and lunchtime meals, and sweet snack items can be eaten at any location, but the baked goods—including morning rolls, cakes, and eclairs—are also available to go. The tender croissants and buttery brioches are winners, and the cookie selection is particularly good, with small rounds of intense flavors like cappuccino. Roger once ordered a box of fresh madeleines to accompany a class he was teaching on Proust's *Swann's Way* and Three Lions' proved up to the task.

Topia, Ltd.

Mailing address: 25-6 N.W. 23rd Place, No. 269, Portland, OR 97210; phone: 230-1986. Open by appointment

The city's most elegant cakes come neither from a restaurant kitchen nor a storefront retail establishment. At Topia, Ltd., Polly Schoonmaker creates magnificent-looking desserts that are as delicious as they are visually stunning. She is a perfectionist with an obsession for details, and she fills orders for large and small occasions alike. If your plans demand a gorgeous, knock-'em-dead finale to a meal, or a stand-alone dessert, Schoonmaker and Topia will deliver, both figuratively and literally.

Her cakes show an attention to detail—a pretty box tied with a ribbon, a fresh flower placed just so. Schoonmaker enjoys matching a wedding cake to a wedding dress, replete with Swiss dots and lacy trim or a spectacular painted surface. Her frosting finishes are mirror smooth, with just the right detail to set the Topia cakes off from any other. Prices are what you'd expect for custom-made, exquisite cakes, but when only the best will do, Topia, Ltd. is what you want.

Zero

See listing on page 15 for location and hours.

We were delighted when Zefiro restaurant opened a retail shop. Two doors down from the restaurant's entrance, in what previously was the office annex, a pistachio-green shoebox has been transformed into a charming shop. A fantastic, dreamy wall mural that evokes images of old maps with quirky sea monsters sets off the glass cases that display a number of Zefiro's most popular items, including some of the best bread around.

But the real focus of this operation are the silky smooth ice creams and outstanding baked goods created by pastry chef Michelle Dennis. Dennis's stellar baked goods are creative and don't suffer from over-sweetening. Cakes and tortes (whole or by the slice) are available year-round, and interesting creations such as a cornmeal crostada (tart) with fruit and rich chocolate cakes appear now and then. In the winter, when ice cream sales are slower, more baked goods line the shelves.

Zero isn't a place for hanging out or for settling in with your ice cream or bakery item, but that doesn't stop the small space from filling up with folks who want to enjoy that great Zefiro flavor.

AND KEEP IN MIND...

Little Wing Cafe

529 N.W. 13th Avenue, phone: 228-3101.
Open Monday through Friday, 7 a.m.–6 p.m.; Saturday, 10 a.m.–4 p.m.

At one time only a wholesale operation called the Little Italian Cookie Company, supplying its chewy-crunchy quaresimali squares (a marvelous cross between a biscotti and cookie) and delicate butter cookies around town, Little Wing Café now offers a number of bakery items.

Mother Dear's Tasty Pastries

438 N.E. Killingsworth Avenue, phone: 287-7655.
Open Monday through Friday, 6 a.m.–6 p.m.; Saturday, 9 a.m.–6 p.m.

You'll find a small selection of humble cobblers, pastries, and cakes strong on sweet warmth and homey goodness. In particular, the deep-dish peach and apple cobblers are delicious.

The Food Lover's Companion to Portland

PRODUCE

I t's no secret that Oregon offers an extraordinary abundance of great produce. The combination of moderate, moist winters and warm, late summers promises a gardener's dream of fruits and vegetables both exotic and familiar. We're the lucky recipients of wonderful wild greens, some of the best berries on the planet, luscious pears capable of being made into world-class pear brandy, and earthy, woodsy mushrooms. From the too-short appearance of June strawberries to the later multitude of peaches, corn, tomatoes, cucumbers, and pumpkins, the Portland area boasts wonderful and accessible produce.

In recent years, scores of small farms have sprung up in the region, dedicated to harvesting the outstanding boysenberries, chanterelles, and arugula of our land. Whether from a farmers' market, a U-pick farm, a roadside stand, or a greengrocer, the plump, juicy peaches, nectarines, plums, and berries generate many of our summer pleasures.

Fruit shows up in marrionberry cobblers, blackberry-Pinot Noir sauce for local lamb, and wild raspberry salsas, chutneys, and vinaigrettes. Cooks turn the sweet cultivated blueberries into syrups, butters, and of course, great pies. Other home chefs preserve raspberries and blackcaps, or make them into cobblers and tarts. Together with Washington, we grow 90 percent of the nation's raspberries. We have succulent wild berries as well as cultivated ones. We are blessed with two valleys—the Hood and the Willamette—that produce a remarkable range of apples. Good cooks eagerly await the appearance of the Walla Walla sweet onion, so mild you can eat it raw without tears or fear of bad breath. The Anjou pears of the Hood River area and the Comice of the Rogue River Valley help make our state the third largest producer of this luscious fruit, which couples so well with Oregon hazelnuts, Oregon blue cheese, and Oregon Pinot Noirs. And let's not forget the local strawberries— heralds of summer and of berries still to come.

We are also mushroom country. Eager hunters stalk the moist forests at the base of Mt. Hood, searching out chanterelles, porcini, and morels, while Oregon's Asian farmers prize their shiitake and matsutakes. We are also growers of humble and rare greens. The wild salad has come of age, and no respectable market can get away with less than a dozen or more leafy greens, from mustard to arugula to anise hyssop.

At the local markets, you'll see snowy cauliflower, achingly violet Japanese eggplants, deep emerald spinach, pale jade fennel, and rows of bell peppers in a spectrum of black, purple, red, orange, yellow, and green. Ruby blood oranges often show up, darkly sinister next to red bananas. These days, every greengrocer is a Picasso of produce. And it's not unusual to find Meyer lemons cheek by jowl with tropical beauties like tomatillos, mangoes, and papayas.

But with all the enthusiasm for local, seasonal produce, it's easy to forget that we are able to bring in fresh, properly harvested goods from everywhere, and with great speed, stretching the seasonal possibilities: it's fine to enjoy the array of soft fruits our late spring and summer bring, but it's no crime to get good strawberries at other times as well.

What's new in Portland—or perhaps a throwback to older days—is the produce market as an autonomous unit, not just part of a larger store. Many produce merchants carefully select from independent growers or small co-ops, or do their own buying from wholesalers, rather than relying on the

THE MELON DRILL: *A Greengrocer at the Wholesale Produce Markets*

It's early morning at the largest produce wholesaler in town, where boxes of fruit are piled on pallets up to the thirty-five-foot ceiling. Though it's already 90 degrees outside, here the temperature is so low you understand why Dante set the lowest level of hell on a frozen lake. **Don Kruger**, owner of **Kruger's Specialty Produce**, the foremost produce stores in Portland, and his assistant buyer, **Patti Hill**, erstwhile chef at Bread and Ink Café, are launched on the melon drill. Kruger cuts open cantaloupe after cantaloupe, searching for an acceptable piece of fruit. Nothing satisfies him. "Garbage, it's all garbage," he scowls. Hill agrees, and they open yet another case, cutting crescent moons out of several melons. The slips (the place where the fruit was attached to the vine) indicate that this lot was harvested too soon. "The flavor's not bad, but they'll never ripen. This batch will go to the cheapo fruit stands." Then another disappointment: "Bad cants are all over the place, like a plague. These taste sweet enough, but in two days they'll just be mush. Junk, junk." One final attempt: "Not a bad taste, but there's no 'finish'. Cantaloupes should be like good wine, with the taste coming after you. This is just dead." Kruger decides his stores will go without cantaloupes for today.

Kruger is the only retail greengrocer who visits the distributor every day and insists on tasting each item he contemplates buying. "I can tell a lot from appearance, but you have to eat to be sure." Apricots, cherries, plums, peaches, berries, papayas–Kruger's got a method that works for all produce: pick the best-looking fruit in the box and if it's inadequate, move on; if it's good, then pick the worst-looking piece; if it's tolerable, buy the lot and go home with a smile.

mega-companies to supply them. As a result, our greengrocers have more control over what they sell, and we all benefit. Supermarkets may have gotten more interesting (Fred Meyers carries tomatillos and fresh shiitake), but the difference in quality between the produce of those stores and that of the small produce people is still considerable.

The easy availability of farm-fresh produce in the greater Portland area makes living here an extra delight. U-pick farms offer an opportunity to snare the freshest produce possible right off the vine. Farmers grow many varieties of fruits and vegetables, including unusual ones rarely seen at even the most specialized of greengrocers. Expect to find (and pluck) such treats as tart Montmorency cherries and unusual species of peaches, corn, and berries.

Each spring, The Tri-County Farm Fresh Guide Association publishes a guide to U-pick farms that is distributed with *The Oregonian*. You can also

---

Meanwhile, Hill is off on a treasure hunt for vegetables. She's already got the Kruger touch, though she joined the company just over a year ago: "Look at this fennel; it's elongating, trying to break into flower." She opens a box of artichokes, squeezes the globes, and listens for the telltale squeak, a sign of freshness. Withered leaves make no sound. These artichokes are sadly silent, and Hill boxes them up. Then we're on to the corn. We pull back the husks, and gnaw our way through the kernels—raw corn is surprising good, but not good enough for these two.

Then it's off to another distributor, a considerably smaller warehouse where Kruger continues to hunt down some corn without success. Finally he lights on his melons—a batch that's a tad immature, but with sweetness shining through. Hill explains: "The taste is embedded in the fruit despite its greenness; you have to trust that the crisp, cleanly breaking texture will ripen well. If it's there, it will develop—the fruit won't acquire flavor, it has to be latent."

"Only one percent of the food-buying public really knows what is good. My job is to make sure they get it and to educate the rest about great fruits and vegetables," says Kruger. To this end, he exercises his perfectionism, getting outstanding products, whether from Canny or Canberra. Do Northwest chauvinists raise eyebrows at such importations? "Some people are purists," he notes, "they'll only eat what is available locally. I love local, but I'm a global guy. I celebrate the seasons of the world."

find a copy at libraries, AAA offices, and Powell's Books. Twenty-four hours a day, a "Ripe and Ready Hotline" (226-4112) announces the produce that's ready for picking. And the Oregon State University Extension Service can also answer questions about the availability of local produce (254-1500).

Kruger's Specialty Produce

See listing on page 111 for locations and hours.

The arugula is bright and crunchy, the apricots positively creamy, and the vine tomatoes, grown so that each one ripens at exactly the same moment, look and taste perfect. Tables and cases are laid out with an artist's eye: bright yolk-yellow Meyer lemons play off against scarlet hothouse tomatoes; corn-husks are opened to show the kernels, and Batavia lettuce is splayed to reveal the deep-hued, tightly packed core. Welcome to the stores with the most resplendent, flavorful and freshest produce in the city.

Pete Peterson, the majordomo at the Macadam store, spends the day bran-dishing his knife: cutting open a peach to make sure everything is flawless, inspecting the lettuces and clipping frayed ends or blackened tips that mar them, recommending items to customers who have come to value his advice. He knows his customers and what they want—when a couple said they pre-ferred Italian eggplants to any other, he made sure that the store had a supply on hand. Peterson enjoys educating his customers on how to look for the ideal orange-flesh melon, how to choose the perfect cantaloupe. Having just received a shipment of Hawaiian ginger, he breaks off a piece: "Smell that oozing sweetness; no Indonesian ginger can touch it."

Because he is able to purchase directly from the small grower who stops by with their wares, Peterson often tastes the fruit before buying it. It is this care and devotion to market freshness that marks the Kruger's style. Kruger's will stock things that other greengrocers often can't get: *haricots verts*, wild huckle-berries, deep purple Peruvian potatoes, and tender *frisée*. And look for the largest selection of fresh herbs in the city. The arrangements alone are a plea-sure to behold.

Nature's Fresh Northwest

See listing on page 11 for locations and hours.

Here's the region's largest selection of organic and sustainably grown pro-duce, many of the producers of which are committed to stewardship of the land. The displays are picture-perfect and always inviting, and you sense that the produce people fuss a lot over their wares. Prices are not particularly low, but the quality is top-notch. Nature's is generous with its samples of fruit, so you can tell just what you're getting. The greens are crisp, and there's a nice balance between the conventional and the exotic. A number of hard-to-find items show up consistently: Asian pears, fresh figs, endive, kumquats, okra, and sunchokes. Especially at the newer stores—Division Street and in Vancouver—the abundance is impressive: in season you're likely to find a half-dozen or more varieties of tomatoes. Nature's sells Evert-Fresh produce-storage bags, which dramatically prolong the freshness of your vegetables.

Sheridan Fruit Company

See listing on page 20 for location and hours.

This store was founded in 1917 as a fruit stand, and produce has always been its mainstay. One guarantee of quality stems from the fact that the Sheridan Fruit Company operates a wholesale produce business as well, and so has control over what comes into the store. Sheridan uses many small, local growers, some of them specializing in organic crops.

While everything looks fresh and attractive, the displays are functional and straightforward—this is not a museum of produce, and aesthetics takes a back seat to solid, no-nonsense presentations. Above almost every basket of vegetables is a card listing that item's nutritional value and brief instructions for cooking; so, for okra, "Fry in bread crumbs for a tasty appetizer," or for escarole, "Braise with meats." One of the chefs in town most committed to fresh fruits and vegetables, Indigine's Millie Howe, has been buying her produce here for twenty years, so something must be right. Since the lamented demise of Sheridan's great rival, Corno's, it's the best bet in the part of town known as Produce Row.

Strohecker's

See listing on page 25 for location and hours.

Here's predictably fine fresh produce, from the locally grown organic oak leaf lettuce to the imported French white asparagus at an unconscionable $14.95 a pound. Strohecker's carries items not always available around the city, like fresh figs, tiny delicate French beans, and baby bok choy. All the potatoes—and there's quite a range—are shown in wicker baskets, giving the lowly

B erries are part of the Oregon myth. Every summer, our farm stands and markets become overloaded with boxes of blue, red, purple, and black berries. Those of us who live amongst this bounty take for granted the remarkable range and abundance of berries. Food lovers in other parts of the country only dream about such indulgence.

If you are blasé about berries, consider the many types available here in the summer months. Oregon strawberries, indeed, are unlike the plump and pretty California variety: ours are a bit smaller and deep red through and through— no white core. Once you've eaten an Oregon berry, no other will do. (Unfortunately, most varieties of Oregon strawberry appear only in mid-June and are very weather-dependent.)

After June, the berry business gets serious. You need a map to navigate the produce markets and a field guide to all the different varieties available. Many berries look remarkably alike, and yet taste very different. Below we list the most commonly found blackberries and raspberries—sometimes called caneberries because that's how they grow. Don't overlook the wild berries when they're available. Huckleberries are grown in the higher altitudes and resemble smaller, dense blueberries, but are shinier and darker, with a very tart taste. Currants—both black and red varieties—have a short season in this area and are hard to find. Farmers' markets are a good source for these delicate berries—you'll likely find them in clusters still attached to twiglike stems. Gooseberries look like pale green, miniature grapes and have a tart/sweet flavor that is best when turned into jam or a light fool dessert.

RASPERRIES

RED: There are at least a dozen June varieties and three or four fall-bearing ones. Flavor: sweet-tart. Season: late June through July and again in the fall.
BLACK: Also called blackcaps. Smaller than the red variety with a slightly drier texture, blue/black in color. Flavor: sweet-tart. Season: first few weeks of July.
GOLD: Hard to find; newly developed by Washington State University. Flavor: sweettart. Season: fall.

BLACKBERRIES

LOGANBERRY: Red raspberry-blackberry cross; deep red in color, elongated shape. Flavor: very tart. Season: mid-June to early July.
BOYSENBERRY: Blackberry-raspberry cross; red purple color, large size. Flavor: sweet- tart. Season: mid-July through August.

EVERGREEN BLACKBERRY: Glossy black, round shape. Flavor: sweet. Season: early August to mid-September.

MARIONBERRY: Chehalem-olallie-blackberry cross, developed in Marion County; Purple to glossy black color, elongated shape. Flavor: sweet, with a traditional blackberry flavor. Season: mid-July to mid-August.

TAYBERRY: Raspberry-loganberry cross originally developed in Scotland by the Tay River; purple color. Flavor: like a loganberry but sweeter. Season: early July.

OLALLIE: Youngberry–black loganberry cross; shiny black. Flavor: tangy sweet. Season: July.

OTHER VARIETIES: Shawnee and Cherokee are shiny black with a sweet flavor; Kotata is black, seedless, and sweet.

With this abundance of fruit, much of which is shipped out of state, Oregon claims a number of large commercial operators creating jams, jellies, and syrups on a large scale. But a growing number of smaller fruit "craftspeople" are emerging. There are roughly 300 independent preserve and jam makers in the state. One of the best is **Sharene Justin** of **Brookside Farms** near the Oregon coast, who makes dozens of her fruit spreads available at the Beaverton Farmer's Market and by mail-order. Besides the usual marionberry (her most popular), blueberry, and raspberry varieties, she buys odd berries from Bauman's Farm in Jervis as well as from growers in the Willamette Valley to turn into such unusual jams as tayberry, Aurora berry (a marionberry-loganberry cross), and brandywine (a hybrid of red and black raspberries). She'll hunt down tiny wild thimbleberries from the coast as well as golden-orange salmonberries. We think her best spread is the luscious wild huckleberry, smooth and fruity. Because Brookside products contain so much fruit relative to sugar, gaining a very intense and naturally sweet flavor, Justin cannot use the term "jam" (which the USDA says must contain at least 65 percent sugar): instead she calls her products "spreads." She cooks in small, controlled batches, making only four pints at a time, so she's constantly at the stove to produce her annual yield of 10,000 jars. The results capture Oregon summer for the rest of the year. She also does impressive berry syrups. To order, write Brookside Farms, 33815 Salmon River Highway, Grand Ronde, Oregon 97347, or call 879-5404.

tuber an aristocratic air. Strohecker's discerning customers know what they want, so the turnover is frequent and the dewy-fresh local produce arrives soon after picking. Special orders are always possible if you want something rare, but Strohecker's prides itself on being correctly in season rather than making possible the unseasonable.

At one end of the produce case you'll find the largest pick of dried mushrooms in the city: packets of boletus, portobellos, lobster mushrooms, yellowfoot, hedgehog mushrooms, chanterelles, cèpes, black trumpets, and matsutakes—a treasure of fungi when the season's over and nothing but hothouse buttons remain on the shelves.

Talarico's

See listing on page 80 for locations and hours.

Talarico's two produce concessions, in Burlingame Grocery and in The Market Place, are superb. The purple, orange, red, yellow—and occasionally black and white—bell peppers glisten seductively; the fruit appears as perfect as that in a Dutch still life; the wild mushrooms always feel fresh and spongy. Gary Talarico makes sure any item showing the slightest sign of aging is instantly removed from the shelves. We especially admire the berries, which are never cheap here but are bursting with luscious flavor and juice. The holiday offerings are timely: look for persimmons starting a bit before Thanksgiving and great cherries for Fourth of July pies. We've never been disappointed at either of Talarico's outlets.

Zupan's

See listing on page 93 for location and hours.

Among the large stores, Zupan's has one of the best selections of produce. We don't know any other place that carries both *kiwano* (a horned, yellow, African fruit which, when cut open, reveals glossy sections of pale green seeded flesh with the flavor of lime and cucumber) and *cherimaya* (a fruit from Peru and Ecuador called "sherbet fruit" because of its texture and a flavor like a combination of pineapple, papaya, and banana). Another unusual item regularly stocked by Zupan's is broccoli rabe, a bitter green with tiny yellow buds that's wonderful sautéed with olive oil and garlic, then showered with Parmesan. Everything looks terrific at Zupan's. Some of the produce is organic, from the farms outside Portland; some is trucked in from Eastern Washington; some flown in from Holland.

Impressive depth characterizes the produce here: eight varieties of chilies, ten kinds of apples, nine different wild mushrooms. All are carefully stacked in bins, baskets, and boxes, row after row producing one of the nicest displays in town. If you need more information than the helpful clerks can offer, you may peruse a produce-buyer's guide that will give you instant, encyclopedic knowledge about arugula or marionberries, chayote or ugli fruit.

Urban Bounty Farm

Mailing address: 3206 N.E. 14th Avenue, Portland, OR 97212; phone: 249-0357.

Down a long gravel road cut through a forested glade in the Johnson Creek basin in southeast Portland, the foliage breaks temporarily to reveal a meadow with an acre of crops, looking as serene as a garden in the Provençal countryside. This is Urban Bounty Farm, part of the Community Supported Agriculture movement since 1993 and the only such farm right in Portland. Beth Rasgorshek and Marc Boucher-Colbert, owners and principal farmers, work the soil, pulling up crops for the weekly delivery to several urban pickup locations, where members will take home anywhere between 5 to 30 pounds of vegetables at a time, depending on the season. For $400, you purchase a subscription membership, guaranteeing a minimum of 200 pounds of produce over a twenty-five-week span. Urban Bounty grows more than forty crops; most members sign up just for the summer program, but there's a separate one for winter's cabbages, cauliflowers, potatoes and squash. You never know exactly what you'll have on a given week, but surprise is part of the fun.

All the crops are organically grown, and everything is as low-tech as can be: on a warm day the crops are washed in an improvised pool, covered with wet burlap, and boxed in a grove of sheltering trees

Raindance Garden

6212 S. Sconce Road, Hubbard, phone: 651-3501.

This is another produce-by-subscription operation, a much larger one originating on a gorgeous country farm, though most of the subscribers are Portland residents. Charlotte and Chuck Kangas cultivate thirty-seven acres, and, like other Community Supported Agriculture farmers, use no herbicides, pesticides, or chemical fertilizers. They pick their crops at the peak of freshness, and deliver a set amount to a pickup point in each quadrant of the city, where their numerous and happy customers gather their share.

S it down with mycologist Lars Norgren in his Produce Row warehouse, where the packing crates burst with black trumpets, hedgehogs, and matsutake and the sorting tables are crowded with porcini, and he'll give you the history of French mushroom growing, delivered with a scholar's knowledge and a morel-lover's passion. On the morning of our conversation with him, he'd been out gathering a handful of chanterelles for his breakfast omelette. An inveterate forager, he recently picked mushrooms in the forests of Russia. He began his career a decade ago, when he bagged 30 pounds of golden chanterelles in one afternoon and sold them to restaurants eager to introduce Oregon's forest resources.

On this day, Norgren hopes to move almost a ton of chanterelles through his warehouse. He doesn't employ regular pickers, but those freelance foragers who know the forests, especially around the Tillamook Burn and in the fog zone just off coastal beaches, find their way to him. While we are talking, a Laotian couple arrives with several unsolicited crates of Lobster mushrooms, a brilliant orange fungus that gladdens Norgren's heart and will show up the next day at Peak Forest Fruit's stand in the Portland Farmer's Market. Almost 75 percent of the mushroom pickers in the region are Asian, mostly Cambodian and Khmer refugees. Though there are rumors of turf battles in the woods, Norgren says that the forests are basically free of territorial disputes, the greatest violence being the pulling of massive portobellos from stubborn soil.

It comes as a surprise to learn that Oregon occasionally imports wild mushrooms from as far away as Africa. But when local weather conditions are not so

AND KEEP IN MIND...

Food Front

See listing on page 19 for location and hours.

Not all the produce here is organic, but most of it is, and you can be assured of freshness and good taste. Food Front handles a wide range of green things, including an impressive choice of herbs.

good, Norgren is likely to buy international varieties from several sources, including Mitsubishi of Japan, the largest mushroom company in the world. Still, Northwest fungi tend to be the tastiest, particularly when conditions are right, which they mostly are given the damp, mild climate. Peak Forest Fruit is the major conduit for Oregon mushrooms, sending some 85 percent of its produce to the best restaurants and stores in town.

As head of Oregon's largest wild mushroom distributorship, Norgren comes by his calling honestly, for his forebears worked in the woods: his grandfather wrote books on the Swedish timber industry; his father followed a career in soil science; and his mother studied forestry. If ever someone were destined to have his livelihood depend on the forest and the richness teased out of its soil, that person is Norgren.

The mushroom revolution in Oregon occurred a few years ago when, thanks to local Japanese growers, shiitake and oyster mushrooms began appearing alongside the conventional cultivated varieties. Then came chanterelles, with their elegant mild taste, rich coloring and funnel shape. Next we grew to love porcini (also known as cèpes or boletus), both the firm fresh kind and the even more pungent dried kind, best used in soups and sauces and as flavoring. Now the omnipresent and meaty portobello is lending its bosky flavor to chicken dishes and serving as the anchor to vegetarian wild mushroom stews.

Norgren's mushrooms are everywhere these days, and he's delighted to have helped make Portlanders wild for the wild.

Sauvie Island Market

17100 N.W. Sauvie Island Road, phone: 621-3489.

Open June through October, daily, 9 a.m.–7 p.m.

This is an enormous produce stand—a shed, really—with the freshest berries, greens, corn, tomatoes, root vegetables, and what have you, plucked right from the vines and the good earth of Sauvie Island.

Chapter 15
TAKE-OUT AND DELICATESSENS

The Portland delicatessen tends to be a place that combines various take-out foods with a version of what the French call *charcuterie* (mostly cooked and cured meats) and what the Italians call *salumeria* (hams, salamis, sausages, pâtés, smoked meats and the like). In this city, the deli focus has shifted from a preserve of smoked fish or cured meats (the New York style) to a shop giving equal billing to sandwiches, grilled and roasted vegetables, marinated chicken, kabobs, quiches, casseroles, even Vietnamese springrolls. Jars of pickled tomatoes may appear on the countertop, but more often you'll find goat cheese marinating in herb-infused extra-virgin olive oil. The Portland delicatessen is upscale and international rather than an ethnic enclave, with a central focus on sandwiches.

Most shops in Portland that offer deli-type fare also do a heavy trade in quick-fix meals. You'll as often find ready-to-heat dinner options as quick-stop lunches or New York-style sandwiches. Merchants are eager to ease meal preparation for busy people, so you can purchase lasagnas, roasted meats, casseroles, and component parts for almost any type of dinner.

Don't hesitate to sample anything you're inclined to buy. Some things look better than they taste; your palate is a better guide than a clerk's adjectives. If you're buying turkey meat, see if it comes from a real turkey, not from a turkey roll (artificial meat to us). Don't hesitate to invent your own personalized sandwiches: say Brie, Westphalian ham, and sliced Bermuda onion on dark bread. And you shouldn't limit your horizon to delis and take-out emporia: many ethnic markets are great sandwich sources. In Vietnamese markets look for French baguettes with roast pork or chicken showered with cilantro, shredded carrots, and hot green chilies, and in Greek markets, search out spectacular sandwiches of *gyro* (spit-roasted lamb or beef).

Campbell's Bar-B-Q

8701 S.E. Powell Boulevard, phone: 777-9795.
Open Tuesday through Saturday, 11 a.m.–10 p.m.

When one of our friend's sons entertained a visiting French teenager and the family wanted to show him real American food, Campbell's was their destination. This 1950s-style roadhouse offers the hottest hot sauce in town to douse over the wonderfully smoky ribs, links, and chicken (medium, mild, or smoky brown sugar varieties are available for the lily-livered). Side orders can disappoint, but the sweet potato pie is everything it should be and more: richly caramelized and ambrosial. Everything here is also for take-out.

Chef's Underground

2574 N.W. Thurman Street, phone: 242-0550.
Open Monday through Saturday, 10 a.m.–6 p.m.

A restored Victorian is home to both this lower-level take-out shop and the restaurant upstairs, Waterzoies. At the small deli, four or five sandwiches are always available, including a solid jerked chicken variety. Salad selection is pretty standard, with choices such as Caesar, potato, and mixed greens. But the real plus is the ability to order meals to go directly from the Waterzoies menu. Any of the menu items can be prepared for take-out, including the Mushroom Chicken Pie, Salmon Salad Melt, Garlic Chicken, Grilled Portobello Mushrooms, or Orange Pecan Snapper among the options. (The Waterzoies selections aren't available on Monday, as the restaurant is closed.)

Cheshire Cat

See listing on page 21 for location and hours.

Cheshire Cat stocks the usual deli meats available in Portland: Molinari salamis, roast beef, hams, turkey breast, and so on. Though the beef is listless, the pastrami is decent, peppery, and very lean. (You *must* get it heated.) The young lady behind the counter asked us, in an *Annie Hall* moment, if we wanted mayonnaise, lettuce, and tomato on it! Have it on dark rye, with a film of creamy horseradish or mustard, and get a side of Paula's Potato Salad. Another suggestion: black bread, a slab of country pâté, and a smear of Dijon, with a few cornichons from the counter jar and you'll have the momentary illusion you're in Paris, though Cheshire Cat for some reason doesn't serve sandwiches on baguettes. The salads here are also a good supplement to a simple supper.

Chuck Hinton's Rib Express

3328 N.E. Killingsworth Street, phone: 288-3836. Open Wednesday through Thursday,
11:30 a.m.–9:30 p.m.; Friday and Saturday, 11:30 a.m.–11 p.m., Sunday, 1 p.m.–7 p.m.

On the sidewalk outside, the thirty-five-gallon drum's hickory smoke draws neighborhood people from blocks away. Inside, a dark funky counter's single purpose is to dispense "Q" of heart-warming authenticity. No tables here—take-out is the only option. The hot sauce is just right: slightly tangy, not blistering strong, and with just a hint of sweetness. The sampler is a good way to test the range, as it includes one pork rib, one beef rib, one link, and one wing. The barbecue ranch beans are mighty good, as is the potato salad.

Czaba's Bar-B-Q

5907 N. Lombard Street, phone: 240-0615. Open Monday through Thursday,
11 a.m.–9 p.m.; Friday, 11 a.m.–10 p.m.; Saturday, 12 noon–10 p.m.

Michael Brown's nickname reflects his great head, round as a casaba melon: his classmates kindly dubbed him "Czaba." His barbecue shop—an improvement over the kettledrum he formerly parked near the University of Portland campus—looks more like a 1940s luncheonette, complete with booths and a funky counter. Takeout from here is a delight, because the ribs are as good as they come: meaty tender pork fueled by a wicked, tangy apricot-based sauce. Dirty rice, rarely seen in town, is a Czaba's staple. And the cabbage salad, crunchy with almonds and with a touch of tartness, is unusually good. Take out any of these down-home treats, and don't forget the dynamite Buffalo wings.

Elephants Delicatessen

See listing on page 8 for location and hours.

Elephants is the premier delicatessen in Portland, a busy palace of culinary hedonism. The deli does a thriving business for those not just too tired to cook, but those who want extraordinarily good take-out. The *charcuterie* is splendid, from "gypsy salami" made with crushed red pepper to fresh herbed pork to a good selection of summer sausages. Especially because of their terrific breads, wide choice of cooked meats, and selection of condiments, Elephants will make up great sandwiches, enhanced with their excellent spreads.

Vegetarians will find one of the better meatless sandwiches in town, made on delicious olive bread and combining ricotta and feta cheese, roasted eggplant, fresh spinach, and sun-dried tomato.

Regular dinner options include the popular chicken verde enchiladas, cold sliced beef or pork tenderloin, roasted vegetables, and wild rice. Dinners for two can be packaged from the changing roster of weekly menu items (prices around $25), and creative dishes like Moroccan Chicken, Coq au Vin, Panzanella, Braised Cabbage Rolls, or Tomatoes Provençal can be purchased by the pound. Popular summer features at Elephants are their prepared picnic baskets: three combinations are available, from $23 to $35 (each for two people), and the basket is yours to keep. A great idea for Chamber Music Northwest concerts. Gift baskets are also available—you can customize your selection or go with their idea for a wedding basket, candy basket, or "Taste of the Northwest" basket crammed with hazelnuts, smoked salmon, berry jellies, and local chocolates.

At holiday time, Elephants offers complete dinners, from roasted bird, stuffing, and mashed potatoes to pumpkin or pecan pie.

Kitchen Venus

1932 N.E. Broadway, phone: 288-FEED (288-3333). Open Monday through Friday, 10:30 a.m.–9 p.m.; Saturday, 10 a.m.–9 p.m.; Sunday, 10 a.m.–6 p.m.

Formerly only a take-out stop, this homey, kitchey space—crammed with old-fashioned signage, refrigerator magnets, and furniture straight out of "Leave It to Beaver"—has expanded into a sit-down dining spot. But prepared food to go is still the mainstay for many who come for goods Granny would be proud of. Enticing platters of meatloaf, roasted chicken breasts, sausage lasagna, layered baked polenta, and teriyaki drumsticks are crammed into an old fashioned display case. Vegetarian tamales, stuffed calzone, quiches, salads, garlic mashed potatoes, and chicken enchiladas fill out the selection. Sandwiches are both comforting and interesting, including meatloaf, chicken and pesto on focaccia, tuna Niçoise, and smoked turkey. Tall layer cakes, cup cakes and Rice Crispie treats are swell sweets to take home. Kitchen Venus food looks and tastes like homemade: nothing is too fancy or elegant, but everything is tasty and reliable.

Nature's Fresh Northwest

See listing on page 11 for locations and hours.

Creativity sparkles at these health-conscious groceries. The take-out selection runs the gamut from Chicken Verde Enchiladas (the must-have entrée for take-out), Squash Enchiladas, Szechuan Noodle Salad, Turkey Meatloaf, and a trio of lasagnas all the way to Barbecued Tofu. The choices change frequently and keep getting better. Burniece Rott—the former award-winning chef at Nature's defunct Santé restaurant—is now in charge of prepared foods and her ability to meld interesting ingredients has impressed us.

Otto's Sausage Kitchen and Meat Market

See listing on page 55 for location and hours.

A fixture in the neighborhood since 1929, Otto's makes its own bologna, roast beef, peppered ham, bacon, ham hocks, and fresh sausages, and cures some sausages as well. The hams are dry-cured, not water-injected, resulting in a denser texture and cleaner taste.

The sandwiches can be excellent. You may design your own from a variety of good meats or dive into their combinations. The Mad Otto is a luscious monster of pepper ham, turkey, and sausage with feta, provolone, cream cheese, and pepperoncini; the only defect is that it's served on a soft, cold, and tasteless roll. Ask for it on a baguette or dark rye. Otto's is a fine place to use for picnic headquarters: in addition to a range of sausages, they have a huge selection of mustards, a very good macaroni salad, and smoky baked beans. At the entrance, you'll see a display of wicker baskets just right for hauling your loot.

Pastaworks

See listing on page 12 for locations and hours.

We come here often to supplement the output of our kitchens. Pastaworks' chefs consistently turn out interesting, high quality foods. Sandwiches are ready-made on focaccia slices or house rolls, with such fillings as tomatoes, fresh mozzarella, and basil; Black Forest ham and gruyere; or roasted vegetables. Their salads usually sport an Italian influence: Bread Chunks with White Beans, Roasted Vegetables, or Orzo and Vegetables. Savory roast chicken quarters give off an herby perfume. And the *spanikopita*—more typically found in Greek markets—are the best version we've encountered, large crisp phyllo triangles stuffed with feta, onions, and spinach. They are fabulous.

In the cold case you can find the fixings for an easy pasta supper: loads of packaged fresh pasta including three or four inventive raviolis, and a super selection of sauces such as peanut, *puttanesca,* spicy sausage, *romesco,* pesto, and Alfredo.

Look in the freezer case for delicious tamales from Café Paul, Oregon's best regional Mexican restaurant. Even the hors d'oeuvre selection is wonderful. The great range of olives, cured meats, and cheeses, as well as the dips and spreads in the case, let us entertain without worry. It seems as if Pastaworks gets a shelf of its own in Lisa's refrigerator.

Ron Paul Charcuterie

See listing on page 16 for locations and hours.

Once largely a charcuterie of smoked meats and fish, Ron Paul now offers a number of well-prepared main dishes and salads to go. The attractive display cases show off very pretty food, including a smooth smoked salmon mousse, salads galore (Tuscan White Bean, Szechuan Noodle, Niçoise Potato, Curried Chicken), quiche, Southwestern Casserole with Feta, Grilled Vegetables and Salsa Verde, and a great Mushroom Strudel. Sandwiches include a fresh ahi tuna burger, shrimp salad sandwich, and a classic, hot open faced turkey. And the baked goods, especially the cookies, are stellar. During the Thanksgiving and Christmas seasons, whole meals, fancy or simple, can be ordered for the family table.

Strohecker's

See listing on page 25 for location and hours.

There's no question but that Strohecker's deli section is one of the best around, right up there with Elephants Delicatessen. The quality is exemplary, and the prices, while hardly cheap, are not exorbitant for what you get. A summer selection might feature an elegant, pale-pink, Chilled Fresh Tomato Soup with Light Cream and Basil. Accompanied by a Shrimp and Lobster Mousse, it is worthy of the hereafter. Other wonderful choices include a rough-cut venison pâté, and a glorious galantine (stuffed poultry that's poached and chilled) of duck liver, duck meat, and pistachios. There are French hams, a silky Black Forest ham, and liverwurst spiked with pistachio nut meat. The selection of Italian meats is outstanding, and excellent sandwiches can be made to order.

A platter of grilled and marinated vegetables resembles a scattering of Persian jewels, and the wild rice salad is memorable. Only one thing looked better than it tasted: ravioli bathed in an orange roasted pepper sauce simply wanted for flavor. But this lapse was more than compensated for by the salads, from Chunky Chicken to Greek Pasta and French Potato. Mom-style meatloaf is sold by the slice. Pretty seasonal tarts such as tomato and Goat cheese can be purchased whole or by the slice. Poached salmon is a staple, and ethnic flavors appear now and then, with glass noodle dishes, stir-fries, sushi, springrolls, enchiladas, and fajitas frequently on the menu. The rotisseried chicken is a perennial draw: it's superb.

Talarico's

See listing on page 80 for locations and hours.

There are more items in the deli case of Talarico's newest store than at the Burlingame Grocery outlet. Many of the takeout items are similar, but requests for low-fat or fat-free goods have been so great that The Market Place store makes its salads with olive oil or mustard instead of mayonnaise. The kitchen turns out a good Smoked Salmon Fettucine, a satisfying Honey-Mustard Potato Salad, and an unusual Prime Rib Pasta. In the summer you'll find attractive arrangements of cold roasted and marinated vegetables.

The meatball sandwich is delicious: a generous number of meatballs are crammed into a baguette and doused in tomato sauce. The Italian meat selection is strong, and features *finocchiona*, the marvelous fennel-infused salami that is popping up everywhere these days. Among the specialty sandwiches, one combines prosciutto, turkey, mozzarella, and pesto on a baguette. They'll also make up any combination of meats and cheeses.

Woodstock Wine and Deli

4030 S.E. Woodstock Boulevard, phone: 777-2208.
Open Monday through Saturday, 10 a.m.-7 p.m.

This is the favorite deli of the Reed College community, no humble claim. Reedies have opened such important Portland restaurants as Genoa, Indigine,

L'Auberge, and Jo Bar, have written acclaimed cookbooks, and have started the first coffee-roasting store in Portland. Both of us are Reedies. Rest assured that the patronage of the Woodstock Deli by hollow-eyed scholars is nothing short of a reliable recommendation.

The deli's central visual feature consists of several walls of wine, with tasting tables running down the aisles and wine cases piled everywhere. You can drink anything with a deli meal for no corkage fee, and you'll find one of the largest beer selections in the city.

Excellent soups, chili, and salads are made on-site and change daily. The tabouli is first rate, as is the cold Indian Cauliflower and Potato Curry. Several entrées stand out: Veggie Lasagna and flavorful Black Bean Polenta. The standard lineup of Italian meats is always available, as is a selection of pâtés. The sandwich combinations are decent, especially the moist turkey. There's a nice selection of cheeses as well, including Canby's excellent Tall Talk goat cheeses.

Zupan's

See listing on page 93 for location and hours.

The deli section is literally center stage at Zupan's, a large, open rectangular counter filled to the brim with good things. The excellent Boar's Head brand meats are lean, without any artificial colors or flavors, and include a sweet maple honey-glazed ham, a smoky Black Forest ham, and very lean pastrami. The cheese counter is full enough so that you can supplement your sandwich with lots of choices.

You'll always find several hot take-outs, including a chicken from the rotisserie, barbecued chicken wings, and old-timey macaroni and cheese. In the summer, casseroles give way to the usual pasta salads, as well as *torta rusticana*—brioche pastry surrounding layers of salamis and cheeses. About a third of the deli products are made on-site, including a chunky black bean salsa and an artichoke-jalapeño dip. Beneath hanging balls of provolone the counter displays jars of stuffed cherry peppers and trays of fire-engine-red roasted bell peppers. There's even a selection of beefsteak and mushroom, or cottage pies, which do well on St. Patrick's Day.

AND KEEP IN MIND...

Downtown Deli and Greek Cusina

404 S.W. Washington Street, phone: 224-2288. Open Sunday through Thursday,
7 a.m.–11 p.m.; Friday and Saturday, 7 a.m.–1 a.m.

Gyros are the big draw here, made of lamb, beef, or chicken and stuffed into pita bread. Other Greek specialties like *spanikopita* and fried calamari can be had to go.

Edelweiss

See listing on page 54 for location and hours.

Look for a good selection of premade salads, deli meats, sandwiches, and ready-to-eat sausages.

Fetzer's

See listing on page 55 for location and hours.

Hot, cooked sausage links, sliced meats, and cheeses are supplemented by made-to-order sandwiches.

Foti's Greek Deli

See listing on page 56 for location and hours.

Great gyros are the highlight of the comprehensive Greek menu at this grocery-cum-takeout store.

Mad Greek Deli

See listing on page 57 for location and hours.

Here are American-style sandwiches and great Greek desserts, all available to go.

Martinotti's

See listing on page 26 for location and hours.

The deli case is stocked with cheeses, meats, and spreads for tasty sandwiches to eat here or take out.

The Food Lover's Companion to Portland

Part 2

FARMERS' MARKETS
AND FOOD FAIRS

Chapter 16

FARMERS' MARKETS

In the past few years the farmers' market movement in the Portland area has taken off like rocket lettuce under a July sun. By "farmers' markets," we mean open-air markets operational only in the late spring, summer, and early fall. Most of the markets have both organic and nonorganic produce, and everything is spanking fresh: growers often pick that very morning. Cutting out the middleman not only keeps prices low, but hastens the peach to your plate.

Vendors are chosen by the markets' managers, and most come from farm areas just outside the city, so they can get their produce there quickly. Many of the vendors are recent converts to the land, refugees from urban turmoil; you don't see many third-generation Italian farmers continuing family traditions. You'll find usual and unusual fruits and vegetables, but also hand-crafted breads, homemade pies, goat cheeses, jams and relishes, plants, herbs, and flowers. The draw is obvious: besides the great produce and products, prices are very reasonable, the mood is festive, and you get free samples and lots of spirited and informed conversation from the vendors. You're likely to get a discourse on the difference between a marionberry and a blackberry, or a lesson in how to cook portobello mushrooms. And a farmer will cut open that tomato to show you the very meaning of sweetness.

Beaverton Farmers' Market

S.W. Fifth and Hall Boulevard, Beaverton, phone: 643-5345 .
Open early June through October, Saturday, 8 a.m.–1:30 p.m.;
mid-June through September, Wednesday, 3 p.m.–7 p.m.

By a few minutes past opening, everything at the Beaverton Farmers' Market is jumping to the sounds of a senior citizen country-western group. With nearly one hundred vendors, this is the largest farmers' market on the West Coast, much like a European town market but with a crucial difference: you are invited to taste virtually everything. All morning long, you'll receive samples of hazelnuts, goat cheese, organic cucumbers, jams, and peaches. You'll get straight talk from **Tall Talk Dairy** Farm about its *chèvre*, or from **Jim Mickelson** about his tayberries (a cross between raspberries and loganberries and named for the River Tay in Scotland). One fellow we've dubbed "the **Professor of Cherries**" will hand you in sequence a young, yellow tart cherry, a plum-colored one full of juicy fruit, then a wrinkled, slightly dried one that looks over the hill but whose taste is the most intense of all; all of this followed by a lecture on the relation of appearance to flavor in the cherry family.

The growers come from everywhere in Oregon and southwestern Washington, and all products are grown, produced, or collected in the region. Most of the vendors are regulars, but some twenty-odd booths rotate among sellers of a single crop with a short season.

There are tiny stands, like that of the **Hasuikes,** who modestly tout their wild blackberries. And there are large stands, like that of **Gathering Together Farm,** which grows organic produce, including peppery arugula and *tat soi,* a Chinese vegetable like bok choy, only better. You never know exactly what a grower may show on a given Saturday, but **West Union Gardens** will probably arrive in July with gooseberries and basil you can scoop up by the handful; they're especially proud of a late fall raspberry, a serendipitous treat for those in September mourning for the end of the berry season. Like a number of the vendors, West Union Gardens has a U-pick farm and a produce stand that sells fresh from the fields; ask the vendors about the possibilities for such midweek restocking.

Dundee Hills Farm features kiwi products, including jam, spreads, vinaigrette, and pancake syrup with a bright, clear flavor. **Meadowcharm Farm** does a chocolate milk that will send you back to childhood bliss, a "farmstead" cheese that's been compared to gouda but is better, and nonhomogenized "creamline" milk.

There's but one stand for meat: **Kelly's Sheep Station**, growers of lamb in McMinnville, which carries frozen shanks, ribs, kebobs, sausage, legs, steaks, racks and chops at very fair prices. **Brookside Farms** has an immense selection of butters and jams, from cranberry to flowering plum to quince-marionberry, and we're looking forward to the honeydew marmalade and the blue elderberry preserves.

If you get hungry, **Fetzer Deli** grills nitrate-free bratwurst and beer sausages, and **Portland Pretzel Company** does a fine twister. On your way out be sure to cruise the street lined with numerous purveyors of good-looking plants and flowers.

Gresham Farmers' Market

Roberts Avenue between 3rd and 5th Streets, Gresham, phone: 727-9828.
Open mid-May through October, Saturday, 8 a.m.–2 p.m.

This is a fairly small affair, with food vendors competing with craftspeople who peddle everything from well-made squirrel feeders to beanbags sewn from tiny American flags. The market seems like a bit of a throw-back to the 1960s: there's a granola vendor and stoneware pottery dealer. When the fresh berries vie for your dollars with baby's old sneakers that have been turned into miniature planters, you wonder if the priorities are straight. It's curious, since Gresham is close to the rich farm country of Hood River and environs. Still, there are a number of produce stands in the several blocks that constitute the market, and they do a lively business. (We're intrigued by an event called the Weird Vegetable Contest.) But for our money, the best stand belongs to **Dot's Specialties**. Dot's bakes a cherry pie topped with a flaky crumb crust and a luscious marionberry pie with sour cream.

Portland Farmers' Market

1200 N.W. Front Avenue (at Albers Mill), phone: 705-2460.
Open May through October, Saturdays, 8 a.m.–1 p.m.

Portland's version has sweet intimacy and charm, and shopping here is a Saturday-morning pleasure. If you're having guests for dinner that night, leave part of your menu unplanned and make your choices *selon le marché*, as the French say. But in France if you so much as pick up a plum the vendor will snarl at you, "*Ne touchez pas!*"; at the Portland Farmers' Market, you'll be begged to sample whether you buy or not. The appeals of the market are dewey-fresh produce, reasonable prices, and very sociable interactions with the thirty-five or so growers.

Among the treats during the spring are the shelled fava beans from the jauntily named **Singing Pig Farm**, and sacks of mesclun liberally sprinkled with edible rose petals, Johnny jump-ups, pansies, and calendulas. The farmer, Steve Rogers, supplies produce to the city's best restaurants from his urban field, where he raises purple peppers, albino beets, ground cherries, frisée, and Sweet Million cherry tomatoes, among scores of other crops. If you are lucky—and flush—you might be able to purchase his Treviso radicchio, a hybrid selling for $40 a pound. But even more mundane items, like marbled yellow-and-orange Old Flame tomatoes, are superb. This may be the best produce at any farmers' market.

THE FRUITS OF MEMORY

Linda and **Larry Addison**, gardeners and foodmakers from Hood River, peruse old cookbooks in search of recipes for their jams and marmalades, which hark back to pioneer days. They raise the fruit and cook themselves the extraordinary condiments and spreads that they jar under the **Rainbow Gardens** label and sell each year at the Portland Farmers' Market.

They began their research with *Maids and Matrons*, a 1921 cookbook given to Linda by her Kansas grandmother, who had ventured west by covered wagon. Linda started with recipes for homemade breads, insistent on replicating them without modification, except for safety standards. A turn-of-the-century volume called *Twentieth Century Cooking and Remedies* was her next source. It had fascinating instructions for condiments tucked away on slips of paper— recipes that were suited to the wild fruits and berries of Oregon—and soon Linda began to make them, using such exotic species as "ground cherries," a tiny wheat-colored fruit that grows in a lanternlike husk. Eventually she created a marmalade combining commercially unavailable cherries and late-harvest peaches. "Older people try some of the marmalade," she says, "and if they tasted it when they were children, you can actually watch the memory happen on their faces."

After two years of experimentation, Linda was ready to market her "savory line" of fruit-based cooking sauces. There's a zesty black cherry sauce with ginger, better than soy sauce and great with white fish and even strong meats like

You'll find several excellent bakers on site, including a company called **Sweet Organic**, which turns out Grand Marnier and almond tarts, and another called **Slices of Life**, which does a sour pecan loaf and another with figs, dates, and apples.

At the far end of the scene, there's a gathering every Saturday at 10 A.M.: Portland's top restaurant chefs give demonstrations, equipped only with two butane burners and a chopping board. This is the only entertainment you'll find—no clown shows, no zither concerts. The focus is strictly on things edible and horticultural.

If your hunger can't be assuaged by nibbling on the samples, **Salvador Molly's** turns out tamales laden with freshly made tomato salsa that are delicious and in tune with the healthy tone of the market.

venison. Her plum sauce has a deeper flavor than sweet-and-sour sauces and delivers a powerful thrust of back heat after you've savored the tartness of the rich fruit—spectacular on cold roast pork or turkey sandwiches.

In an 1890 cookbook, Linda found a recipe for Apple Vanilla Honey (which is not really honey but a jam), reproduced from a yet earlier American treatise of 1739. To make it, she boils sugar and vanilla beans, then marinates local apples in cider, and finally plunges the cold apple-cider mix into the now-caramelized bubbling sugar mass, producing what she calls a spectacular thermal reaction so "explosive" it reduces the apples to a smooth texture. The result is a fragrant, aromatic mix that's sweet, mild, and ambrosially delicate. It looks like golden honey, but is smoother and runny with apple mash, and you can demolish a jar in minutes if you're not careful.

Linda won't even look at any cookbooks written after the Depression, for they emphasize convenience over skill, and she prizes skill, even *inconvenience*. After all, she patiently translates recipes that dictate five inches of hearth flame under a copper kettle or "half an egg shell of cream." "I have to figure out how big her hens were," Linda sighs.

The Rainbow Gardens line is not available in stores, because Linda wants personal contact with her customers. She sells at the Portland Farmers' Market and at regional country food celebrations. But you can mail-order the products direct from her home at 407 June Street, Hood River, Oregon 97031, phone: 800-435-3941

Sauvie Island Market

17100 N.W. Sauvie Island Road, phone: 621-3489.

Open June through October, daily, 9 a.m.–7 p.m.

This popular market does not have vendors who bring their produce into a central arena; much of the produce is raised on the 200 acres adjacent to the market that are either worked by the Grandee family, who own the market, or are leased to other growers. In season, some thirty items are available, starting with strawberries in June; going through raspberries, marionberries, boysenberries, and blackberries in July; corn, beans, and tomatoes in September; and ending with apples, pears, squash, and pumpkins as the market closes down in October. The Grandees sell everything from apples to zucchini, and well over half of that abundance comes from Sauvie Island.

Nothing fancy here—just a large, open shed with a concrete floor. You feel you've come right to the farm. The market is a favorite destination for weekenders on their way back from Sauvie Island's beaches, though many shoppers make the fifteen-minute trip from Portland, especially to buy the berries, which have pride of place. The Grandees normally have different varieties of each berry, thus extending that berry's length of season.

Sauvie Island Market has periodic celebrations, from a strawberry festival in late spring to a pumpkin festival in mid-fall. On weekends, you can buy sausages and grilled hamburgers in the shed, which will keep you fortified while you shop for beans, cucumbers, jars of fruit butters and mustards, raspberry-chili jellies, and bulk walnuts and hazelnuts. In high season, the huge corn bins are refilled at a frightening rate, as tons of ears come rumbling in from the fields. You can even pick flowers for a small fee: gladiolas, lilies, and zinnias are in abundance.

Owned by the same family, **The Berry Basket** is a half-mile down the road toward the bridge. In addition to the name-sake crops, it inevitably has gorgeous peaches, apricots, and cherries.

AND KEEP IN MIND...

People's Farmers' Market

3029 S.E. 21st Avenue, phone: 232-9051.

Open May through October, Wednesday, 2 p.m.–7 p.m.

This is the only completely organic farmer's market in the city. It's confined to a small lot next to the People's Food Store Co-op, and there's a decided neo-hippie atmosphere to the proceedings.

FOOD AND WINE FAIRS

Beyond the suburbs, the area around Portland retains a charming, small-town, bucolic feel. During the summer, it seems as if each little community outside the city sponsors a food festival of some sort, a celebration of bounty and spirit. There are strawberry festivals and crawfish feeds and sausage bashes. Year-round, interesting food and wine fairs have become local institutions. Annually, we learn about apples, party with Greeks, indulge in wine country celebrations, and feast on all things Italian.

We try to avoid the big commercial extravaganzas such as The Bite and ArtQuake: these downtown weekend extravaganzas offer restaurant-run booths selling snacks with mass appeal. Fine food isn't the focus, and we've never found the assortment of spring rolls, elephant ears, or buttered corn to be reason to brave the hordes of people.

Festa Italiana

At various locations in the Portland area including Ponzi Vineyards and Pioneer Courthouse Square downtown Occurs usually during the last week of August

Traditional arts and food dominate this week-long festival. A celebration of the Catholic Mass at St. Philip Neri Church in Southeast Portland inaugurates the events. The artsy stuff that follows is always a kick: a bocce ball tournament and party takes place at Ponzi Vineyards in Beaverton; a celebrity grape-pressing exhibition is foot-stompin' fun, and puppet shows, lectures, and fine operatic concerts continue through the week.

But we especially enjoy the food, of course. Booths are set up in Pioneer Square for the final festival weekend, and almost every Italian restaurant and caterer in town participates. David Machado—the creative chef of Pazzo Ristorante who is half-Italian and half-Portuguese—always whets appetites with his Pioneer Square noontime cooking demonstration.

Gourmet Apple Tasting

Portland Nursery, 5050 S.E. Stark Street, phone: 231-5050.

Occurs usually during the first and second weekends of October

Every fall, this wonderful retail nursery rearranges its botanical kingdom and sets up an apple-tasting extravaganza. For two weekends, small apple growers bring samples of their specialties for tasting and discussion. You can buy many of the varieties from labeled wooden bins or walk around to the back of the property and help yourself to freshly pressed cider.

Spending time here gives you a free education about apples. The nursery provides an informative crib sheet listing every variety of apple present and its characteristics. Under a permanent tent, long tables are arranged in a circle, with plates of apple slices and descriptive labels set out every few inches. We've tasted slices we fell in love with only to discover how rare that variety is in the Pacific Northwest. If you're lucky to become attached to a particular apple and find the orchardist present (or their business card displayed), you might be able to purchase apples directly from the grower. Many Willamette Valley growers will sell a limited number of apples of an unusual variety directly to the public.

We've discovered Empire, Galer, King David, and Arkansas Black apples here, and we've made pilgrimages to the Yamhill Valley to buy apples in a follow-up to apple-tasting day at Portland Nursery.

Greek Festival

Greek Orthodox Holy Trinity Church, 3131 N.E. Glisan Street, phone: 234-0484.

Occurs usually during the first weekend in October

A little retsina or ouzo and the crowd can get wild, but never out of hand. Eating is the primary activity at this annual festival, but drinking and dancing are popular as well. For three days, the parking lot of the Greek Church becomes an outdoor taverna. All of the food is made by the enthusiastic people of the parish. Inside the special tents, sausages, gyros, souvlaki, and beverages are dispensed in good humor and rapid order. At mealtimes, suits and jeans co-mingle, occupying the few seats inside and around the tent. The feeling is chaotic and lively: Greek music blares through the air and everyone has a good time. Lisa's husband was once filmed for the evening news as he was juggling sausages and beer on his way to a table.

Closer to the church building, long tables display irresistible desserts: tray after tray of baklava, sticky honey balls, cookies, squares of delicate pastry, twisted pretzel-like sweets, and numerous other confections not normally available at retail shops. We, like many others, sometimes come just to buy an assorted box to take home.

All food must be purchased with script: vendors sit dispensing chits at strategic spots. No money, neither dollars nor drachmas, can be directly exchanged for something to eat. Inside the church hall, you'll find a more formal meal service. Tickets can be purchased for these lengthy, delicious feasts. When the retsina flows freely, diners get involved in the entertainment.

International Pinot Noir Celebration

P.O. Box 1310, McMinnville, OR 97128, phone: 503-472-8964 or 800-775-4762.
Occurs usually during the first weekend in August

Each summer, more than 500 food and wine aficionados gather at pretty Linfield College in McMinnville for this worldclass event. The focus is the Pinot Noir grape, the varietal best known as French Burgundy, but more and more seen as Oregon's wine strength. Pinot Noir producers—from Oregon, California, New York, France, Austria, Germany, South Africa, Australia, and New Zealand—join wine lovers for three days of wine tasting, seminars, wine spitting contests, Yamhill Valley touring, and of course, *major* eating.

The festival has earned a reputation for fine dining. That's quite a trick to pull off, since the college's kitchen is not as well equipped as most restaurant kitchens. And more than 600 meals need to be served at once. Most years, a nationally known guest chef or two join a handful of area superstars and loads of kitchen volunteers—some who are also well known chefs in their own right—for three days of frenzied food preparation. The results are splendid, with meals both elegant and deliciously complicated.

As this is an obligatory event for serious wine drinkers around the world, the tickets (sold as an expensive package, except for a Sunday public event) go fast: last year, all tickets were gone within six days of release. If you're interested in attending, the first step is to get on the mailing list. Once notification of the summer wine party hits your mailbox, you should call in your credit card number at once. Housing is limited—college dorms or area bed-and-breakfasts—so for area residents day-tripping is the best option. All activities are held on the campus, except for event-sponsored excursions.

Ramble, Tramp and Plod

Witness Tree Vineyard, 7111 Spring Valley Road. N.W., Salem,
phone: 503-585-7874. Occurs on many Sundays between May and October

Under a 200-year-old oak tree, on a hill overlooking a magnificent vista, a picture-perfect spot serves as the site of country picnics sponsored by one of the Salem area's better wineries.

A Portland restaurant—usually Paley's Place, one of our favorites—provides an elegant picnic lunch, and Witness Tree Vineyard supplies the wine. That in itself should lure folks to these Sunday events ($35 per person). But the real fun is going into the cellar with the winemaker and tasting wine from the barrels before the wine is bottled. You get a great education in the art and technique of making wine.

After you've tasted a number of wines, you face a steep hike to the picnic site. The reward is at the top, under the old spreading tree, where tables set with silver await your pleasure. The view is terrific and the lunch makes for a lovely, lingering afternoon.

Part 3

WINE AND BEER

Chapter 18

WINE AND BEER

B etween the Oregon wine industry and microbrewery phenomenon, Portland residents have been treated to homegrown, world-class beverages. In the Yamhill Valley Pinot Noir grapes produce wine that not only competes with the best of the French Burgundies, but in some vintages has surprisingly surpassed them.

The Oregon wine industry is relatively young. A few ambitious pioneers planted grapes in the early 1970s, ignoring snickering and raised eyebrows. When David Lett's Eyrie Pinot Noir beat out French wines at a blind tasting in 1978 in Paris (it emerged the number two pick), the wine world was stunned. Oregon vintners—and their wines—were coming of age.

As in the Côte d'Or in France, Pinot Noir is our premier grape, although Pinot Gris, Chardonnay, Cabernet, and a few other miscellaneous varieties are also grown. The relationship between Burgundy and Oregon was further solidified when Domaine Drouhin, one of the most respected wineries in France, opened a satellite operation in Dundee. Their wines are highly rated and consistently delicious. The area's other wineries—in particular Eyrie, Archery Summit, Rex Hill, Ponzi, Erath, Cameron, Sokol-Blosser, and Beaux Freres—have all earned national, and in some cases international, reputations.

Buying wine in Oregon offers a unique advantage. Of course, you can purchase bottles (and cases) at very good prices from a number of Portland area wine shops, but take the opportunity to go directly to the wineries to taste and buy. The drive through Yamhill County—our wine country—is bucolic and charming, with great picnic sites. Talking directly with winemakers at winery tasting rooms offers a chance to learn how the wine was made and why it tastes as it does. And the informal world of Oregon wine is anything but stuffy and pretentious.

Beer making is a subculture in these parts. The local scene boasts no fewer than a dozen microbreweries, each turning out relatively small numbers of handcrafted beers. Many pubs and restaurants serve on tap at least one brew from the bigger beer boys such as McMenamins and Widmer. Bottles from small brewers, including Portland Brewing, Bridgeport, Full Sail, and Pyramid, line many supermarket shelves.

The influence of these two cottage industries can be seen in almost every retail grocery. But merchants, happily, are not altogether nationalistic: you can easily find the best of Bordeaux, Burgundies, Italian varietals, Chilean wines, and Australian wines, and other international choices and beer offerings around town are equally global. Burlingame Grocery, for example, stocks more than 300 labels.

The Cellar Door

921 S.W. 16th Avenue, phone: 221-7435.
Open Thursday afternoon and by appointment

While The Cellar Door stocks no inventory, it offers customers access to an unusually broad selection of wines at very competitive prices. Clients can sample wines on Thursday afternoon and borrow books here. Co-owner Karen Hinsdale is often asked to sell partial or whole collections of fine wine and offers those unusual bottles to her clients, too, at fair prices. And she holds "dock sales" of wines she brings in from France.

Hinsdale is one of the foremost names in wine sales in the region. In a former life, she sold wine through a major distributorship, Henny-Hinsdale, working directly with California and French vineyards and châteaux. Though she has played several roles in the local wine community during a twenty-year period, she continues to maintain her longtime relationships with distributors and wineries around the world. She has a strong bond with the French Bordeaux producers and ships containers of their estate-bottled wines to Portland for benefit dinners and wine-tasting events.

With Wendy Lane, an advertising and public relations executive, Hinsdale launched The Cellar Door: since Hinsdale was continuing to bring in out-of-state wines and so many people were asking her to locate fine wines for home consumption, Lane and Hinsdale decided to market their connections as a personalized wine-buying service. Two of their aims are to demystify wine and to help people begin wine collecting. They learn the wine tastes of clients, help develop wine preferences, and even consult about building wine cellars.

The Cellar Door's strengths lie in the personalities of its owners. Their detail orientation is evident in the computer database they use to fill out profiles of clients. To watch them in action is a lesson in persistence: Lane and Hinsdale are masters of working the telephone, scouting for availability and price.

Harris Wine Cellar

2300 N.W. Thurman Street, phone: 223-2222.
Open Monday through Saturday, 10 a.m.–6 p.m, Sunday, 11 a.m.–4 p.m.

The name of this dark wine shop is appropriate: the cavelike space is as musty as a basement. Rows of racks hold single bottles, and two back rooms—even darker than the main space—store more cases. This old-fashioned shop opens onto a large restaurant that does such a brisk lunch business that often during midday hours nobody is available to help wine customers.

Sydney Thomas and her husband, Art, now operate the shop opened by Sydney's father in 1961. It stocks wine from around the world but the largest inventory is French: Art's favorite wines are the lush red Bordeaux. The better and higher priced wines aren't necessarily displayed; you need to ask to see the hidden bottles. The Thomases keep old, great bottles a secret for the knowledgeable, who will really appreciate them.

Wine classes have always been a strength of the store. The beginning class covers wines of the world. Specialized classes include "Bordeaux," "France in Your Glass," "Italy" and "Spain," and run serially in eight-week blocks. Partylike, invitational wine tastings are held two or three times a year. On those nights, all inventory is discounted 20 percent. Otherwise, discounts apply only to straight cases (20 percent) or to mixed cases (15 percent).

Great Wine Buys

1515 N.E. Broadway, phone: 287-2897.
Open Monday through Saturday, 10:30 a.m.–6:30 p.m.; Sunday, 12 noon–5 p.m.

Rachel Starr prides herself on finding "really good wines that aren't overpriced" for her storefront wine shop along busy N.E. Broadway. When she

Wine writer **Matt Kramer** bristles when asked why, as a nationally recognized wine columnist and author of four "Making Sense of …" wine books and one cookbook, he lives in Portland, Oregon. "Portland's not provincial. That's snobbery," he says and goes on to assert that talent can live anywhere and that he chooses to be here.

Matt Kramer came to Portland to attend Reed College and, like many Reedies, never left town. After a brief career in public policy, Kramer, who always loved to eat, became obsessed with learning how to cook. An opportunity to write about food (for the brand-new *Willamette Week*) presented itself; he switched careers and has never looked back. His restaurant reviews in the late 1970s were the most avidly read column in *Willamette Week*, and his demanding standards of excellence set the tone for Portland's restaurant explosion. Wine was hardly an interest of his at that time. "I was cowed by wine," he says, "all those connotations of sophistication, with fancy words and foreign names." But while he was on vacation, the newspaper decided to add wine coverage to his beat, so Kramer was unexpectedly plunged into the world of wine.

Gradually, Kramer's wine writing began to eclipse his food and restaurant writing. By 1984, wine defined his professional world, though food never really disappeared from it. "There's a tremendous division between food and wine writers, with some exceptions, of course. It's rare to see the two subjects mixed." But Kramer is successful at both: by 1984 he had moved to *The Oregonian*, penning a weekly food column in the Sunday magazine and a wine column in the main paper.

Though Kramer stopped writing about food soon after, he recently returned to his first love: his cookbook on the cuisine of Piedmont is soon to be published. He chose the Piedmont because the area is Italy's most lush region and its cuisine offers a great complication of flavors, a trove of raw materials. Kramer's interest in ingredients extends to wine. He argues that "there's no alchemy in wine making. All of the ingredients must be 'gold ore.'"

Kramer claims that the nature of cookbook writing is very formulaic and not analytical enough for him. He prefers the philosophical edge of wine writing, so he makes wine his primary focus, although he still loves food and loves to cook. Kramer is very blunt about his weekly column in *The Wine Spectator*.

"These guys don't hire me, Matt Kramer. They want the creature Matt Kramer, the *character*, the voice. This guy's controversial, irreverent. He takes the critic's stance. I don't always know where this character comes from." So one Kramer column rails against restaurants for serving wine in ordinary glasses instead of good crystal like Riedel. Another bemoans the lack of women wine collectors, and the next month almost every letter to the editor is from a female wine collector who was offended. In fact, more letters to the editor respond to Kramer's columns than to any other feature of the magazine.

But when you make the mistake of asking Kramer about living in Portland, you'll feel his own wrath, not that of his persona. You'll also hear an impassioned championing of Portland as a sophisticated wine market. "I'm amazed at what gets sold in Portland! I follow the weekly sales lists from each of the wine distributors, and the wine purchased in Portland is very international, strong on Burgundy and Italy. The sophistication is astounding." He adds that Portland is hardly a provincial market. The range of easily available good wines is boggling. Kramer gives the example of Lemma Distributors, the Portland-based firm that handles the bulk of French Bordeaux and a good number of Italian wines. According to Kramer, Lemma's inventory has resulted in the largest book of wholesale wines in America—200 single-spaced pages.

And what sells best in Portland? Italian wines. Portland is the second largest Italian wine market in the United States, after New York. And we're talking about wines in the $30–$40 range. How come? Kramer claims there are several reasons for this remarkable interest: a good importers/distributors (Lemma and Columbia), a major influential merchant (Pastaworks), his own writing about Italian wines in *The Oregonian*, and the fact that Italian wines taste good in our climate.

Many Oregon vintners are disappointed that Kramer doesn't spend more time writing about the Oregon wine scene—after all, Kramer is a nationally respected wine critic whose books wind up on every "must-have" list of wine books. A common complaint is that he's in a position to bring deserved attention to Oregon and, as an Oregonian, has a responsibility to do so. But does a New York wine writer repeatedly promote or discuss Long Island wines? Does a San Francisco wine author only write about Napa Valley wines? Kramer exhorts: "I write what I want to write. What I think is important."

opened her store in 1983—it is now the oldest independent wine shop in Portland—her focus was wines for under $5. A more reasonable current goal is $10, but prices keep creeping up. As a result, Starr focuses on value over price.

If she has any regional emphasis, it's probably Oregon and the Northwest. She's been warming up to German, Alsatian, and Rhine wines recently, and she's always had a love of Champagnes. Most world regions are represented, but California gets no particular recommendations from her.

Starr teaches introductory wine classes once a month, and John Poston, former sommelier at The Heathman restaurant and at The Plaza in New

APPLE BLOSSOM TIME AT CLEAR LAKE *or Le Trou Portland*

Steve McCarthy, perhaps the finest maker of *eaux-de-vie* in America, is owner of **Clear Creek Distillery** as well as its sales rep, bookkeeper, forklift operator, and bottler. When we go to see him, he's hunched over a beaker of Grappa like an alchemist at his alembic, scrupulously reducing the proof of the brandy from 80.20 down to 80.00. After ten years of attempting to match the great European clear brandies, McCarthy is finally getting close to what he had always envisioned but had barely hoped to achieve.

Clear Creek is a hands-on business and a quintessential Oregon affair. As McCarthy, a lawyer and head of Tri-Met in a previous life, explains, he takes pleasure in a kind of old-fashioned "making," doing something difficult and seeing it come out just right. He is a fanatic about quality, overseeing every aspect of the process, from the initial selection of fruit from his family orchards in the Hood River Valley, to the distillation process, when he "coaxes the flavor out" to achieve "pure mist of pear."

When McCarthy realized that Oregon winemakers were blazing a trail by using unattractive soil for grapes and turning out fine Pinot Noirs, he decided to see whether other Oregon fruits could be put to "higher" uses. After traveling in Normandy and Alsace to study the process of producing *Poire* William and buying the necessary equipment in Europe, he began to try his hand with the same pears in Oregon, called Bartletts. McCarthy's cherished goal was both to make use of the bounty of Oregon farms and to craft fine *eaux-de-vie* that even French masters would acknowledge as the equal of their brandies. Success with both goals means that his distinctive slim bottle with its crystalline brandy is now a familiar sight all over town.

A brandy release is much like a particular vintage year of a wine: when McCarthy makes a new batch, it's almost like creating a whole new product, with

York, teaches classes on specialized regions. Formal tastings take place Friday evenings; more casual sipping is done on Saturday. Daily, different wines are available to purchase by the glass.

One of Starr's unusual marketing efforts is matching wine and food with the dinners she coordinates at such restaurants as Winterborne, Ron Paul, and Merchant of Venice. Occasionally, Starr conducts vineyard trips to learn more about local wines. Her informative monthly newsletter outlines educational programs, best buys, and sales. That's also where you can note the shop's motto: "No Snobbery Allowed."

---

the opportunity to improve, not simply to replicate, what was done before. Last year, he produced only 1,000 cases of pear brandy for nationwide distribution.

Recently, McCarthy released a blue plum brandy, but before it's gone he'll be back, pouring, sifting, distilling, trying to improve it. McCarthy makes a very Italian Grappa from the pomace, or residue, of grapes after their pressing, producing several varieties, each with its distinctive taste, from Muscat, Pinot Noir, Pinot Grigio, and Gewürztraminer grapes acquired from Oregon's best vineyards. And he's developed a splendid raspberry *eau-de-vie* or *framboise*, and a fine *kirsch*, or cherry brandy.

Only a select number of restaurants carry such an elegant product. In Portland, these places tend to have serious owner-chefs, as at Zefiro, Wildwood, or Paley's Place, or chefs who understand the virtue of fine brandy, like Philippe Boulot at The Heathman. We've even seen Clear Creek *eaux-de-vie* on New York menus. Of course, Clear Creek bottles are available in state liquor stores, but not many of them carry the entire line. The best chance of finding a broad representation of McCarthy's skill at the still are at the O.L.C.C. stores at S.W. 10th Avenue and Salmon Street, S.W. 5th Avenue and Washington Street, and the one at Strohecker's.

McCarthy is happy with his new *eau-de-vie de pomme*—it took him a decade of experimenting by mashing Golden Delicious apples and fermenting and storing the result–but even so, he is still tinkering with it the way good scientists are wont to do. This apple brandy rivals the great Normandy Calvados, familiarly known as *le trou Normand* ("the Normandy hole"), since it's famous for burning an opening in your throat between courses, allowing you to continue eating rich Normandy fare. Will McCarthy's new apple *eau-de-vie* be *le trou Portland*?

Liner & Elsen

202 N.W. 21st Avenue, phone: 241-9463.
Open Monday through Saturday, 10 a.m.–6 p.m.; Friday, 10 a.m.–7 p.m.

Matthew Elsen and Bob Liner make wine buying enjoyable. These two partners don't take much seriously—including themselves—except for wine. Humor dominates their shop, evidenced by witty comments, quirky wine signs, and offbeat merchandise. It's the team L & E electric-blue bowling shirts

OUR STEIN RUNNETH OVER

Over the last ten years, Portland has become a beer-making capital. Brew pubs and microbreweries have become the corner soda fountain for this generation. What makes one community rise to beverage stardom? That's easy to answer for wine, since particular varieties of grapes grow only in very particular soil and in the right weather conditions. Oregon is fortunate to have a large and sophisticated wine region because of its propitious weather patterns, soil conditions, and geography. Great wine is made here because of great grapes in a perfect environment and because of the wine pioneers dedicated to producing fine Oregon wines.

But the availability of hops doesn't necessarily brew a beer community, any more than lemon groves create a lemonade empire. It takes an entrepreneurial spirit as well as an interest in handcrafted goods and small-scale productions. Home brewers have always been around, just like amateur winemakers. Portland, it would seem, fosters all the right component parts.

Winemaker Dick Ponzi created **BridgePort**, Portland's first brew pub (see page 167). The **McMenamins** empire soon followed, allowing two brothers to open a slew of neighborhood brew pubs across the city, culminating with their Edgefield Lodge complex: a combination movie theater, bed-and-breakfast, brew pub, and fine restaurant (Black Rabbit). **Widmer** came next with two brewing facilities; draft taps of their many beers appear in a wide range of facilities around town. **Portland Brewing** and **Full Sail Ales** round out the roster of the "major" small brewers in Portland. Many more small microbrewers have appeared on the scene, giving beer fans a real choice of fine handcrafted beers.

As a result, the days of limited selection or big-brand dominance are gone. Every self-respecting pub has at least five microbrews on tap these days. **The Dublin Pub** (6821 S.W. Beaverton-Hillsdale Highway, phone: 297-2889) sports 104 taps of primarily Northwest beers, with additional—more global—selections in bottles. It holds monthly beer tastings. **Produce Row** (204 S.E. Oak

and Big Pinot Noir boxer shorts for sale that look both out of place and right at home. The wines are anything but offbeat.

When Liner & Elsen started out together in 1990, Burgundies were their specialty. The two rode the wave of big wines (1989 and 1990 vintages) while the supply lasted and then expanded their reach around the world. They now keep about 400 labels in stock. You won't find a lot of the more commonly marketed, national brand wines here. Liner & Elsen attempt to carry a unique selection of goods, handpicked for taste and price, from small producers and the big guns.

Street, phone: 232-8355) offers an impressive twenty-seven taps and more than 150 different labels of bottles. **Kell's** (112 S.W. Second Avenue, phone: 227-4057) local draught beer totals twelve taps, with a few Irish beers thrown in to satisfy the international crowd.

Seasonal changes can be charted in the beer community as much as in the restaurant world. Winter brings strong ales and "winter warmers," notably BridgePort's Winter Brew, Widmer's *Winternacht*, Nor'Wester's Winter Weizen, Portland Brewing's Jubel Ale and Icicle Creek, Full Sail's Wassail Ale, and Star Brewing's Elfin Ale. Summer's crop of specialty beers usually feature lighter beers, many with berry undertones.

A good number of the local brews are bottled for retail sale. Most self-respecting grocery stores stock a healthy selection. Keep in mind that when the law changed in 1985 to allow beer consumption at the site of manufacture, it also made possible the opportunity to bring a container directly to a microbrewery to get it to go.

*M*cMenamin's **Blue Moon** brew pub on N.W. 21st is a college fraternity tap room for the twenty-something crowd. It's a huge space with blue, green, and red tubes of neon glowing eerily on old beer posters and advertisements for vintage rock groups: Jethro Tull, Santana, Albert King at the Fillmore. A few naked tangerine-colored bulbs cast a warmth on picnic tables and benches, and down the length of the fifty-foot bar a lineup of spouts leads to kegs of beer concealed in the wall, some thirty different styles from the major microbreweries in town. The names of additional special beers are chalked up on the big green signboard behind the bar, alongside pastel drawings made anew each day. You experience a bit of visual overload here, especially with the psychedelic wall paintings that suggest a major time warp, but the crowds pour in, relishing a place that looks as if it had been here in their infancy. It wasn't.

cont'd

Value is an L & E theme. Wine prices are a bit better than those of their competitors, and case purchases receive a good discount. Service is the house motto (along with "No Dancing"). Each day, four reds and four whites are offered for tasting—in 2-ounce (more or less) portions. The now-common Friday tastings offered around town originated here and are still offered on first and third Friday evenings and each Saturday.

Wine-appreciation classes, offered about three times a year, sell out quickly. Unscheduled tastings and classes are held for visiting winemakers and for special releases. At holiday time, the Luxury Vintage Champagne class provides a wonderful education about fine bubblies. L & E's monthly newsletter is a hoot, full of good deals, new release data, and the tasting calendar. The guys also dispense sixty seconds of wine wisdom four times a week on KOTK-radio. Two days a week, during morning and afternoon drive times, Liner says they "get to say stupid things fast" on the air.

Blue Moon is casual and friendly; if you show interest in a beer you haven't ordered, the server is likely to bring you a free sample. Food is strictly on the relaxed side: Black Bean Garden Burger, Pizza Bread, Taco Salad, and mean French Fries. But you've come for the brew, such as hearty India Pale Ale, amber-colored Hammerhead, or Ruby—a pink ale brewed from whole raspberries that's less sweet than you might imagine.

In a newly restored brick warehouse on North Russell just off Interstate Avenue, the **Widmer Gasthaus** presents another face of the local brew pub scene. Stainless steel tanks holding the company's beer are visible through large dining room windows. The gorgeous bar boasts three ceramic stands from Munich bearing five taps apiece, and the renovated interior gleams with polished wood throughout, from the oak floors to elegant pillars flanking the bar counter. The brick walls set off the warm glow of the dining rooms and the sparkling open kitchen. The clientele is more establishment here, though hardly sedate. The Gasthaus simply provides a comfortable ambiance, reminiscent of gracious old German hospitality rooms at breweries.

Widmer spells its drinks "*biers*," and the Gasthaus serves only its own brand. The Hefeweizen, a clean-tasting wheat beer, is the company's most popular. We're fond of the Oktoberfest, a malty fall amber-colored brew, and when a rich and deep beer is called for, the winter Festbier, which utilizes chocolate malts. The Widmer beers marry well with such favorite dishes as Smoked Salmon on Potato Pancakes with Red Onion Compote and Capered Sour Cream, and the wonderful German sausages.

The shop stocks wine books and periodicals galore, from general information volumes to books on specific varietals. Wine glasses from Riedel and scads of wine paraphernalia—openers, racks, labels, and even Vino, a wine board game—sit forlornly in the corner, pushed out of the way by the rows and rows of bottles and boxes.

Pastaworks

See listing on page 12 for locations and hours.

It should be no surprise that the focus of the wine inventory at Pastaworks is Italy. The selection is remarkably deep—about 500 labels —and the display fills more space than any other department at either location. When owners Don Oman and Peter de Garmo first started, they only sold a small sampling of wines, and most were Californian—what they knew best. One evening, someone gave them a bottle of 1977 Selvapiana Riserva to drink. They fell in love with it and learned that "oak and body aren't everything."

Spanish wines also get a healthy amount of shelf space here, and the stores promote local wines as well. The older wines tend to be kept at the Hawthorne Boulevard store, where there's more space. Twenty percent discounts are offered for single-label case purchases.

Tastings have been sporadic and spontaneous, but with the recent remodeling of the Hawthorne Boulevard space, Pastaworks hopes to do more formal tastings and classes, especially to focus on food and wine combinations. Staff already get training in matching food and wine.

Portland Wine Merchants

1435 S.E. 35th Avenue, phone: 234-4399 and 800-344-VINO.
Open Tuesday through Saturday, 10 a.m.–6:30 p.m. (except Friday, 10 a.m.–8 p.m.)

This neighborhood wine shop opened in 1994 to fill a void in the Hawthorne area. The owner is a California refugee who also owns a wine distributorship in the San Francisco Bay Area. Portland Wine Merchants often beat Oregon shops on price, since the California market is more competitive and it's cheaper for Rory Olson to bring his wine wares up from California than to buy them here.

As of this writing, Olson was offering the silky Domaine Drouhin of Oregon 1993 Pinot Noir at a full $3 a bottle less than any other wine merchant in town. Other wines gets the same rock-bottom pricing, although the selection is a bit thinner than at some shops. Olson admits that he doesn't carry everything, but rather "a little something of a lot." Basically, he picks and chooses what he knows and likes and is able to sell a lot of California wines otherwise unavailable in Oregon.

The prices are competitive nationally, too, since 40 percent of his retail sales gets shipped to New York or the Bay Area. Olson runs ads in *The New York Times,* among other places.

The blackboard lists daily wines for tasting, a weekly schedule of tastings, hot deals, and good values, echoing the monthly newsletter. Four-week classes on wines of the world, and on matching wine and food, take place throughout the year.

Strohecker's

See listing on page 25 for location and hours.

This Portland Heights grocery maintains a long-established wine department that's the largest in town with over 3,500 labels in stock. Wayne Strohecker and wine manager Robert Kanzaki oversee a sophisticated wine program that includes futures sales, promotions on prerelease specials, fall Beaujolais Nouveau releases, and consulting for weddings, parties, and private-cellar building. Sales are split an impressive fifty-fifty on case versus single-bottle sales. This place moves a lot of wine.

Twice a year, usually in September and February, sales bring in a swarm of people anxious to take advantage of the 20 percent discount applicable to all single bottles. Case purchases (one label) are normally discounted around 18 percent, and mixed cases get a 10 percent price break.

Wandering through the partitioned space on the lower level doesn't reveal all the wine. A locked back room holds the "library" wines—the old Bordeaux vintages that collectors covet. This basement's basement holds even more wines in packed cases, as backup inventory and storage for the many special orders.

Kanzaki says that Oregon wines in particular practically fly out of the place and that he ships them all over the country. He really knows the native grapes: he serves on the Oregon Wine Advisory Board and has won many awards for his retail wine selection. The Champagne range is impressive, including a nice showing of older vintage bottles. Ports and sherries are also well represented.

As important and impressive as the holdings are, shopping for wine at Strohecker's never feels stuffy or rarefied. Both Wayne Strohecker and Kanzaki are knowledgeable and eager to assist you in wine buying. A good selection of wine books is displayed: you can use the house copies for reference or buy your own. There's a generous beer selection located upstairs in the main part of the store.

AND KEEP IN MIND. . .

Burlingame Grocery

See listing on page 83 for location and hours.
A wonderful wine selection and personalized service.

Cheshire Cat

See listing on page 21 for location and hours.
Good value and a broad assortment of wines and beer.

Martinotti's

See listing on page 26 for location and hours.
A remarkable cellar holds hard-to-find old Bordeaux, but at prices far higher than any of the competition.

Riccardo's Vin Italy Enoteca

16045 S.W. Boones Ferry Road, Lake Oswego, phone: 636-4104.
Hours vary, but help is available at the restaurant across the parking lot
This small wine store companion to Riccardo's restaurant sells a limited but choice selection of Italian wines at reasonable prices. Tastings on Saturday afternoon include appetizers from the restaurant.

Ron Paul Charcuterie

See listing on page 16 for locations and hours.
This deli/restaurant is also a reliable retail wine and beer shop, with an interesting choice of bottles, including a strong Oregon presence.

Woodstock Wine & Deli

See listing on page 140 for location and hours.
An impressive wall of wine and regular, well-attended tastings.

Wizer's

See listing on page 32 for locations and hours.
A long-established cellar with a deep collection of aged Oregon wines.

Dick and Nancy Ponzi used to grow grapes near their home in Los Gatos, California. Dick was an engineer, designing Disneyland's amusement park rides. But wine was really the Ponzi's love. They researched where Pinot Noir, Reisling, and Chardonnay grapes grew best. Like Christopher Columbus looking for the New World, they studied maps and explored possibilities: Burgundy was too cool for them; Mendocino too close to home. They had been to Oregon often—Nancy's parents lived in Gaston—and grew intrigued about the similarity of its climate to Burgundy's. But they knew of no grape industry in Oregon. Undaunted, in 1969 they packed all their worldly possessions into a flatbed truck and headed north with their three kids to grow grapes.

At first, Dick taught engineering at a community college, while Nancy looked for suitable land. (They ultimately bought 100 acres in Beaverton.) While teaching, Dick happened to meet a bookseller who, coincidentally, was also growing grapes—David Lett, Oregon's wine pioneer. With Lett, Dick Erath, and Richard Cory, the Ponzis formed an informal group that met regularly to teach themselves about making wine.

In 1970, David Lett produced his first Eyrie bottling (the 1975 Pinot Noir is legendary), and in 1974 the **Ponzi** label appeared. Oregon had a wine industry! And the Ponzi's had a family enterprise: the Ponzi children grew up at the winery, and learned to love the art and technique of making wine. Unlike other Oregon wine offspring—and more like the Burgundian tradition—the Ponzi children have chosen a life in the family business.

By 1983, as the Ponzi vineyard started to make money, Dick Ponzi was itching to find another challenge, one that would be compatible with the winery.

He sniffed around for a creative opportunity and grew curious about beer making. Only the big boys made beer locally—Blitz Weinhard, Bohemian, Rainier. But trailblazing is a Ponzi trademark; that Oregon law forbade the sale of beer at the place of brewing didn't hold Ponzi back one bit. In 1984 he opened **BridgePort BrewPub**, the first microbrewery in Oregon. His company produced a handcrafted beer, more expensive than the commercial competition. In part because of his visibility with wine sales, Ponzi didn't have much trouble selling kegs and bottles of his beer to restaurants and taverns. His bigger challenge was on-site sales.

He felt that the old law should be changed. In the 1985 Oregon legislative session, Ponzi spearheaded that effort and was successful. Beer sales were now allowed at breweries, and brewpubs were born. BridgePort was the first and it got so big—exporting bottles and kegs to eight states and always seeking wider exposure—that the Ponzi family was able to pull back and let staff run the operation. BridgePort became so self-sufficient and successful that the Ponzis sold it in the fall of 1995.

What does that mean for the ever-expansive Dick Ponzi and family? He wants to give his wines greater international exposure. With Ponzi wines already available in Great Britain and Italy, he hopes for stronger worldwide visibility, especially for his wonderful award-winning Pinot Noirs and Chardonnays. The Ponzi crew will also plant more of their 100 acres—only 40 acres are currently under cultivation. The Ponzi's are intrigued by Italian varietals and have started to plant Nebbiloa, Dolcetto, Pinot Blanc, and a few Piedmont grapes, inspired as much by their Italian heritage as by the growing conditions.

Part 4

KITCHENWARE, TABLEWARE, AND BOOKS

Chapter 19

KITCHENWARE AND COOKING UTENSILS

Y ou don't need a copper sauté pan to brown chicken pieces properly, or a *bain-marie* to keep sauces warm, but they help. Lots of cooks do remarkably well without impressive equipment, though the goods abounding in cookware shops make it hard to resist fine German cutlery, French fluted tart pans, or even the well-balanced oyster knife.

Must you indulge yourself beyond the basics to be a superior home chef? Hype abounds of course; you don't need a $400 Beraducci cheese grater to produce the right amount of Asiago for your pasta. On the other hand, you'll discover that fine cookware from All-Clad eliminates any chance of uneven hot spots in the cooking surface. And it's a pleasure to have a perfectly balanced boning knife or a well-hefted rolling pin or a hand-mixer that doesn't get clogged in the batter. Having a good cleaver and a seasoned wok will make you feel more authentic cooking Chinese food.

Besides, there's great pleasure in exploring a fine cookware store. In addition to presenting displays of handsome equipment, the store can be a kind of school: you'll learn about the proper use of a knife, how to keep it sharp, and how to distinguish the function of one blade from another. A good store opens up your repertoire: buying a fine Belgian waffle iron instantly expands your breakfast options; a good juicer of apples turns out drinks that put even unfiltered cider in the shade. And having the right tool for the task inevitably imparts confidence, whether it's a heavy baguette pan, a fish poacher, or a copper casserole. There's a secret little pleasure in knowing you can produce a bone marrow spoon if called upon when you serve *osso bucco*, or being able to put your hand on citrus-fruit peelers, zesters, and curlers just when you need them.

Cloudtree & Sun

112 N. Main, Gresham, phone: 666-8495. Open Monday through Thursday, 10 a.m.–6 p.m.;
Friday, 10 a.m.–7 p.m.; Saturday, 10 a.m.–6 p.m.; Sunday, 11 a.m.–4 p.m.

Cloudtree & Sun is chockablock with stuff: jalapeño catsup, cactus and Snakebite salsas, and mango grill sauce sit next to Crabtree and Evelyn lotions; garden fountains and birdbaths are next to trout platters; and recipe card boxes next to picnic hampers. A third of the store is devoted to gift items—candles, pillows, picture frames, and the like—another third to tableware (the designs tend toward country or Victorian), and a final third to cooking equipment. Cloudtree is quite decent in its selection of the latter, especially its range of the omnipresent Calphalon. Anything unusual here? Well, a very large choice of cooking thermometers and a shelf of kitchy teapots. It's fun to explore the nooks and crannies of the shop, and often you'll unearth a nice item, such as a pretty glazed-tile trivet.

The clerks and owner Mary Jo Hessel couldn't be friendlier, and if you get hungry while shopping, the very pleasant Main Street Grocery, under the same management, is next door; you can walk through to it.

Cook's Corner

11777 Beaverton-Hillsdale Highway, Beaverton (at Beaverton Town Square),
phone: 644-0100. Open Monday through Friday, 9 a.m.–8 p.m.;
Saturday, 9 a.m.–6 p.m.; Sunday, 12 noon–5 p.m.

A general cookware store, Cook's Corner has an impressive selection of gadgets. We were also taken with the bottles for storing vinegars and herbed oils—they are corkable, the glass is marked with old-fashioned etching, and they come in several colors. Another item stocked in many styles is the pepper grinder: you'll see it in woods and crystal acrylic (one is shaped like a pyramid, another like a perfume bottle); there's even a set made from sink faucets. Cook's Corner specializes in pot racks, including several in oak. There's a Souper Strainer for degreasing gravies and stocks, ceramic roller pins, and a sheet of printed labels for your spice jars.

Their kitchenware prices range from inexpensive to moderate. A good part of the store is devoted to wedding presents, including crystal, vases, and some nifty picnic baskets.

Decorette Shop

5338 S.E. Foster Road, phone: 774-3760. Open Monday through Saturday, 9 a.m.–5:30 p.m.; 109 Tigard Plaza, lower level, Tigard, phone: 620-5100. Open Monday through Saturday, 9 a.m.–5:30 p.m.

If you're about to get married and want to make your own wedding cake, Decorette is your place. Tell Carol Winner what fantasy you have in mind, and she'll show you the basics: how to fill the layers of your cake with ready-prepared Vienna cream, how to use pillars to raise the tiers, and how to make buttercream flowerettes. She'll even teach you how to spray paint your own edible design right onto the icing. If you want something other than a traditional bride and groom on top of the cake, you can buy a pair of cuddling wedded dogs, a brace of cows contemplating bovine bliss, or even a spun sugar man in front of a television set.

In one of the most charmingly anachronistic shops around, you'll find everything imaginable to construct your own confection. You can buy soccer ball cake pans to shape a cake for your favorite goalie; you can pipe whipped cream into hundreds of different-sized decorating tips, buy dozens of styles of sprinkles, or food coloring in more colors than Crayola ever dreamed of. There are checkerboard cake sets, candy-making sets, thousands of chocolate molds, and an ample bookshelf featuring tomes on icing.

Decorette holds classes on all aspects of cake and cookie making; the titles of the classes invoke worlds most of us never knew existed: "Introduction to Gum Paste," "Air Brushing Your Cake," and "Rolled Fondant—Beginner, Advanced." Prospective brides can study the art of personalizing toasting glasses and decorating cake knives.

424 S.W. Washington Street, phone: 227-2087.

Open Monday through Friday, 9 a.m.–5:30 p.m.; Saturday, 9 a.m.–5 p.m.

This venerable establishment has been in Portland for 125 years, and cutlery has occupied the George family since the early nineteenth-century in Hamburg, Germany. In this narrow, charmingly old-fashioned shop, knives of all kinds abound, from hunting to Swiss army to tools for woodcarving elves, but the kitchen knives are the most impressive. Carl George, great-grandson of the founder, will explain why, if you're a serious cook, you might want a number of paring knives, each engineered for a different task. The range of boning or filleting instruments is also striking, and even more so the lethal-looking bread knives. And you simply cannot do without a cleaver or two—a light one for mincing vegetables, a heavier hitter for dealing with whole roasting fowl.

Of course Germans are standouts at making cutlery: Henckels and Trident are the master brands, and George and Son sports a wide selection, all gleaming upon the wall. Any chef worth her *julienne* carries a personal valise of blades; James Beard often dropped in when he was in town to check out the latest piece of cold Toledo. There's also a decent selection of steak knives.

For those who want the sharpest knives and do not mind drying them as soon as they've been washed, George & Son carries an unusually good selection of all-carbon French knives. The store will also sharpen your knives, returning them to you in a renewed, reinvigorated state, or you can shop the huge assortment of sharpening stones and devices to keep your knives honed to perfection.

Be sure to note the gorgeous hardwood knife cases in a variety of sizes and shapes, most set at 45 degrees for ready display and the right handling.

Kitchen Kaboodle

N.W. 23rd Avenue and Flanders, phone: 241-4040.

Open Monday through Saturday, 10 a.m.–6 p.m.; Sunday, 12 noon–5 p.m.

N.E. 16th Avenue and Broadway, phone: 288-1500.

Open Monday through Saturday, 10 a.m.–6 p.m.; Sunday, 12 noon–5 p.m.

8788 S.W. Hall Boulevard (Progress Square), Beaverton, phone: 643-5491.

Open Monday through Saturday, 10 a.m.–6 p.m.; Sunday, 12 noon–5 p.m.

Clackamas Town Center, upper level, phone: 652-2567.

Open Monday through Saturday, 10 a.m.–9 p.m.; Sunday, 11 a.m.–6 p.m.

While much of Kitchen Kaboodle's business these days is in furniture, their kitchenware and tableware selections are unsurpassed. The colorful displays make for pleasant shopping, and the sheer sweep of merchandise can easily entice any avid cook and entertainer. You know it's summer when colorful citronella candles appear in terra-cotta bowls. The season also brings out oodles of summer glasses and iced tea pitchers, some in brilliant Mediterranean hues.

The Broadway Kitchen Kaboodle boasts a garlic corner full of presses, mills, peelers, roasters and storing jars; a pasta section replete with a variety of hand-cranked and electric pasta makers that mix, knead, and extrude the dough to any shape; and a pizza nook bulging with wheels, paddles, rimmed baking stones, and even jars of herbs prepared especially for the pies.

The stores have an enormous range of colorful Indian dishtowels, more aprons than Julia Child could wear in a lifetime, and more mitts than Yogi Berra ever used. There's little by way of equipment that you won't find here, and the choices are very extensive, especially the large number of bowls (check out the Chantal line), canisters, and wooden implements arranged in large white jars, good themselves for storing spoons, whisks, and ladles. We were impressed by the range of Cuisinart pots, especially the gorgeous stockpots with steamer and pasta cooking inserts. The Calphalon selection is the largest in town; we like almost everything in the line. The fish poachers are especially prized.

There are nice little green marble mortars and pestles, fine for grinding your own peppercorns when you prefer them with a rough texture. If you are a bread nut, there are cutting boxes for precise slicing, oak roll-top bread boxes, and a stunning array of white toasters.

As for tableware, Kitchen Kaboodle carries a good selection of glassware in the middle price range, enlivened by deep cobalt blue glasses and plates from Mexico. Be sure as well to note the lovely pasta bowls and fruit bowls, in colorful patterns both geometric and whimsical.

Many cooks delay their purchases until January, when Kitchen Kaboodle holds its major storewide sale and everything is discounted at least 20 percent.

Kitchen Resource

1438 N.W. 23rd Avenue, phone: 227-2070. Open Monday through Saturday, 10 a.m.–6 p.m.

Kitchen Resource doesn't attempt to compete with The Kobos Company or Kitchen Kaboodle (see listings in this chapter), but it does have some fine items worth perusing. There's a choice assortment of baking rings in every possible size, all from France, and a vast selection of tart pans for the avid baker. The All-Clad cookware is handsome and, with its thick gauge, cooks evenly and conducts quickly. One of the store's specialties is its beautiful baskets—be sure to check out the charming wicker garlic baskets designed for proper ventilation, they are shaped like bulbs themselves. Don't overlook the cedar planks used for baking whole salmon in the mode originated by Pacific Northwest tribes. One of Kitchen Resource's more unusual items is a conical strainer for making apple sauce; after employing this tool, you'll never again be satisfied with jarred apple sauce. They also carry a fine selection of white bistro ware.

The Kobos Company

See listing on page 38 for locations and hours.

Along with Kitchen Kaboodle, Kobos is the premier store in town for the serious home cook, and many of the professionals buy here. David Kobos was a forerunner in bringing high-quality kitchen equipment to Portland, though the store began as a pioneering coffee emporium, and you can enjoy watching coffee being roasted every Saturday on several of the premises.

To understand how serious Kobos can be, it's instructive to examine the Rosle brand of small utensils. Kobos is one of only three stores in America carrying this stunning line of German-made implements, all designed as a result of ergonomic research. They're beautifully balanced and tooled. Even the humble zester feels solid in the hand, as do the melon scoops and the potato peeler. These instruments of almost surgical precision do not come cheap—$36 for the spatula and $23.50 for the zester—but are worth every pfennig.

Kobos has numerous shelves of gleaming white tableware, although these days the Cordon Bleu egg cups come from Beijing, not Paris. There are treasures everywhere: an Endurance asparagus steamer with a mesh insert and numerous baking materials, including Madeleine molds, just the ticket either for kitchen decor or to make buttery cookies accompanying your Japanese tea as you dip into Proust.

Kobos has more gadgets than any other store in town, walls and tables full of them, including the midrange line of Good Grip utensils, which feature rubber handles. There's a decent selection of copperware, tons of Calphalon, and a fine choice of overhead racks for displaying your pots and pans.

Because Kobos began life with coffee, there's a very sizable collection of espresso machines, French presses, and all the other equipment needed for intense caffeination. Not to be neglected is a section of humbler items:

mounds of brightly colored dishtowels, cobalt blue soap dishes, and scrubbing brushes in every conceivable style and bristle.

The recently opened shop on N.W. Vaughan Street is an exciting venue, not least because of the giant roasters on site. During the week you can watch coffee beans being roasted several times daily, and three different varieties of beans will be chosen from each day's batch for immediate sale—you can't get them fresher than this.

Oregon Retinners

2712 N. Mississippi Avenue, phone: 287-7696.
Open Monday through Friday, 7:30 a.m.–4:30 p.m.

You should never cook in a copper pan if you can see copper beneath the tin lining, where the latter has begun to flake away. The chemical reaction that occurs when heated copper comes into contact with food is, except for sugar, potentially poisonous. If you spot telltale signs of copper on the cooking surface of your equipment, the solution is to take it to Oregon Retinners. For $2.50 per diagonal inch (measured from where the bottom of the pan meets the side up to the top of the opposite side), they will completely retin the inside of your pan. They do beautiful work, but bank on a month's wait.

Portland Cutlery Company

536 S.W. Broadway, phone: 228-2030.
Open Monday through Saturday, 9:30 a.m.–5:30 p.m.

Another Portland institution of long standing, this store has sold elegant cutlery for over ninety years. Like George and Son, Portland Cutlery carries an impressive range of kitchen knives, naturally featuring the two German giants of the breed: Henckels and Trident. Tony Trotti, who has been here for almost forty years, will show you the newest wrinkle, ceramic blades that are actually harder than steel and never dull. Portland Cutlery stocks game and poultry shears and a goodly number of cleavers. Cheese knives are among the specialties of the shop, the blades etched so that cheese won't stick; they slice cleanly through even the softest of triple crèmes. You'll find all kinds of steels (often mistakenly called "sharpeners"), some even fabricated from industrial diamond dust. If you bone whole fish with any frequency, you owe it to yourself to pick up a flexible blade for filleting, for it enables you to separate the meat from the backbone with delicacy and grace.

Like George and Son Cutlery, Portland Cutlery also has a knife-sharpening service; but whereas the former establishment charges by the time it takes to put a new edge on the blade, Portland Cutlery charges 35 cents per blade inch.

Williams-Sonoma

700 S.W. 5th (Pioneer Place), phone: 225-0607. Open Monday through Friday, 9:30 a.m.–9 p.m.; Saturday, 9:30 a.m.–7 p.m.; Sunday, 11 a.m.–6 p.m.

This national store, known to many through its pretty mail-order catalogs, boasts an airy perch on the top skylit level of Pioneer Place Shopping Center. While Williams-Sonoma carries a goodly range of utensils and cookware, all of which are well chosen, it does not quite have the professional feel of either Kobos or Kitchen Kaboodle, but rather a Martha Stewart home-entertaining ambiance. Williams-Sonoma thrives on gastronomic accessorizing, and you'll be struck by the colorful seasonal displays. The salespeople are knowledgeable, patient, and helpful: let a clerk explain their nifty Bread Baker and you'll be hooked.

Even the well-equipped cook can find items that suddenly appear indispensable: crème brûlée irons, or Charlotte and brioche molds. One visit turned up four different sizes of ice cream scoops. On a more frivolous note, we've spotted realistic French paper leaves to place under cheese or on a buffet table. We like the terra-cotta onion roaster and the "onion cellar" of the same material—a canister for storing bulbs in a dry, dark environment.

There's a good selection of black cookware from Calphalon and colored cookware from Chantal. We were also drawn to the deco mesh soda siphon, for imparting glamour to any drink, and to the replica of the famous 1935 Waring Blender, which now comes in green, blue, black, and white, as well as chrome. Among the best bets in the shop: an impressive choice of dishtowels, some Portuguese, some French, and all in tasteful stripes or antique designs representing various accoutrements of the table. As summer comes on, you'll see outdoor hurricane lamps that look like train lanterns and a full display of well-designed grilling implements. The tableware here is bright and cheerful. We're especially impressed by their serving pieces and their colorful napery.

AND KEEP IN MIND . . .

Most of the Asian groceries (see listings on pages 45 through 51) have good selections of woks, bamboo steamers, Chinese earthenware casseroles, cleavers, and other utensils for the Asian kitchen.

HOTEL AND RESTAURANT SUPPLY HOUSES

H otel and restaurant supply houses represent an often-overlooked source of cookware. Several local stores are open to retail trade, and though one doesn't see many nonprofessionals stocking their home kitchens (less than 5 percent of customers tend to be "domestic" customers), these stores are treasure-troves of the mundane and the extraordinary.

Supply houses typically sell in dozens and by the case, but except for glassware and dishes you can generally purchase individual items. Of course you'll see equipment you couldn't use even when hosting your kid's Little League team: a Hobart 8-quart mixer with a hook to knead dough for two dozen loaves, Robot Coupe processors that shred 50 pounds of cabbage in eight minutes flat, or mammoth Chinese ranges, weighing in at a ton and containing tub-sized woks atop gas burners of 80,000 BTUs.

But hundreds of items are perfectly fit for home use, and part of the pleasure of shopping here is imagining how the institutional function of an object might be reinterpreted on a smaller scale. If you want to wow your kids, turn a nook of your kitchen into a ballpark concession stand with an old-fashioned hot dog cradle-steamer. Items that look commonplace in ordinary hash houses take on a sort of industrial chic in the home kitchen. A King Size Can Punch and Bottle Opener (the St. Peter's of church keys) is impressive, and if you host excessive dinner parties, you can produce a specially designed doggie bag. Ice cream lovers may purchase a gorgeous stainless Hamilton Beach Milk Shaker, an old-fashioned scooper, a paper-straw dispenser, and a dozen ribbed ice cream soda glasses or tulip sundaes. You can put a toothpick dispenser on the breakfast table, or an after-dinner mint machine, which drops chocolate creams one at a time, in your foyer. You can impress guests with a 3-gallon iced-tea dispenser in high-impact plastic or a fountain service that delivers syrups, fruits, and toppings for your frozen yogurt, an inspired gift. You can also buy preset menus, fun for house guests at breakfast time.

A metal-tipped bottle is perfect for splashing sesame or chili oil onto Chinese dishes; a grated Parmesan dispenser turns your kitchen into a pizza parlor. Many objects have an unexpected beauty: you'll discover mesh strainers as graceful as butterfly nets. A hundred different pastry tips, sporting stars, crescent moons and crosses, are displayed in a box that might pass for a Joseph Cornell assemblage.

Bargreen Ellingson

2112 S.W. First Avenue, phone: 224-9427.

Open Monday through Friday, 8 a.m.–5 p.m.; Saturday, 9 a.m.–1 p.m.

Whereas Boxer-Northwest and Kalberer Food Service Equipment (see below)—the two oldest restaurant supply houses in Portland—reside in the old commercial zones of northwest Portland, the showroom of Bargreen Ellingson is just a whisk's toss from RiverPlace and the aeries of Portland Towers. A Tacoma-based company, Bargreen opened its Portland branch three years ago and chose to locate in a gentrified urban-renewal neighborhood. It's an upscale kind of place, and residents of the neighborhood occasionally outfit their kitchens here.

One of the boons of such stores is the range of sizes you'll find for any given item, especially in stock pots and roasting pans of all descriptions. Because Bargreen's buys in bulk, its prices are very reasonable compared to those in domestic shops; lobster crackers, for example, are only $2 apiece. Most of the equipment is more basic than frilly. Keep in mind that this is not a discount house and that most of the brands are not what you'd see in places like Kobos or Williams-Sonoma.

But there's a functional beauty in many of these objects, such as the mandoline, a finely calibrated device for slicing everything under the sun, or the conical China Caps, a stock strainer with a solid wooden pestle to push all the juices out. It's fun shopping here, if only to buy a pair of black-and-white chef's pants for inspiration.

Boxer-Northwest Company

438 N.W. Broadway, phone: 226-1186. Open Monday through Friday, 8 a.m.–5 p.m.

Boxer-Northwest (formerly Boxer-Marcus) is a long-running hotel and restaurant supply store in town that sells to the public. Established in 1919, it claims to have more walk-in trade than Kalberer and feels a bit more workaday than its rival.

You'll find ice cream "dishers" with an "ergonomically improved thumb tab" for easier scooping next to ice cream spades and old-fashioned scoops. In another section you'll see yellow plastic mustard dispensers, fine for a picnic or camping it up at home. For those who are prone to break drinking glasses, Boxer-Northwest is an excellent locale to stock up on glassware in bulk (minimum of two dozen) at a 35 percent discount.

Wearever cookware is king here. We like the look and feel of the omelette pans, which seem properly hefty for good sliding and flipping of the eggs. Even if you have an aversion to Tupperware, you might go for the heavy clear plastic containers they have here. There's a very cool fudge server with a pump for an industrial look. And if you want your teenagers to respect table etiquette, you just might improve matters by picking up a "No Shoes, No Shirt, No Service" sign for a mere 89 cents.

Looking for durable kitchenware? Nothing is missing here, from poultry shears to whisks in a dozen sizes to flour sifters—all considerably cheaper than you'd pay at gourmet cookware shops and often of better material, for when you sling hash you've got to have sturdy equipment.

Kalberer Food Service Equipment
234 N.W. Fifth Avenue, phone: 227-1161. Open Monday through Friday, 8 a.m.–5 p.m.

Kalberer, the oldest and largest restaurant supply business in Portland, has an elegant showroom crammed with interesting objects. The clerks may be a bit surprised to see a customer not of the trade, but even the guy who handles the national restaurant accounts can find time to show you around. Check out the Redco wedgers, cutters, slicers, and cubers—they all look like medieval torture instruments but have a far more benign function. The Insta Dice, for example, will cube a potato into hundreds of uniform little pieces three times faster than you can by hand. Put this machine on your counter, along with the Wedgemaster (perfect for tomatoes) or the Crowncutter (just the thing to make a crown-shaped top on a half a cantaloupe), and you've got labor-saving devices-cum-conversation pieces.

Kalberer boasts an enormous selection of glassware. The glass beer mugs come in many sizes and shapes, including one formed like a Western boot. In the back room you can find mesh rubber bar matting that comes by the foot and in several colors, a good idea if you store glasses upside down. While we're on barware, you'll find genuine Waring blenders, streamlined juice extractors, and deco Hamilton Beach drink mixers.

If you do much Chinese cooking, you're in Hunan heaven: rice cookers, bamboo steamers, dim sum nested steamers, rice scoops, Chinese fish shears, even a bird's-nest skimmer. Why not buy a white chef's hat in cotton with a Velcro closure: perfect for showing off around the wok or the Weber? And if you're really daring you can purchase a mini movie-house popcorn machine or a nacho chip dispenser.

The really serious cook should inquire about restaurant ranges adopted for home use. These black, welded steel stoves are generally equipped with six burners and have ovens that can hold a 25-pound turkey. They last a lifetime and deliver an inferno of power—even on the showroom floor it's thrilling to stand at the controls. Kalberer carries both Wolf and Garland ranges, and though only the commercial kinds are on the floor, the store can order domestic models.

Chapter 20

TABLEWARE

P ick up any cookbook with color photographs, and chances are the food is on dinnerware chosen for heightened aesthetic appeal. Two recent books remind us of how the right china complements the food on which it is served. *Monet's Table* recreates the meals the Impressionist painter enjoyed at Giverny. One photograph catches the morning light as it streams into the chrome-yellow dining room, illuminating some buttered toast on the plates Monet designed, in canary yellow with bands of cornflower blue. In a different vein, *Pacific Flavors: Oriental Recipes for a Contemporary Kitchen* dazzles with dinnerware that plays against the very contemporary recipes: thus, a fillet of Salmon in Ginger Butter rests on a plate of red, orange, yellow, chartreuse, and sky blue punctuated by crisscrossing dabs of black.

Many major designers, artists, and architects have turned to tableware— it's amusing to see how Michael Graves's postmodern buildings are echoed in his pottery. People nowadays mix and match their table settings, so that a set of simple white bistroware might be punctuated by a striking Laure Japy plate of resplendent hues. You can purchase reproductions of Monet's china if you wish to emulate the meals the painter shared with Rodin, Degas, and Renoir, or you can buy magnificent majolica serving platters from Connie Kiener, one of the best ceramic artists working in Portland.

La Bottega di Mamma Ro

940 N.W. 23rd Avenue, phone: 241-4960. Open Tuesday through
Saturday, 10 a.m.–6 p.m.; Sunday and Monday, 11 a.m.–5 p.m.

Mamma Ro's factory in Italy supplies a few U.S. boutiques bearing her name. This shop vibrates with bold colors, all the dinnerware organized into poppy red, tulip yellow, hunter green, pure black, Alpine white, and French blue. For anyone who wants basic shapes and lots of color choices, this is an ideal place to stock the cupboard. There are canisters, casseroles, and saucepans in "the best RED in the industry" as the catalog proclaims, as well as spaghetti bowls, soup tureens, and onion keepers in all the hues.

We're charmed by the country collection, which comes in a sponged or speckled look. Despite the designation "country," some of the colors are sleekly sophisticated when mixed and matched, especially a rectangular dessert plate of peppermint pink sitting atop a rectangular dinner plate of granite gray: the appeal is pure 1930s elegance. There's also a line of terra-cotta cookware for a more rustic look.

Carl Greve Jeweler

731 S.W. Morrison Street, phone: 223-7121.
Open Monday through Friday, 10 a.m.–6 p.m.; Saturday, 10 a.m.–5 p.m.

While the ground floor is wall-to-wall with gold and gemstones, upstairs there's a world for those who entertain and put special effort into the appearance of their table. This crown jewel of Portland's tableware shops has been in the Greve family for four generations and carries every famous line you can think of: Waterford, Hermès, Baccarat, Lalique, Tiffany, and Cristofle. You know a store has caché when it is called upon to outfit the dining room of a local CEO's yacht.

The sales help is both attentive and unobtrusive; they begin by offering you tea, coffee, or sherry. Wander through these hushed precincts and you'll see a wealth of gorgeous objects: Kosta Boda art glass and hand-painted crystal-clear plates, as joyous as a confetti parade; Orrefors candlesticks with blue and silver dots; and a cookie jar designed by architect Richard Meier for Swid Powell, looking like a medieval turret. There are lobster platters and charming dishes for melted butter in the form of Dungeness crabs, a wall of Bernardaud Limoges, and a case of antique silver pieces mostly in English plate.

Among the more offbeat (and inexpensive) finds are place-card holders, which come in a variety of quirky designs. Other relatively modest items include tablecloths, placemats and napkins. Don't let the high-end items frighten you from browsing; there are inexpensive treasures tucked away everywhere, and even some of the most beautiful items are less than you might imagine. Those architect-designed pieces from Swid Powell are surprisingly reasonable.

Cook's China, Crystal and Silver Shop

8538 S.W. Apple Way, Beaverton, phone: 292-4312.
Open Monday through Friday, 10 a.m.–5:30 p.m.; Saturday, 10 a.m.–5 p.m.

This store houses a vast repository of traditional tableware, with all the famous names in place: Lenox, Royal Doulton, Denby. Cook's draws many customers by discounting almost everything from 20–50 percent off list (even on special orders), the sole exceptions being Waterford crystal and Nambé hollowware.

Even though Cook's displays the latest designs from numerous manufacturers, not much will disturb conservative tastes. Most of the dishes would feel right at home at an embassy party. There are lots of gold-rimmed plates and impressively solid wooden chests to store flatware. Innumerable tables display appropriate settings, all of them looking quietly dignified. Of course, you also have catalog resources at your disposal. The experienced staff acts with impeccable courtesy; you have the feeling most of them have been to the soirées whose tables they helped create.

Dansk

700 S.W. 5th Avenue (Pioneer Place), phone: 274-2119. Open Monday through Friday, 9:30 a.m.–9 p.m.; Saturday, 9:30 a.m.–7 p.m.; Sunday, 11 a.m.–6 p.m.

Dansk was the quintessential brand name associated with the Danish modern craze of the 1950s and early 1960s, and most everyone assumed the company was based in Denmark; the sleek, bold designs echoed Viking ships, its very name means "Danish" in Danish, and its famous first designer was Jens Quistgaard, a Dane whose flatware designs are in the Museum of Modern Art. But the company is thoroughly American.

This shop in Pioneer Place is what the Dansk people call a "lifestyle store," as distinguished from Dansk's many outlet stores, which sell discontinued items and seconds. It straddles the line between highly formal tableware and the everyday, though there's no reason not to use the classically modern stemware, the colorful bubble glass bowls, and the trim hand-forged stainless for all your meals. The store still stocks the designs that made Dansk famous: the deep, oversized, wooden salad bowls, the aerodynamic-looking stainless serving pieces, and the deep blue pottery, a color that crops up in the textiles for the table. There are new items, but Dansk has lost none of its timeless grace or its cool, startling, and sophisticated modernity.

Dieci Soli

304 N.W. 11th Avenue, phone: 222-4221. Open Monday through Saturday, 10 a.m.–6 p.m.; Sunday, 11 a.m.–4 p.m.

Next time you're shopping at Powell's, venture over to this charming store nearby, stocked with French and Italian country pottery and linen. The name is Italian for "ten suns," and plays on the owner's daughter's name, Tennison. Appropriately, the Provençal table linens depict sunflower bursts of yellow splashed on geometric patterns in blue, recalling country bistros in southern France. Most of the ceramics, tablecloths, and napery at Dieci Soli are informal in style, and many prices are modest to boot.

Many of the ceramics come from Italy, most from the Umbrian town of Deruta. The distinctive mark of Deruta ware is its designs, which are at once childlike and sophisticated, mostly in floral patterns that echo patterns 200 years old. There are cookie jars, pitchers, and large fruit bowls, some decorated with griffins that traditionally guarded the gates of Florence. Don't miss the Italian tiles based on floral Renaissance motifs—they make colorful trivets.

Plat du Jour

529 N.W. 23rd Avenue, phone: 248-0350.
Open Monday through Saturday, 10:30 a.m.–6 p.m.; Sunday, 12:30 p.m.–4:30 p.m.

Plat du Jour boasts one of the most varied collections of dinnerware in town. You'll find traditional English Denby, Royal Crown Derby, Wedgwood, country garden pottery from Portugal and Italy, Gien Faience from France, and a splendid assortment of Fiesta ware (if the purple Fiesta is still available, grab it, for it's about to be discontinued and will become a collectible item). Don't miss the Laure Japy Limoges ware depicting bold parrots, if you wish to dream of jungles at the table.

A nice touch is the massive display board of flatware, all the pieces attached by Velcro so you may take them down and feel their heft. Plat du Jour shows elegant stemware, including Orrefors's clown flutes for amusing Champagne sipping; but to create the illusion you've just won the big prize, think about their Nobel line of Champagne glasses, modeled after the crystal used for laureate-toasting by the king of Sweden.

There are items designed by major American architects: very understated white-on-white plates from Richard Meier, splashy patterns from Robert Venturi, and the postmodern classical line of Michael Graves. The shop also carries china and crystal by Christian Dior and Ralph Lauren.

Pottery Barn

700 S.W. 5th Avenue (Pioneer Place), phone: 225-0773. Open Monday through Friday, 9:30 a.m.–9 p.m.; Saturday, 9:30 a.m.–7 p.m.; Sunday, 11 a.m.–6 p.m.

One of the many national chains in Pioneer Place, Pottery Barn is familiar to shoppers through their catalogs. What you'll find here are inexpensive, unassuming pottery, glassware, and accessories for the informal table. The look in dinnerware is fresh and youthful, right for cautious, budget-conscious singles and newlyweds. There's a wealth of deep cobalt Mexican glass. Among the nicest items are heavy green serpentine utensil jars and round slabs in seven- and twelve-inch diameters, perfect for serving cheese. These stone pieces resemble fine marble. We were impressed by the picnic baskets, which hold four plates and four sets of silverware; the wicker is woven of grey, beige, and putty straw and is set off with leather straps—just the thing in which to carry potted shrimp, Stilton cheese, Champagne, and strawberries with clotted cream to your next picnic.

The Table Gallery

921 S.W. Morrison Street (The Galleria), phone: 274-1902. Open Monday through Friday, 10 a.m.–8 p.m.; Saturday, 10 a.m.–6 p.m.; Sunday, 12 noon–5 p.m.

A pleasant shop in the Galleria, The Table Gallery handles a small range of china, stemware, and flatware. The most beautiful selections in the shop are by Sasaki, a Japanese company whose work is inspired by designs from Kenya, Peru, and North Africa. The Peruvian plates are especially striking, in patterns that resemble the Byzantine decorative work of Gustav Klimt, in vivid orange, metallic gold, brick, black, and snowy white. Note also Sasaki's Onde vases, dramatic vessels in chartreuse and cracked lavender. The store features periodic sales, with 20 percent off all stemware when you buy four or more pieces, and the same discount on all flatware and chinaware when you buy four sets or more.

Twist

30 N.W. 23rd Place, phone: 224-0334.
Open Monday through Saturday, 10 a.m.–6 p.m.; Sunday, 11 a.m.–6 p.m.

Twist is the outstanding shop in Portland for gorgeous contemporary design in tableware. Owner Paul Schneider has assembled a group of artists whose work is extraordinarily beautiful. Walking through this dazzling shop is diversion enough from whatever drabness may afflict your life, but Twist eschews mere glitz or high-style for its own sake. Some of the most beautiful pieces constitute the dinnerware by Luna Garcia, whose white terra-cotta looks at once earthy and suave, in solid eggshell colors of cream, cinnamon, moss green, and deep pastels, with soft ripples in the glaze that define the handcrafting.

Some of the stellar work comes from Portland ceramicist Connie Kiener, whose grand majestic bowls and museum-quality platters echo Italian majolica ware: she features fruits, vegetables, and fish swirling in concentric patterns, pieces that suggest harvest fertility and Northwest bounty.

There's a line called Droll Designs featuring plates with bold pears, leeks, and tomatoes—they make stunning accent pieces. Pears in a very different style are found on David Wilder's plates, which echo eighteenth-century French engravings, backed by a cracked gilt glaze with fragments of a French text. We greatly liked the knives and forks by Michael Aram in a delicate yet rusticated twig style. Twist offers endless pleasure and temptation.

Urbino

521 N.W. 23rd Avenue, phone: 220-0053.
Open Monday through Saturday, 11 a.m.–6 p.m.; Sunday, 12 noon–5 p.m.

Urbino specializes in handmade ceramicware, some imported and some by talented American designers. One of the most striking lines of serving platters and bowls is executed by Hillary Harris, who uses bold vegetable forms, such as deep black eggplants, floating on a light ground rimmed with dramatic white polka dots. There's a Cassis line of French country pieces, mostly done with centuries' old geometric patterns from Provence. Asian art makes a striking appearance in the shop: we especially like the Japanese nailhead trivets, in hexagonal or round shapes, in black or jade green. These dignified pieces suggest a Zen quietude. Urbino carries a set of extremely pretty cutting boards made of bird's eye maple and finished with soft edges—almost too nice to cut upon.

Vessels, Inc.

2605 N.E. Martin Luther King, Jr. Boulevard, phone: 249-1952.
Open Tuesday through Saturday, 10 a.m.–6 p.m.

Vessels advertises itself as "tableware with meaning," the meaning being that African tribal motifs makes bold, aesthetically powerful statements and blend beautifully with contemporary table design. This serendipitous shop has established a reputation for original artifacts of very high quality. It opens into Steen's Coffee House and is but a step or two from Doris' Café. Vessels carries a selection of ethnic and Afrocentric products as well as works by African American artists. There are lively hand-painted wine glasses by Athene Hampton, who also manages the shop, and flatware with swirling metal tribal designs, surprisingly comfortable to hold, by a Cuban woman from Florida. We admire African olive wood servers with cow bone handles and patterns made by herbs and root dyes, wooden vessels from Kenya (they make handsome fruit bowls), and placemats of mud cloth in strong black and cocoa abstract patterns. One of the most beautiful aprons we've ever seen, scintillating in black, green, brick, and gold, is made from Kente cloth used in Kenyan ceremonies.

Virginia Jacobs

2325 N.W. Westover Road, phone: 241-8436. Open Monday through Friday,
10 a.m.–7 p.m.; Saturday, 10 a.m.–6 p.m.; Sunday, 11 a.m.–5 p.m.

A small, elegant shop specializing in gorgeous linens, Virginia Jacobs carries tablecloths and napkins from some of the world's finest lines. They are displayed in wooden armoires and with tableware from Patrick Frey of Paris, whose simple and charming plates complement the nappery. You'll find sumptuous Egyptian cottons, placemats with silk bows, and linen cocktail napkins. There are stunning pewter serving spoons and forks from Carol Boyes: if you've ever wanted a whimsical design on your curry and rice spoons (guaranteed to enhance your Indian fare), this is the place. There's a cache of antique sterling, as well as several surprisingly contemporary patterns from Deruda ware. Objects for the table are chosen for a quiet, restrained effect.

Zell Brothers

800 S.W. Morrison Street, phone: 227-8471.
Open Monday through Friday, 9:30 a.m.–5:30 p.m.; Saturday, 9:30 a.m.–5 p.m.

Zell Brothers is another top-of-the-line shop for tableware, though the store that once was a family business has since been sold to a national chain. Nevertheless, it retains its dignified, gracious air and is a grand repository for every major brand name you can think of. Though Carl Greve is the only store in town that has access to a complete line of Tiffany crystal, flatware, and china, Zell Brothers does very well with all the great names; they are also the exclusive local seller of Herend, the exquisite Hungarian hand-painted china. Here's the place to come if you want a traditional chafing dish, a punch bowl to serve fifty, or a silver platter to bear a baron of beef. This is also the place to see the pulsating designs of Versace's plates for Rosenthal, the tailored tableware of Ralph Lauren, or Hermès dinnerware, looking just like their heraldic scarves. Paloma Picasso's glass designs are also shown here.

In the center of the third floor stands a wooden cabinet displaying the famous blue-and-white pottery from Spode, many pieces based on eighteenth-century designs, which in turn were influenced by Chinese porcelain. These make marvelous collector's items but are entirely functional: if you're a serious coffee drinker, think about the jumbo cup (really a massive coffee bowl) and saucer with a romantic scene of Roman ruins, a design in continuous production since 1816. You'll also find such wonderful pieces as a marmalade pot, a ginger jar, and a water pitcher, done in all the great Spode Georgian, Victorian, and Italian designs.

Twice a year Zell Brothers offers 20 percent discounts on all purchases.

AND KEEP IN MIND. . .

Dazzle

704 N.W. 23rd Avenue, phone: 224-1294.
Open Monday through Saturday, 10 a.m.–6 p.m.; Sunday, 11 a.m.–5 p.m.
Since Dazzle's merchandise is neither for the conventional nor for the timid, be sure to ask for assistance from the flamboyant owner Faviana Priola, who will point you to candle holders bearing teapot and cup motifs, a cookie jar in the shape of a kitchen sink, or elegantly beautiful objects, such as cobalt-blue frosted bottles, ideal for serving liqueurs.

Chapter 21

FOOD AND WINE BOOKS

*P*ortland is a haven for the devoted collector of cookbooks, food history books, or anything to do with food preparation. The largest bookstore in the country is here, as well as the largest cookbook store in the world, and they are not even in the same place. We once encountered an out-of-towner camping out in the food section of Powell's, who looked as if she would happily remain for the duration. When we told her there was another store in town with over twice the number of food titles, it was as if, in the midst of lunch at Chez Panisse, she was informed that Julia Child had invited her to dinner.

Long gone are the days when cooks were satisfied with *The Joy of Cooking, The Betty Crocker Cookbook,* and *Fanny Farmer's.* Although these works are good references, serious cooks now own separate volumes about each of France's major gastronomic regions, several Italian cookbooks, and a book on Thai cuisine. There's a series on the favorite dishes of Proust, Cézanne, and Monet; there are numerous works on the cuisine of the Caribbean; and virtually every dish, from adobo to zabaglione, has its own scribe. The prose in many cookbooks has improved dramatically, perhaps under the influence of those great food writers, Elisabeth David and M. F. K. Fisher. We spend almost as much time reading our cookbooks as using them.

There's a national competition for cookbook writing in a range of categories sponsored by the James Beard Foundation, and there are Julia Childs awards from the International Association of Cooking Professionals. Portland authors have fared well with each. One of our favorite cookbooks is by Portland writer Janie Hibler: *Dungeness Crabs and Blackberry Cobblers.* A nominee for a James Beard award, it is a treatment of the heritage of Northwest cooking from Native Americans to European settlers to more recent Asian immigrants. The book is illustrated with wonderful historical photographs and has marvelous recipes from Geoduck Clam Chowder to Cascade Mountain Huckleberry Tarts. Karen Brooks, long a fixture on the local food scene, has compiled an engaging collection of recipes by Portland's best restaurants and home cooks entitled *Oregon's Cuisine of the Rain.* One of its invaluable chapters is a long discussion of regional ingredients called "The Taste of Oregon." Caprial Pence, co-owner of Westmoreland Bistro and Wines, has produced several fine and popular cookbooks, one based on her award-winning television cooking series (see page 200).

As for writers on wine, Portland has two of national stature. Heidi Yorkshire recently garnered a nomination from the Julia Childs Awards for her charming introductory book on the art of wine appreciation, *Wine Savvy*. Matt Kramer is engaged in a major series of books entitled *Making Sense of Wine*; he has done a general study of wine and another exclusively on Burgundies (see page 156). Kramer has also been asked to write the first chapter ever on wine for the newly revised *Joy of Cooking*, a project to which Janie Hibler is contributing material on game, desserts, and various Northwest recipes.

Portland has become so food conscious that most of the small, independent stores carry a good stock of food- and wine-related books. Check out such places as **Annie Bloom's Books, Broadway Books, Twenty-Third Avenue Books**, and **Looking Glass Books**. Of course most cookware shops dedicate a corner to cookbooks. But for wealth of selection, used as well as new titles, and rare items as well as this year's culinary bestseller, nothing can match Powell's Books for Cooks.

Barnes and Noble Booksellers

1231 N.E. Broadway, phone: 335-0201.
Open Monday through Saturday, 9 a.m.–10 p.m.; Sunday, 10 a.m.–9 p.m.

This national store has a fine food and cookbook selection, roughly on the scale of Borders. Near the cookbook section are several overstuffed chairs and tables where you may browse and salivate. The emphasis appears to be on Americana, which seems appropriate for an all-American chain; but ethnic titles and national cuisines are strongly in evidence as well. Perusing the shelves, we noticed that Barnes and Noble has an especially rich choice of books on breakfasts and brunches, a good thing, since we can all use inspiration to renew our morning options. One reason to think about a cookbook purchase here is that the store offers a 10 percent discount on all hardcover books, and 30 percent on all *New York Times* bestsellers, though it's unlikely that Julie Sahni's *Classic Indian Cooking*, although one of the most indispensable of cookbooks, will ever leap into this company.

Borders Books and Music

708 S.W. Third Avenue, phone: 220-5911. Open Monday through Thursday,
9 a.m.–10 p.m.; Friday and Saturday, 9 a.m.–11p.m.; Sunday, 10 a.m.–7 p.m.

Borders has appropriately placed the food books and cookbooks next to its café. In a pleasant alcove you'll find comfortable armchairs and a couch for your literary repast. Along a fifty-foot wall stretches a very respectable display of cookbooks, from French on the left to Diet Plans, Calories, and Fiber/ Sodium/Heart on the right. If you're undecided between several books of Italian recipes, this is a good place to contemplate their relative virtues, since you can reflect at leisure, latte in hand.

There are a wealth of books written by celebrity chefs—perhaps the newest trend in the cookbook world—and Borders usually has a display of the winners of the prestigious James Beard cookbook competition.

Powell's Books for Cooks

3739 S.E. Hawthorne Boulevard, phone: 235-3802. Open daily, 9:30 a.m.–7 p.m.

With almost forty thousand titles, Powell's Books for Cooks is the largest cookbook store in the United States, perhaps the world. The shop's very presence in Portland speaks volumes about the city's fervent interest in food. There are impressive sections on all the world's cuisines, and numerous books from every conceivable region and ethnic group in America. Where else could you find an entire section on the cuisines of Bali, Laos, and Cambodia; or one on Pennsylvania Dutch/ Amish/ Shaker cooking; or books on the classic cuisine of Soviet Georgia? And where else would you locate the scholarly *Oxford Symposia on Food,* or collector's items like *The Gun Club Cookbook, The Army Baker: Baking in the Trenches,* and *A Date with a Dish: A Cookbook of American Negro Recipes*? Patty Merrill, the creative force behind Powell's Books for Cooks and its former manager, has established an astonishing store.

It's no surprise that Italian cookbooks have pride of place, since Powell's Books for Cooks is linked to Pastaworks by a passageway. Nine shelves of Italian cuisine cover everything from village festivals to trattorias to the favorite dishes of Venetian gondoliers. The French section is also impressive, ranging from Richard Olney's treatises on French food to a volume oxymoronically titled *French Cooking in Ten Minutes.*

There's a vast section on baking, a large one on professional cooking (including books on ice carving), books on food preservation, others on condiments and savories. There's even a section on food and sex, where you'll discover *Cooking in the Nude, The Fabulous Sex Organic Diet,* and that salubrious coupling, *The Kitchen Casanova* and *Venus in the Kitchen.*

Perhaps most interesting of all is the collection of rare books. The store abounds in fascinating out-of-print items, such as Dali's sumptuously illustrated *Les diners de Gala,* signed James Beards, and nineteenth-century recipe collections. So serious a place is Powell's Books for Cooks that it produces a mail-order catalog of rare, sale, and new books several times a year. Is there another cookbook store anywhere that has its own curator (the erudite food scholar Johan Mathiesen)? The store also occasionally sponsors signings and conversations with such well-known cookbook authors as Paula Wolfert and Molly O'Neill. In short, Powell's Books for Cooks is one of the literary and gastronomical glories of Portland.

Powell's City of Books

1005 W. Burnside Street, phone: 228-4651.
Open Monday through Saturday, 9 a.m.–11 p.m.; Sunday 9 a.m.–9 p.m.

Powell's is now the largest bookstore in America, and it contains a food and cookbook section rivaled only by Powell's Books for Cooks. The main Powell's collection contains a groaning board of culinary literature: four banks of shelves holding books in every conceivable category of taste, including herbs and spices, tofu and soy foods, cheese, picnics, and beer making. Of course American regional and national cuisines take most of the space, and you can discern their relative importance and reputation by noting shelf allocation: French cooking gets six shelves, Italian four, British a mere one, ditto Korean. As for domestic consumption, California leads the way, tied with the Southwest, while Alaska—caribou cuisine?—gets a few linear inches.

Powell's always has good sale tables; one of the reasons for shopping here is their wealth of inexpensive out-of-print and used cookbooks. The Northwest section is impressively full, and there's an eye-catching bank of oversized, coffee-table food books. Those familiar with Powell's entrance display case of quirky titles will recognize a similar penchant inside, with such amusing books as *The Phony Gourmet, How to Repair Food*, and *Baking Soda Bonanza*.

Not to be missed is the superb stock of wine books. Powell's also has an impressive list of gastronomic literature (including everything written by M. F. K. Fisher), books on food and history, and anthologies of food quotations—excellent resources for showing off at dinner parties. The culinary reference section contains numerous volumes of every conceivable food topic, including catalogs of culinary institutes, food mail-order houses, and master indices to cookbooks.

If you're not seeking a rare cookbook and you wish to browse through books on collecting silver or medieval Italian history as well as the vast culinary holdings, Powell's main store is for you. You can also drop into Anne Hughes's coffee shop, have a pastry, and scan cookbooks at leisure before making your choice.

AND KEEP IN MIND...

Kitchen Kaboodle

See listing on page 171 for location and hours.

Kitchen Kaboodle offers a solid collection of cookbooks, featuring many elegant and coffee-table food books. It holds an annual sale in January, when cookbooks are 20 percent off.

The Kobos Company

See listing on page 38 for location and hours.

The Kobos Company doesn't maintain a huge stock of cookbooks, but what they have has been carefully chosen and includes most of the indispensable titles.

Williams-Sonoma

See listing on page 175 for location and hours.

Their own colorful, well-written, and stylish series, *The Williams-Sonoma Kitchen Library*, covers a wide range of dishes, food categories, and holiday entertaining.

Part 5

COOKING CLASSES
AND CATERERS

COOKING CLASSES

Chapter 22

Even as golf pros return to their teachers for a swing diagnosis or to perfect a new trick with the sand wedge, professional cooks sometimes take lessons to improve their technique or to learn a new cuisine. Of course we amateurs go to cooking classes to enjoy a meal, to watch a great pro at work, and to learn the foundations and basics of cooking—how to make French sauces, how to bone a lamb. In some classes you merely observe and taste, in others you get down and get floury. There are cooking classes where you can learn to decorate cakes with buttercream designs, others that focus on more complex matters, say the cuisine of Catalonia or of the Caribbean. Some sessions are reminiscent of high school Home Ec classes, others provide the chance to spend time with celebrity chefs.

Portland is awash with cooking classes. They're held in restaurants, in stores, and at public institutions. No kitchenware shop worth its sea salt lacks a demonstration kitchen, luring customers with the promise of becoming an instant Bocuse. Even when they're largely demonstrations, Portland cooking classes tend to be interactive, with lots of participation from students. Not for us the formalities of the Cordon Bleu, with deference paid to semi-divine chefs. Our example might have been set by James Beard's famous Gerhart classes, which by all accounts were good-natured, lively, and robust affairs, with sheer enjoyment of good food and a commitment to culinary demystification. All the while you can give yourself over to gastronomical monomania: discussing preparations, recounting great meals, relating cooking stories, obsessing over the dish that's underway. Good talk is the bread and butter of cooking classes.

Atwater's Food and Wine School

111 S.W. 5th Avenue, phone: 275-3600.

This is clearly the school with the best view in town. Thirty flights up, Atwater's offers a series that meets monthly, alternating food and wine classes to raise awareness of how they complement one another. Demonstration meals are prepared by chef Mark Gould, Atwater's young and talented cook. After the lesson, which includes tips about techniques, hints about where to find ingredients, and suggestions on how to make the most of seasonal foods, Gould serves the dinner he's just made. Local winemakers and experts conduct the wine classes, which highlight vintages from specific regions: Tuscany, Alsace, Germany, Champagne. Individual classes are $50, and the entire twelve-month cycle goes for a nondiscounted $600.

In Good Taste

408 S.E. 3rd Avenue (Sheridan Fruit Company), phone: 236-2113.

Gayle Jolley runs the best and most expert cooking school in Portland, hands down. In Good Taste is tucked into a corner of the Sheridan Fruit Company, between meats and wines, and always draws big crowds. Jolley, a lively, effervescent presence, does the bulk of the instruction, and with her experience teaching Thai, Vietnamese, Indian, French, Mediterranean, and American regional cooking, she covers all the bases. She's been catering manager at the Heathman and Vintage Plaza hotels, as well as at Pazzo's. She has assembled a first-rate stable of regulars, including Amelia Hard, erstwhile owner of Genoa; Heidi Yorkshire, author of the award-winning *Wine Savvy*; and Chris Arnerich, former owner of Delevan's and a renowned baker. In addition, Jolley has lured several major Portland chefs to offer classes, among them Cathy Whims of Genoa, David Machado of Pazzo, Cory Schreiber of Wildwood, and Caprial and John Pence. She has also managed to get a few stars from outside, including Madeleine Kumin.

Jolley herself offers a series of foundation classes of French cuisine: sauces, bisques, soufflés, crusts. The Portland chefs tend to feature favorites from their own restaurants; here's a chance to see how to concoct what you've already enjoyed or to learn what you've been missing. Jolley and Hard together teach a series of Italian regional classes, and there are always terrific specialty classes: one on dumplings (not your grandmother's weighted sinkers, but ultra-contemporary dumplings, such as Shrimp and Cilantro Potstickers, and Peach Dumplings with Caramel Sauce), another on Afghan fare, yet another on Catalan grilled food. One of the classes in greatest demand is Yorkshire's "Wine Savvy Basics"; she teaches the elements of tasting, describing, and pairing wine with food.

What characterizes the cooking here is a combination of simplicity and sophistication, a sense of serious passion for great food, and a belief that food reflects the deepest qualities of a culture.

Kitchen Resource

See listing on page 172 for location and hours.

The kitchen in the back of this pleasant cookware shop is the site of classes that continue through the year. There's no special motif or national cuisine dominating the schedule, but a very eclectic set of offerings ranging from a wild mushroom menu to a lesson in gnocchi-making. An occasional off-beat class pops up, such as one called "An Evening Breakfast," for night owls who need a 3 A.M. fix of scrambled eggs. Or one called "Virtual Vegetarian," which, despite its title, is not for on-line fans of lima beans.

A number of fine local chefs show up, including Caprial and John Pence of Westmoreland Bistro, and Stephanie Pearl Kimmel, who long ran Eugene's Excelsior Café and now heads the King Estate (Winery) kitchen. Most of the classes, which are demonstrations rather than hands-on sessions, range from $35 to $55. There's a healthy emphasis on seasonal classes: "A Spring Menu" features such nice French *plats du printemps* as Baked Asparagus Custard, Fricassee of Chicken in Light Cream, and Strawberry Tart.

Noodles School of Food at Nature's Marketplace

8024 E. Mill Plain Boulevard, Vancouver, Washington, phone: 360-695-8878.

This is Nature's Fresh Northwest's first excursion into cooking classes, and they have launched the new school in their newest store with an impressive lineup. Classes change continually; in general they feature specific foods (seafood, cheeses, chutney), holiday celebrations (Christmas desserts), and national cuisines (South American). Given Nature's orientation toward healthy eating, it's no surprise that Noodles School of Food occasionally

Fifteen hungry students are gathering around the large tiled table that fronts the work area of Sheridan Fruit Company's demonstration kitchen. We're here for **Amelia Hard**'s cooking class, "The Cuisine of Venezia," tonight's offering at **Gayle Jolley**'s celebrated **In Good Taste cooking school**. The table is set with pink and pale green place mats, and scattered about are bottles of olive oil, packages of Bob's Red Mill polenta, and several Italian cookbooks opened to sections on Venice. Everyone is buzzing, some about recent trips to Italy, others about remembered Italian meals, others just introducing one other and making small talk.

It's barely 6:30 P.M., and Hard, former owner of Genoa, long Portland's outstanding Italian restaurant, gets us into our seats as she talks about the Venetians' love of seafood. Jolley is helping her colleague this evening and begins by explaining the several wines she's selected to accompany the dinner, which will begin with Mussels Baked with Garlic Bread Crumbs, proceed to Risotto with Zucchini and Bacon, then on to Grilled Monkfish, Polenta, and Radicchio, and conclude with Espresso Granita.

The event is a carefully paced affair, with lots of explanation and demonstration, though it is not a hands-on class. It's more like going to a great restaurant and a fine theater performance at once, with plenty of audience participation (at least verbally) and lively interaction. Hard has prepped several of the more elaborate dishes, like the mussels and the polenta, but she saves a few mussels to indicate exactly what's demanded of the recipe. "I will demonstrate the mussels," she announces, passing around a couple of bivalves to show us why she's chosen them and showing us the bread crumbs, which have been ground to an exact degree of fineness. As she works, she keeps up a teaching patter, elucidating the varieties of Tuscan olive oils (we taste three kinds and learn to evaluate them) and clarifying the debearding process. Questions fly, and Hard, coolly making her way from chopping board to oven to stove, is a mine of information and advice, from the reason why kosher salt is better than commercial (the chemical that allows for easy pouring imparts a metallic taste to commercial brands) to an elaborate theory of risotto cooking methods.

Hard asks us to come up and peer into the pot, to see how the zucchini cooks almost to mush, lending a creamy texture to the arborio rice and infusing it with a richer flavor. Just as we're engrossed in the risotto cooking theory, the mussels arrive on our plates, forty-five minutes into the evening. By now people have gotten quite friendly and lots of good talk has covered the waiting time, during which Jolley has been pouring and explaining the first wine. The mussels are extraordinary, and it's hard to say which is better fare—they, or Hard's wonderfully genial banter.

The risotto is the most complex dish on the menu, and both cooks speak to the question of when it's done; informed opinions abound, from the pro-soupy faction to the pro–al dente. More cooking tips and demonstrations follow: we hear how to choose a great Parmigiano reggiano that's been aged at least eighteen months; we note that the cheese for tonight's risotto is stamped with the date and year of its making. (Ironically, just behind the table, stands a shelf of processed Velveeta and jars of Cheeze Whiz!) The risotto is now done, and everyone sighs as the plates go around. It will be the star of the evening.

We troop outside for the grilling, after a discussion about monkfish, too seldom found in local markets. When we return to the table with our prizes, the entrée is accompanied by concentrated food talk, local foodie gossip, and anecdotes about great Italian chefs. This class is for people who love jabbering about food almost as much as they love eating it.

The granita is simple and a classic, but because whipped cream comes with it, Hard is moved to give a Julia Child-like discourse against the loathed fat police. She's obviously preaching to the converted, and we all nod in agreement.

For three and a half hours it's been a celebrational evening. After some talk about the communal joys of cooking and eating together, there are a few hugs, a wine purchase or two, and some exchanges of phone numbers. And with comfortable satiety, we each disappear into the night.

offers classes in vegetarian cooking. Many of the instructors are buyers from Nature's several departments, and the guest teachers include Heidi Yorkshire of *Wine Savvy* fame. Classes are held in a kitchen and demonstration room near the entrance to the Vancouver megastore.

Northwest Culinary Resource Center

1401 S.W. Yamhill Street, phone: 790-1066.

"We Chop, We Sauté, We Create." So goes the motto of Northwest Culinary Resource Center, and while it probably won't displace Caesar's famous line, it does have a nice ring. Greg Taylor, a gold-medal winner in the International Culinary Olympics and a former instructor at the Western Culinary Institute, heads the school and is committed to a hands-on experience for his students. He offers culinary courses with such themes as "Cooking for Kids," "Wild About Oregon," and "The Basic Gourmet." He will even put together a class featuring a theme menu that you and your food or wine club design for yourselves.

Classes range over a broad spectrum of foods, meals, and preparations, including game, brunch, and smoking techniques. One of the specialties of the Center is its global wine classes, which cover not just the obvious regions of Alsace, Bordeaux, Burgundy, and California, but Australia, South America, and Portugal as well. Two of the most exciting ideas involve classes that begin by foraging in the woods for wild mushrooms and other forest edibles or at the shoreline for coastal foods, and conclude with menus utilizing the harvest or the catch.

Pastaworks Cooking Classes

S.E. Hawthorne store only. See lising on page 12 for location and hours.

Italian cooking naturally predominates in the Pastaworks classes, held at their S.E. Hawthorne Boulevard strore. There's a series featuring French bistro cooking, with separate classes on such regional styles as Provençal or Lyonnaise, and a Spanish series which might have Andalusian fare or Catalonian recipes. The principal Italian cities come in for attention, with menus built around their specialties: Florence, Venice, Bologna, Genoa, Palermo. These classes are often timed to take advantage of seasonal availability: thus, a class on Naples will appear in late summer for the tomatoes so prominent in the cuisine. Mediterranean cooking generally has a significant place; one year featured a series of salads from Morocco, Lebanon, Spain, France, and Greece.

Most of the Pastaworks classes are seriously hands-on affairs: teams of students prepare and present the dishes, with support from the demonstrating cook. All the classes are taught by the school's director, Teri Huggett, who earned her diploma at La Varenne in Paris and has cooked at The Heathman Bakery and Pub, Winterborne, and Jake's.

You can sign up for an individual class (around $40 or $45), or take a series of two or three classes, always with a discount for the series. Since so many of the classes use ingredients stocked by Pastaworks, participants receive a 10 percent discount certificate for the shops and for merchandise from Powell's Books for Cooks.

Pazzo Ristorante

627 S.W. Washington Street, phone: 228-1515, ext. 236.

David Machado, chef at Pazzo's (see page 231), runs a splendid set of classes in the wine cellar of the restaurant twice weekly (Monday evening and Saturday morning) from fall through late spring. It's appropriately called "The Cellar Series," and the ambiance is that of a fine dining room, not a kitchen. Tables are grouped in front of an antique bar, waiters serve the dishes, and wine steward John D'Anna speaks about grapes and vintages while the chef preps at the bar. Of course the focus is on Italian (regional) foods and wines, and students at these demonstrations watch the cooking of and then consume a three-course meal. In addition, the restaurant's pastry chef explains the making of Italian breads and sweets. While it's not a hands-on class per se, anyone may come to the counter and help Machado cut the gnocchi dough or handle other chores. About sixteen fill a class; and each session runs about $55.

Portland Community College

Many locations, phone: 977-4933.

Each fall, PCC puts out a huge catalog of course offerings, including cooking, food, and wine classes. You can sign up for "Basic French" or "Foods of Kenya" (be the first on your block to make *mandazi* and *sakuma*). PCC is one of the best places in town to learn Chinese cooking—there's an entire class on Chinese soups—and breadmaking. There are lots of practical classes, too: "Converting Your Favorite Recipes to Low-Fat Dishes" and "Catering Your

Own Party." If you've been stuck on TV dinners, here's one for you: "Cooking for One or Two—Beyond Frozen Entrées."

Westmoreland Bistro and Wine

7015 S.E. Milwaukie Avenue, phone: 236-6457.

You have to take the Pences on faith. Once a month on Monday evenings John and Caprial Pence spring a surprise: the subject of their cooking classes is never announced ahead of time, and the three dishes for the evening are at their whim and the market's availability. There's no brochure; all is by word of mouth, and the faithful flock to the Bistro. There's a down-to-earth style about the demonstrations, which might include such items as a Warm Spinach Salad with Dried Cherry Dressing, Pan-Fried Ravioli with Roasted Red Pepper, and Plum Upside-Down Cake. There's no attempt to teach in a systematic fashion, say, the fundamentals of Gascony cuisine. Most of the dishes come straight from the restaurant's varied offerings and from Caprial Pence's several cookbooks.

Caprial Pence's television show, "Caprial's Café" (shown on The Learning Channel), won a 1995 James Beard Foundation nomination for the year's Best Television Cooking Show, and viewers of the program will get a good idea what's in store were they to take a class. The level is geared to those who need some coaxing in the kitchen, enjoy a low-key but confidence-building experience, and want the basics as well as a few adventures. Caprial is always homey ("I just use my finger if I can't put my hands on a spatula"), reassuring ("They say it couldn't be done, but we did it!"), and completely unintimidating (she'll never say "*bain marie*" when "water bath" will do).

AND KEEP IN MIND...

Bob's Red Mill

See listing on page 17 for location.

The cooking school at Bob's Red Mill deals almost exclusively with grains, legumes, bread making, and the like.

Uogashi Japanese Restaurant

107 N.W. Couch Street, phone: 242-1848

This restaurant offers a number of courses in Japanese cooking, including making sushi. It takes as long to be a sushi master as to be a samurai warrior, but at least you can make a start.

The Food Lover's Companion to Portland

Chapter 23

CATERERS

Even the most fearless and accomplished home cook sometimes needs a caterer. We still love to entertain, but for larger gatherings, we've been known to call a pro so we don't have to fuss in the kitchen and can mingle with our guests without distraction. For busy professionals, finding time to entertain is always an issue; choosing a caterer means that planning, preparation, serving, and cleanup are no longer worries.

How do you know which caterer to call? The same way we learned. Get the name of the caterer at a function you attended where you especially enjoyed the food. Ask your friends whom they have used—word of mouth is a useful and powerful resource. Or call a caterer from the listings below and ask questions to find out what would be best for your needs.

A good caterer should ask *you* many questions. What is the date? How many people? Where are you holding the affair? What's the nature of the event? What are your food and style preferences? What's the budget? Are there any dietary restrictions? What kitchen facilities are available? The caterer can also arrange for drinks, serving platters, dishes, silverware, glassware, tables, chairs, flowers, music, serving staff, and anything else that will ensure a successful party. Remember that success is determined not only by whether the guests have a good time, but whether the hosts do as well. You hire a caterer to take care of the details, so that you, too, can enjoy your party.

Most caterers work out of a home or commercial kitchen, without office space. Whenever a caterer has a business address, we've listed it for you. But you'll find that most caterers are easy to reach by phone and will meet with you in your home or anyplace that's convenient.

Allan Levine Catering

Phone: 635-4735; at Garbonzo's, 922 N.W. 21st Avenue, phone: 227-4196.
Allan Levine, owner

Allan Levine specializes in kosher catering. Naturally, bar mitzvahs, bat mitzvahs, and Jewish weddings head his list, but he'll serve for any occasion when the need arises for kosher food. Levine ran a kosher restaurant in his native South Africa and more recently owned Cajun Café; any man who served tasso ham and andouille sausage between kosher cooking assignments is a complex fellow indeed. Occasionally he'll transform his own kitchen into a place for dietary regulation. He also does Indian and Middle Eastern fare, the latter in keeping with his Garbonzo's restaurants.

Armadillo Caterers

Phone: 235-4957. Paul Folkestad, owner and chef

Paul Folkestad, an alumnus of the Zefiro kitchen, is a busy caterer, doing everything from weddings to corporate lunches (Weiden & Kennedy advertising agency is a regular box-lunch client) to intimate parties. Some clients hire Armadillo to do a regular monthly dinner. Last fall, Folkestad prepared an elegant seven-course French meal for European Adidas executives. And at a memorable recent wedding, Folkestad's grilled halibut stood up well to the costume party competition for attention.

Armadillo's repertoire is focused on Mediterranean, Asian, and barbecued flavors. The company's bento cart—stocked with skewered kabobs and fresh salad rolls—can be hired for picnics and informal affairs. During the week, the custom-made cart serves the public near Good Samaritan Hospital in Northwest Portland.

Folkestad also enjoys the cooking-with-kids classes he teaches at the Catlin Gable School and dreams about opening a children's cooking school.

Briggs & Crampton

1902 N.W. 24th Avenue, phone: 223-8690.
Nancy Briggs, owner; Gail Yazzolino, manager

Long established as one of the premier catering firms in town, Briggs & Crampton gigs include large charity events, weddings, corporate occasions, and home-based intimate dinners. The kitchen staff is capable and dependable, with many graduates moving on to chef positions around town.

Platters decorated with fresh flowers are a Briggs & Crampton signature. For a recent party at the Pittock Mansion, where seating is limited and kitchen facilities restricted, they pulled off an elegant stand-up dinner for 200—where knives and forks would have been difficult to maneuver—with beautiful passed hors d'oeuvres including Crab and Scallion Puffs and Caviar with Crème Fraîche on Pumpernickel Toasts and a buffet laden with pretty, easy-to-eat finger foods: Sliced Beef Tenderloin sporting a rosy red bull's eye, Grilled Prawns with Plum Dip, and assorted tartlets with chanterelle, roasted vegetable, or lemon-goat cheese fillings. Everything, including the full bar, espresso cart, flowers, and string quartet, was arranged by the caterer. Briggs & Crampton overlooks no detail; as a result, a steep price can be part of the deal.

To sample this caterer's cuisine in a relaxed, gracious, and very private setting, check into their Table for Two. A stunning three-course lunch is served to two diners at noon each weekday at their catering headquarters. The set meal is elegant and delicious. An obstacle even greater than the expense ($75 per person without wine) however, is booking: reservations must be made at least three months in advance and Briggs & Crampton accepts reservations only one day each quarter. A redial button on your phone is a must to get through on the appointed day.

Cuisine Bebe

Phone: 223-7971. Barbara and Jean-Marc Baker, owners and chefs

Small in-home cocktail parties, brunches, and sit-down dinners are the focus of this small caterer. Owners Barbara and Jean-Marc Baker arrived in Portland two years ago from the San Francisco Bay Area, where they worked on their own and with Jeremiah Tower. They make virtually everything they serve, except for the bread and smoked salmon.

Their cuisine leans toward rustic styles and the flavors of Tuscany and Provence, with a little regional American as well. The Bakers describe it as "spontaneous." Presentations are natural and uncontrived, on stoneware and glass platters, with decorations of tropical and local leaves and ivies.

Jean-Marc recently became chef at a local country club but is still involved with Cuisine Bebe's menu planning and execution.

Eat Your Heart Out

2338 S.W. 6th Avenue, phone: 222-6111. Monica Grinnell, owner and chef

One of the most established caterers in town, Eat Your Heart Out was begun by Monica Grinnell two decades ago. It was she who introduced *torta rustica* to Portland, and soon it began showing up on hosts' tables everywhere. "If there's anything that characterizes our catering nowadays, it is not a dish or even a cuisine," says Grinnell, "but a look of abundance and harmonious colors and arrangements." She studied interior design, so the aesthetics of food styling come easily to her. Much of Grinnell's signature look comes from the many interesting serving pieces she's collected over the years. Her tables might be formal or casual, but they always include lots of baskets, flowers, and greens.

Not long ago the Oregon Symphony held a fund-raiser that included tours of a number of architecturally interesting homes. Eat Your Heart Out catered the party at each home, adapting the menu to the house itself. Thus there was a "Casbah" party at a Mediterranean-style house, an American classic garden party at a traditional house, and a Southern menu at a home resembling a plantation manor.

Grinnel has provided a training ground for several cooks who have gone on to success in Portland's food world: Ron Paul cut his teeth and his first *mirepoix* on the chopping boards of the old Eat Your Heart Out restaurant.

Elephants Delicatessen

See listing on page 8 for location. Lisa Turner, Catering Manager

Elephants differs from the other caterers in this book in that it specializes in preset or format menus, designing the event from a list they've put together. Elephants seldom does a sit-down dinner—almost all of its catering is buffet-style. Many of those events are in the public eye, such as the Art Museum receptions after the Portland Arts and Lectures events. Because it has a standardized format and employs a large staff, it can prepare a party on very short notice, often within twenty-four hours. Of course, you can browse the store to get ideas should you wish to put together your own selections.

Elephants also caterers a lunch delivery menu (free delivery on a minimum $30 order): sandwiches, sack lunches, salad entrées, soups, and desserts, all available with a phone call or a fax (224-4097). If you let the delicatessen know a day ahead of time, you'll be guaranteed delivery on the minute. If you call that morning, lunch comes within a half-hour of your specified time. With the twenty-four-hour prearrangement, you can get more elaborate catering: poached salmon, cannelloni, pâté, chilled beef tenderloin, platters of morning pastries, and lox platters.

Food in Bloom

2701 N.W. Vaughan Street, Suite 421, phone: 223-8033 or 223-6819.
Kristin and Jim Harris, co-owners

One of the more venerable caterers in town, with eighteen years of experience, Food in Bloom handles more than 1,500 events a year and has staged as many as twenty-five parties in a weekend. Such a calendar takes serious planning, and the company keeps a full-time staff of two dozen people. Begun by Kristin and Jim Harris, Food in Bloom is the kind of caterer who can elicit congratulations, cheers, and toasts from the guests. Consummate professionals, they give as much attention to the look and feel of the occasion as to the food itself. "Staging" is not just a metaphor: Food in Bloom can provide props to stylize an event, such as faux marble columns hung with lights for a dramatic effect.

At the 1995 Governor's Arts Award Dinner, they served a sit-down dinner for 500, including Stuffed Grilled Swordfish with a *Coulis* of Fresh Tomatoes on a bed of French lentils. They have done a buffet for 2,000 people for a benefit. Such vast settings make a dinner party for 75—the heart of their business—seem like duck soup. They've given English teas on the garden paths of noble old homes, and produced dinners in the shadows on sloping lawns. Food in Bloom has done a lot of Mediterranean cooking of late, but they're increasingly drawn to Southeast Asian cuisines, as they cater for several Pacific Rim trade organizations.

Hands On Café and Catering

8245 S.W. Barnes Road (Oregon School of Arts and Crafts), phone: 297-1480.
Pia Baumgartner, Jack Cook, and Lee Anne Fitzpatrick, owners and chefs

Anyone who has eaten at Hands On Café, the delightful restaurant attached to the Oregon School of Arts and Crafts, knows that the food is cooked with devotion. The place settings are composed of pottery hand-thrown and fired in the ceramic workshops of the school, and fresh flowers adorn the tables. The same attention to detail and aesthetics marks the catering service, and the owners' varied backgrounds contribute to the diversity of the organization. Lee Anne Fitzpatrick spent time in Mexico and South America and lends ethnic culinary flair; Pia Baumgartner grew up in Sweden and contributes classic, continental styles of cooking; Jack Cook specializes in Italian and Northwest cuisines.

Hands On has an impressive range, from Brazilian seafood stews to traditional Thai dishes to Salmon with Blackberry Sauce. Perhaps even more than their cooking, their natural look is famous in food circles. For a Northwest dinner, for example, they'll use baby pears on branches and clusters of Oregon grapes as table decoration; for a Thai dinner, they'll draw from their collection of bright Thai tablecloths garnished with orchids and other exotic flowers and leaves.

Jane Bergin Catering

1706 N.E. 32nd Avenue, phone: 281-0305. Jane Bergin, owner and chef

Jane Bergin reluctantly designates her catering style as "French country," by which she means dishes like potted sage cheese garnished with edible flowers. But press her and she'll tell you about a Southern-style barbecue she did not long ago and a benefit for Oregon Public Broadcasting featuring a dinner with seven courses each from a different country. Although she can't be narrowly categorized, she does lean toward Mediterranean cooking.

Bergin is devoted to seasonal foods, so expect a bounty of Oregon produce and fish if you're thinking of a summer event. Tasso-Wrapped Shrimp, Grilled Swordfish with Papaya Salsa, a seasonal Vegetable Basket with Green Peppercorn Dip have all graced summertime wedding menus. She makes her own stocks, grows her own herbs, and gathers lavish bouquets of fresh flowers for her table arrangements. There's a country spirit in her work, and she's looking to buy a farm with a barn near Portland to stage events in her own venue, a longtime dream.

Leave It to Linda

5910 S.W. 177th Avenue, Aloha, phone: 649-6101.
Linda Venti, owner and chef

Linda Venti cooked on a yacht off the south of France and took classes in Florence from the great Italian chef Giuliano Bugialli. Trekking in Kenya, she came upon *bhajais*, spicy potatoes fried in a batter, in a small Indian restaurant outside Nairobi, and found them memorably delicious. With that background she certainly isn't going to offer cold meat and cheese platters.

Unwilling to settle for the humdrum, Venti aims for authenticity and will eagerly try any national cuisine, including those from different African countries. Many customers come to her without definitive ideas, so she gladly makes suggestions, often from the countries in Asia and Europe in which she's traveled. She fondly recalls a dinner for 400 at the Oregon Episcopal School that featured Thai lamb curry, green mung beans in a pepper sauce, and Balinese barbecued chicken.

Porter's Woodsmoke Bar-B-Que Catering

1513 S.E. 3rd Avenue, phone: 232-8172. Hollis Harris, owner and chef

Hollis Harris's preferred method of cooking is a 55-gallon drum filled with hardwoods lit by wax, a method that transcends your backyard Weber. Harris has catered a number of theme parties, including one with a Wild West motif engaged by a Japanese American Society; everyone—clients and cooks alike—dressed like Wyatt Earp, and guests munched on smoked brisket doused with homemade hot pepper sauces. Harris can handle jerk pork at a Caribbean fete and ribs at a hoedown. Whether you want to celebrate Easter with a roasted lamb on a spit or you're a good ol' boy looking for baby backs and North Carolina pulled pork, Harris can do the job.

Ron Paul Catering

1441 N.E. Broadway, phone: 284-5439. Eric Rose, catering manager

One of the most active and visible caterers in town, Ron Paul has established an enviable reputation by stressing fresh, beautifully presented and simple but elegant food. There are no gimmicks, no emphasis on exquisite serving dishes, no costumed waiters to establish the motif of the event: the *food* is the decor. Ron Paul never confuses catered meals with theme parks.

Ron Paul Catering looks for the spirit of a cuisine, not for the creation of ersatz authenticity. If they are serving Thai food, you won't see Thai tablecloths because, as Eric Rose notes, "We make no attempt to convince you, even in fantasy, that you're in Thailand." Ron Paul events are characterized by artistry in the food, especially their signature platters of roasted summer vegetables arranged in concentric circles as intricate and bejeweled as a rose window in a Gothic cathedral.

Paul was the first Portland chef invited to cook dinner at the hallowed cynosure of American cuisine, the James Beard House in New York. If he can ship sixty-six *ballotines* of pheasant across the country, hand-carry Oregon mussels and pears to the Beard House, and be greeted with applause by a tough New York audience, then catering in town must be a snap.

Paul enjoys suggesting menus and educating tastes, but always makes sure the host feels comfortable with the choice. Every job is created from scratch, and over the years he has rarely repeated a menu. If there's a request for a very unusual food, he'll accommodate that, too. Recently a local Oriental rug dealer requested a Tibetan dinner, and Eric Rose researched the subject as best he could. No yak meat, but the spirit of the land was captured to the dealer's pleasure. Recent jobs have included a dinner attended by Vice President Al Gore preceding a Pacific Northwest Forest Conference and box suppers for the Los Angeles Lakers on their way home after a Blazer game.

Soigné

Phone: 246-1913. Donnis Hilliard, owner and chef

A former kitchen manager for Briggs & Crampton, Hilliard was most recently half of Angel's Food, one of the most respected catering firms in town. When co-owner Twinka Thiebaud—the erstwhile personal chef to Henry Miller in Hollywood—decided to focus her talents on product development instead of catering, Hilliard renamed the business and kept on whisking and chopping. With Angel's Food, Hilliard developed wonderfully full-flavored low-fat recipes that she uses for Soigné. But her emphasis is broader than that: rather than focus on any one cuisine, she prepares whatever a client requests, with the most careful, detail-oriented preparation and presentation. She'll do fried chicken and corn for a picnic and make it the most upscale, elegant picnic imaginable, and she'll happily cater a sit-down, formal dinner. She doesn't print menus or cuisine suggestions, but prefers to meet with clients to discuss possibilities. Hilliard's goal is simple, clean presentation of great food.

Tavola

Phone: 225-9727. Linda Faes, owner and chef

Catering has always been Linda Faes's first love. Even when she owned restaurants—the dessert-focused Paisley's in Northwest Portland and the dearly departed Panini downtown—Faes couldn't stay away from off-site cooking. In 1995, she sold Panini, even though it was a thriving scene for terrific little sandwiches (*panini*), salads, and stellar desserts. She can duplicate that fare for a party, but Faes is accomplished in more challenging cuisines as well, especially those of Asia and the Mediterranean. She makes her platters look casually elegant, using fresh flowers, a bit of lace, or perhaps a piece of ribbon to add dimension to her work. Imagination reigns.

Faes loves to cater dinner parties, and takes great pleasure in freeing a hostess from worries and responsibilities. Lisa hired Faes to cater a luncheon for thirty people and Faes wouldn't let Lisa help with anything. At one point, Faes shut Lisa out of her own kitchen, reminding her that hiring a caterer meant that the caterer did all the work. Faes arranged for the rentals and did all the prep, serving, and cleanup. The mini-sandwiches were all but inhaled by the guests, as were the simple, tasty salads, and berry shortcakes. And Lisa had hoped for leftovers!

Yours Truly

1628 S.W. Jefferson Street, phone: 226-6266. Heather Harvey, general manager

Over fifty years ago, two women who ran a secretarial school decided to open a catering business on the side—hence the name Yours Truly—and it became so successful that the school was soon dropped. Ever since, this establishment has been the darling of "old Portland." Their hallmark is an antique collection of china, silver, linen, and stemware so large that they do not charge for place settings, virtually unheard of in this business. Yours Truly is a bit on the traditional side, but for tasteful and proper entertaining it can hardly be matched. On the other hand, they will barbecue pork and have moved tentatively into ethnic cooking. Heather Harvey also specializes in wedding and specialty cakes, something many caterers will not touch, and has won numerous local prizes for her chocolate desserts.

Not many caterers provide you the opportunity to try their cooking before you sign the contract. Yours Truly runs the Gate Lodge Restaurant on the grounds of the Pittock Mansion, and it's a good place to experiment before you commit. Try the Bengal Chicken Salad, Hot Crab Sandwiches, and prize-winning chocolate.

AND KEEP IN MIND...

Atwater's

111 S.W. 5th Avenue, phone: 275-3629. Jim McInally, catering manager

This swank restaurant with its four-star view over the city offers off-site catering. Expect dishes similar to those at the restaurant: very attractive, formal, and with complicated ingredients and presentation.

Jake's Catering

S.W. 10th (Alder Street), phone: 241-2125. Dorcas Popp, catering manager

Jake's Catering, the catering arm of McCormick and Schmick's restaurant empire, is housed in the Governor Hotel Kitchens. These folks handle grand-scale events, such as the Fred Meyer Challenge (600 meals). Although not cutting-edge, their food tastes good and every courtesy gets extended to clients.

Ron Paul approaches the job of catering with the skills and oversight of a general planning a campaign down to the smallest detail, often transporting materials and people for many miles. The event where we tracked his masterful operations—a wedding for 150 guests— was not exactly halfway around the globe, but was a considerable seventy-five miles from Portland on the grassy slopes of the Columbia.

A huge white tent flaps gently in the wind, the whitecaps in the river lap at hundreds of windsurfers with their brilliant sails, and a woman in a wetsuit with board in tow sidles past the wedding party guests, surfers all, and nobody bats an eye. Behind the tent in the "staging area" Ron Paul bastes free-range chickens, fires up the grill, arranges the already-poached cold salmon, places the fine cheeses next to Oregon summer berries, and puts the finishing touches on his signature platters of cold marinated vegetables (including roasted garlic, potatoes, peppers, stuffed grape leaves, and grilled eggplant). Like a meticulous stage designer, he even supervises the table and floral arrangements.

Napoleon planned his Moscow campaign with less foresight. Paul has scouted the site, determined the location of the tent and its dance floor, and, since there's no access to any building, has ordered portable toilets and set up a generator to power the lights. The prep work at the caterer's kitchens took some five hours, from early morning bread-baking to the moment the racks rolled out to the vans. The salmon and the Crab Puffs have survived the afternoon transportation in iced Styrofoam containers, the champagne retains its chill; and many hundreds of glasses have arrived intact. A sudden crisis: the tapping device for the beer kegs won't fit. Paul is instantly on his beeper, and within ninety minutes his man arrives from Portland with the correct paraphernalia.

As the marriage ceremony finishes, servers stream out of the staging area, bearing Bruschetta with Sun-dried Tomatoes and Pesto, or with Prosciutto and Fresh Pears. On waiting tables lie eight immense salmons, each one outlined in edible flowers and garnished with overlapping cucumber slices in the pattern of fish scales. Everything has been meticulously plotted: backstage there's movement but no consternation, frenzied activity but inner calm. Paul's people have been through this many times, yet everything comes off with an energetic spontaneity.

Any leftovers not claimed by departing guests will go to Blanchette House, a Portland shelter for the homeless. When the last of the dance music dies at midnight, everyone is happy and relieved, and Paul can finally clean up. Since there's no sink on site, dishes get washed down with a hose and buckets— the only primitive touch to a sophisticated bash.

Part 6

RESTAURANTS

RESTAURANTS

We each regularly review restaurants for our newspapers: Roger for *Willamette Week* and Lisa for *The Oregonian.* We go to restaurants as others go the office, but usually with greater anticipation. Still, the life of a reviewer is less glamorous than you may think. Night after night we're obliged to violate the rueful Miss Piggy command: "Never eat more than you can lift." We are condemned to fly in the face of nutritional sanity and often can hardly enjoy the meal for all the note-taking.

But we don't mean to shed crocodile tears. We love to track the growing number of wonderful dining spots in town. In the wake of the food tsunami over the last five years, many splendid restaurants are appearing on the scene and the national press has put Portland on the culinary map. Chefs obviously feel the same way. The bounty of Oregon—our remarkable produce, game, seafood, nuts, and wine—has lured many fine cooks. Starting with Christopher Israel and Bruce Carey of Zefiro, the great migration from California has included Wildwood's Cory Schreiber (a Portland native son who created showy dishes at the Cypress Club in San Francisco), Pazzo's David Machado, and Café Azul chef Claire Archibald (who was raised in McMinnville but established herself at Chez Panisse in Berkeley). Jo Bar's rotisserie consultant learned his trade at Roti in San Francisco. Even Swagat's team of Indian-trained cooks made their first home on the U.S. range in the San Francisco Bay Area.

New Yorkers have also flocked here in recent years. First among these refugees is The Heathman chef Philippe Boulot, a Norman whose skill at The Mark Hotel earned him three stars from *The New York Times.* Vitaly and

Kimberly Paley, the warm and gracious owners of their eponymous Portland restaurant, worked in such New York hot spots as Bouley, Chanterelle, and Union Square Café. Ken Gordon of 28 East owned a successful lower Manhattan restaurant, and Tony Demes, Couvron's architectural chef, also migrated from the New York area.

These chefs have raised the sophistication level for Portland diners, but they joined a stable of Oregon pioneers, creative chefs who toiled here before the rest of the world discovered our food haven: Millie Howe at Indigine; Patti Hill, former chef at Bread & Ink; Greg Higgins at The Heathman and then his own place; Dennis Baker at Café des Amis; Amelia Hard, former chef at Genoa; and June Resnikoff at L'Auberge. Portland's rich ethnic communities—especially Asian—have brought forth terrific Thai, Vietnamese, Chinese, Catalan, Greek, Japanese, and Indian dining spots.

For this chapter, we've picked the places where we dine most often, the haunts we return to again and again, sometimes for the food, sometimes for the ambience. Our list is a reflection of our personal tastes and habits and is not intended to be a definitive dining guide, nor even a list of "the best" in Portland. (Our newspapers annually publish such guides, to which we contribute and which we help edit.) The list here is meant to reflect our own take on the scene (circa September 1995), to guide you through the wealth of dining options available in Portland to spots that are our favorites and may become yours as well.

Alexis

215 W. Burnside Street, phone: 224-8577. Open Monday through Thursday, 11:30 a.m.–2 p.m. and 5 p.m.–10 p.m.; Friday and Saturday, 11:30 a.m.– 2 p.m. and 5 p.m.–11 p.m.; Sunday, 4:30 p.m.–9 p.m. Credit cards accepted

By now Alexis has a fine patina of age, like the weathered marble of the Acropolis. Though we can't remember the last time a new dish appeared on the menu, Alexis simply burnishes its image, getting ever closer to the Greek idea of culinary perfection.

What should the uninitiated order? To begin with there are several excellent appetizers. The sour creamy *Tzatziki* is laden with garlic, enough to terrify those vampires not so far away from Macedonia. *Melitzano* (eggplant purée) is a pungent, smoky affair, with chopped tomato for color. *Saganaki* is a production number: a pan of fried Kasseri and Kefalotiri cheeses flamed with brandy, a kind of Greek fondue that is great to sop up with the chewy country bread. Finally, the Deep-fried Squid, which is never oily, always crunchy, and loaded with the flavor of the sea, is the best calamari in town.

For main dishes, their Moussaka is state of the art. It consists of ground lamb covered with a sinfully rich béchamel. Lamb chops are tender and flavorful (ask for them rare), and the baked catch of the day is always a treat. We're fans of *Garithes Souvlaki*—skewered chargrilled shrimp, nicely done with just a touch of lemon and Alexis's own olive oil. Good selections of retsina keep the proceedings well-oiled. The atmosphere is lively (no need to break plates in order to feel the gusto!), the service couldn't be more attentive, and if Alex Bakouros himself is there to preside, you'll meet the titular spirit of the place. Alexis is a family business, with everyone dedicated to making the restaurant a welcoming, satisfying experience. Though you can't go into the kitchen and point to the bubbling pots to order your dinner (as you often can in Greek tavernas), in most ways Alexis represents authentic Greek dining. Lively Greek music enhances the evening, and the prices are eminently sane. Be sure to attend Alexis's annual Greek Independence Day bash, one of Portland's great public parties. Alexis will probably go on forever.

Assaggio

7742 S.E. 13th Avenue, phone: 232-6151. Open Tuesday through Thursday, 5:30 p.m.–9:30 p.m.; Friday and Saturday 5:30 p.m.–10:30 p.m. Credit cards accepted

For years, we roamed the landscape looking for a great neighborhood pasta joint, and then Assaggio opened. Not only is their tasty pasta plentiful, but the space is absolutely charming, if a bit noisy, and the prices friendlier than a Nordstrom sales clerk.

Most of the food is very, very good: the kind of honest pasta preparations you'd make at home if you had the time and the inclination. Nothing too fancy, nothing too outrageous, just good, solid dishes at prices that won't force you to eat cheese sandwiches all week as a result.

Appetizers or first courses are limited—bruschetta, grilled vegetables, polenta, a few salads. Focus on the bruschetta, a toasted slab of their wonderful house-bread baked, topped with a lava flow of white beans, fresh tomatoes, or sautéed mushrooms. The white beans make a stunning topping, and the generous size of the portion allows two diners to share easily.

While it would take you a while to work through all the mostly meatless options—from simple Spaghetti with Fresh Tomato and Garlic to Bow Ties with a Light Walnut and Cream Sauce—the best deal is the restaurant's namesake, an assaggio (Italian for "sampling") of pastas chosen daily by the kitchen.

All members of your party have to order the assaggio. The kitchen picks three pastas and then sends your way, in a timed sequence, a generous bowl of each one for the table to share. At $10 per person—no more than many of the individual pastas—you get a hefty portion of three different dishes.

Desserts cover the Italian map, from a lovely *tiramisu* to silken *panna cotta* (a molded cold cream with fruit) to a spectacular Chocolate "Salami" (a log of ground chocolate, dried fruit and crushed petit buerre cookies that's surprisingly light and flavorful).

As you'd expect, Assaggio is popular. Reservations are only accepted for parties of six or more. An hour's wait on any night is typical. Our advice is to eat at the counter if you can—or grab five friends, make a reservation, and enjoy yourself.

Atwater's

111 S.W. 5th Avenue, phone: 275-3600. Open Monday through Thursday, 5:30 p.m.–9:30 p.m.; Friday and Saturday, 5:30 p.m.–10 p.m.; Sunday, 5 p.m.–9 p.m. Credit cards accepted

The dazzling city view dominates the scene from Atwater's elegant, thirtieth floor aerial perch. Chef Mark Gould's market-inspired preparations are artful, but not always as consistent as the view. Some things, like a sophisticated surf-and-turf tower of Grilled Foie Gras, Tuna, and Pepper-Crusted Filet—all enrobed in a wonderfully winey port reduction—can work. A delicious Duck Risotto is a perfect marriage of creamy rice and shards of duck confit. But some entrées suffer from confusion; too many ingredients can be more than the palate can process.

The wine list is remarkably deep, especially in old Bordeaux. At least twice a year, Atwater's plays host to Bordeaux release dinners, which we love: they offer a rare opportunity both to drink across a year of wines and vertically through one château, tasting from bottles most of us could never afford, let alone find. Wine is poured generously, and the mood and setting are chic and sparkling.

The dress-up, glamorous atmosphere keeps Atwater's one of the only special-occasion restaurants around. The same stunning view and culinary strengths and weaknesses extend to the handsome blond-wood bar, where you can hear some of the best live jazz in the city and a more casual menu and mood attract a younger, less stuffy crowd.

The Food Lover's Companion to Portland

2601 N.W. Vaughn Street, phone: 223-3302. Open Sunday through Thursday, 5 p.m.–12
midnight; Friday and Saturday, 5 p.m.–1 a.m. Credit cards accepted

For simple dinners, month in and month out, this is one of our favorite places,
a space that's guaranteed to put you in a relaxed and cheerful mood. In summer, the romantic patio offers the best al fresco dining in the city; in winter,
the bar glows with coppery warmth. L'Auberge's bar is a mellow spot, and
everyone seems to unwind here. While the more formal room on the lower
level is certainly handsome, we've always been partial to the cozier area above.

The dishes are traditional bistro, starting with succulent mussels, which
yield lots of good juice. The salads are crisp, the vegetables accompanying
main courses cooked just right (green beans served with a creamy aioli are
properly al dente), and such main courses as Grilled Chicken with *Fines
Herbes* or a Flank Steak with Anchovies show the kitchen's deft touch. Two
desserts that have been on the menu for years should not be missed: the satiny
Chocolate Mousse and our absolute favorite, the Lemon Cheesecake, poached
for airiness. It's so light it feels more like a palate cleanser than a rich sweet.

Things can get rather busy on weekend evenings, but the service is always
accommodating even if sometimes slow. If you've made a habit of seeking
out Asian restaurants on Sunday evenings, think seriously about changing
your ways, for on Sunday, in addition to its regular bistro fare, L'Auberge
serves some of the best ribs around as well as one of Portland's great ham
burgers with spectacular crisp potatoes. And on Sunday at 8:00 P.M., old
movies are shown in the bar dining area.

410 N.W. 21st Avenue, phone: 274-1572. Open Monday through Friday, 11 a.m –
3 p.m. and 5 p.m.–10:30 p.m. (Friday, 5 p.m.–11:30 p.m.); Saturday, 5 p.m.–11:30 p.m.;
Sunday, 5 p.m.–10:30 p.m. Credit cards accepted

There's nothing startling about this country Italian restaurant, which tends to
feature Tuscan and Umbrian cuisine, but the cooking is very dependable and
the place is full of good energy and pulsates at late hours. Basta's boasts an
impressively large and reasonably priced list of Italian wines. Best of all, the
food complements the ambience, which is a triumph of taste imposed upon a
space that might have crushed most designers. (If you can transform a Tastee
Freeze into a trattoria Sienese, you can do most anything.) Basta's gets crowded on weekends, but the area around the bar makes for a lively waiting area.

There is usually a dish of perky Roasted Peppers, which, along with a simple order of room-temperature Spinach with Olive Oil and Lemon Juice, makes a wonderful starter. We also love the paper-thin carpaccio, the beef fillet named for the Italian Renaissance artist Vittore Carpaccio; the red of the beef exactly matches the hues of the painter's palette. Pasta dishes are dependable, and three of them stand out for us: the *Puttanesca, Fusilli* Laced with Shredded *Brasato* (wine-marinated beef), and the scrumptious Egg Noodles with Braised Ragoût of Duck. Polenta with a Light Cream Sauce of Garlic and Sage is excellent, and the rabbit dishes are always delicious. There are hearty stews once the weather turns cool, and the *Brasato* served on its own is much like a homey, tender brisket. If you're lucky, you might catch a special of Pork Stewed in Barbera Wine and Blended with Tomatoes and Basil: the ensemble achieves a burnished mahogany tone and a pungent, savory flavor.

There's no better late-night supper than a plate of pasta, some crusty country bread, and a glass of Barolo, and Basta's fills this bill with *sprezatura*.

Berbati Greek Restaurant

19 S.W. 2nd Avenue, phone: 226-2122.
Open daily, 11 a.m.–2 p.m.; 5 p.m.–10 p.m. Credit cards accepted

Ted Papaioannou runs an ever-expanding operation, but his recent focus on Berbati Pan, the jumping dance joint behind the restaurant, has not diverted his attention from the menu one iota. If anything, it's made us conscious of how good Greek food, especially *mezethes* (appetizers), can be late at night, when Berbati does a rousing business. Papaioannou is a genial host and will gladly discourse on all aspects of Hellenic cuisine. The *Kalamari* are crisp and no one serves better lemon-infused sautéed potato wedges, an interesting starter. All the usual Greek dishes are here, including a smooth, garlicky *Tzatziki,* which is great slathered on the crusty dark bread, and luscious feta-filled *Tiropites.* Our favorite dishes are the lamb chops done to a rare turn with a touch of oregano and lemon; Sautéed Shrimp in a Lemon-Oil Sauce; and the excellent *Stifatho,* a stew made with chicken in a tomato base. The spices are always sharp, tangy, and aromatic, and all dishes are homemade and fresh—essential characteristics of good Mediterranean cooking. Berbati and Alexis are the two best places in town for Greek fare.

The Food Lover's Companion to Portland

Bread and Ink Café

3610 S.E. Hawthorne Boulevard, phone: 239-4756. Open Monday through Friday,
7 a.m.–11 p.m.; Saturday, 8 a.m.–10 p.m.; Sunday, 9 a.m.–2 p.m. and
5 p.m.–9 p.m. Credit cards not accepted

Perhaps the quintessential neighborhood restaurant on the eastside, but one that draws from all of Portland, Bread and Ink Café grew in stature under the hand of chef Patti Hill, whose cooking had an inspired intensity and sublime but simple integrity. Hill is gone, but the café is carrying on in her tradition. There are several features about Bread and Ink that make it a relaxing, affable place: the comfortable green leather chairs, the easygoing crowds, and the generally communal feel, especially on Sunday mornings, when half the tables are reading *The New York Times*. There's a touch of Berkeley or Cambridge about the place.

Breakfast items are good (we wolf down the Home-Fried Red Potatoes), and on Sunday you can get a "Yiddish Brunch" that includes smoked sable, scrambled eggs with lox, blintzes, and assorted sweet pastries. Bread and Ink served Portland's first salad of wild greens—and continues to do so. The guacamole is quite fine, and the pâté is exceedingly well made. Of course, their baguettes are legendary; ditto their Greek rolls and bialys.

At dinner, the café offers five or six entrées, several of which change nightly. Portions are not enormous, but the food is always cooked *au point* and is garnished with style. Duck Legs Braised in Apricot Preserves, Hoisin, and Dark Soy Sauce nestle against a Purée of Gingered Yams. Vegetarians as well as carnivores will enjoy a potato gratin made with Gruyère and fortified with wild mushrooms and roasted garlic. The soups are always a treat, whether a Curried Red Bean or an autumnal Squash Bisque. The *Cassatta di Siciliana* has long been the favorite dessert, consisting of lemon pound cake layered with ricotta, candied orange peel, and chocolate and covered with espresso-chocolate ganache. This is a cozy place to drop into at almost any time of the day, and to return to often.

El Burrito Loco

1942 N. Portland Boulevard, phone: 735-9505.
Open daily, 10 a.m.–10 p.m. Credit cards not accepted

Mexican food at its best exudes spicy flavor or earthy primal tastes. In Portland's once-barren Latino landscape, these fundamentals have become increasingly easier to find. Burritos are the fast food of the moment, and this authentic Latino eatery was one of the first spots to offer these inexpensive great tastes. The soft burritos are mammoth, the kind that take two hands to eat. One comes with batter-fried *chilies rellenos*, refried beans, and shredded beef; another has scrambled eggs and Mexican sausage chunks. Top them off with the salsa of fresh tomato, onions, and bits of jalapeño—and get plenty of napkins and a cold soda to wash it all down. If the tables are occupied (as frequently happens), get your burrito to go and enjoy it somewhere else.

Café Azul

313 Third Street, McMinnville, phone: 435-1234. Open Monday through Saturday, 11 a.m.–2 p.m.; Thursday through Saturday, 5:30 p.m.–9 p.m. Credit cards accepted

Co-owner Claire Archibald spent five years working with Diana Kennedy in Mexico, and before that, ran the upstairs kitchen at the remarkable Chez Panisse in Berkeley. With her sister Shawna, she operates this marvelous small regional Mexican café. We love the simplicity of the place: the clean, fresh, delicious flavors of the cooking and the remarkably low prices. We always start off with the *Gorditas*, small hand-patted tortilla sandwiches that ooze molten cheese and salsa with a deep roasted flavor. Sometimes we construct a great meal just from the starters. Their guacamole is at once smooth and chunky, with a strong onion presence and crowned with bits of tomato; a bowl of warm black beans has crumbled *cotija* cheese on top. Dip the warm house chips alternately in the salsa, guacamole, and beans, and you'll be rewarded with delightful contrasts of texture and flavor. Even though the more complicated dishes like the sultry chicken tart called Tinga Pie are fabulous, we tend to focus on the extraordinary tacos. The most unusual offering is *Rajas con Crema*: fire-roasted pasilla chilies, onions, and cream. Smoky, roasted flavors intermingle with tart and creamy for a startling, wonderful taste. Dining here is a genuine treat, well worth the hour's drive from Portland. Café Azul is a terrific stop on your way to or from the coast, but it's also an excellent destination, smack in the urban center of wine country.

Café des Amis

1987 N.W. Kearney Street, phone: 295-6487. Open Monday through Saturday, 5:30 p.m.–10 p.m. Credit cards accepted

This casual neighborhood bistro is popular, and while the French-inspired cuisine is neither hip nor haute, this place works on many levels. It's at once comfortable, accessible, and romantic, with a helpful, informed staff. You'll be as happy here in jeans as in more formal business attire, and the menu offers both moderately priced and more expensive possibilities.

You can make a handsome meal of the appetizers, especially the chunky Duck Terrine with Pistachios, Dungeness Crab Cakes with Chipotle Aioli, or the earthy Wild Mushroom Ravioli. Soups are among the best in town, creamy and smooth with interesting flavor combinations. The three signature entrées are always a good bet: Duck with Blackberry Sauce, the legendary Filet of Beef with Port Garlic Sauce, or Salmon Troisgros with a reduction of white wine, shallots, and crème fraîche. Periodically, the menu sports new additions: a cured-then-grilled Pork Loin with Cranberry Chutney and Braised Red Cabbage is lovely fall fare, Poussin with Forty Cloves of Garlic is beautifully burnished and arrives showered with roasted garlic cloves; and a thick Cioppino of Northwest seafood floats in a spicy tomato base. Chef Dennis Baker is not obsessed with seasonal foods, but he does weave into his repertoire fresh and interesting flavors. Save room for the tempting desserts: tasty cakes, silken creams, and fruit-based mousses.

Campbell's Bar-B-Q

See listing on page 134 for location. Credit cards accepted

The location of this authentic barbecue parlor—outside Portland's inner core, away from the more likely storefront haunts of the North and Northeast—always surprises us. But once you're inside the pair of ordinary buildings, smoky flavors fueled by fire dominate the setting. The family-friendly experience is also a waist-expanding one: it's easy to overeat here! The temptation of so many succulent barbecued meats makes us weak, and we wind up gnawing on bones and licking the incendiary sauces off our fingers for hours.

Order a combo platter that includes a good assortment of the roster of barbecued meats. Campbell's does chicken, pork ribs, beef ribs, brisket, pork loin, turkey, and hot links—each meat just short of falling apart and being overcooked, and wonderfully smoky and succulent. They offer not one but four strengths of barbecue sauce: mild (a little bland), medium (getting better), smoky brown sugar (good and sweetly hot), and hot. Really hot. Even the staff stares at you when you order, waiting for you to turn funny colors and grab your throat. You will. Mop up with fluffy house-baked rolls or sweet crumbly corn bread. And don't forget to order a few side dishes—most are very good. We love the creamy, old-fashioned Potato Salad, the Baked Beans, and the Sautéed Greens.

Try to save room for dessert. If you can force yourself to swallow just a little more, the homey sweets are mighty good eating. In particular, try the Peach Cobbler or the Lemon Meringue Pie. Or better yet, take one home to enjoy after you've had a chance to recover from your excess.

La Catalana

2821 S.E. Stark Street, phone: 232-0948. Open Tuesday through Sunday, 5:30 p.m.–9:30 p.m. (Friday and Saturday until 10:30 p.m.). Credit cards accepted

Until Portland gets a Spanish restaurant, La Catalana alone must represent Iberian cooking for us. Indeed, the restaurant undertakes that task with considerable success, featuring a cuisine that reaches from the urban sophistication of Barcelona to the isolated hamlets of the French Pyrenees to the craggy coves of the Costa Brava. Their fare combines such seemingly distinct ingredients as rabbit and oysters or shrimp (*Mar i Muntanya*—literally "sea and mountain"), or chicken and snails blended with honey and pears. Catalan cooking, which assimilated ideas from the French, the Italians, and the Moors, is pungent and earthy, driven by such sauces as *allioli* (a mayonnaise-like emulsion of garlic and olive oil that is slathered on grilled meats and fish) and *romesco* (based on hazelnuts, almonds, sweet peppers, and tomatoes).

A tapas menu, available in the summer and only if you ask for it, offers you a choice of delectable small dishes. The appetizers at La Catalana are rustic and spark conversation and good cheer. There's Grilled Bread Rubbed with Olive Oil and Tomato and accompanied by either anchovies or thinly sliced ham; Briny Mussels Broiled with Spinach Mousse and *Allioli* (making a sort of Hispanic version of Oysters Rockefeller); Grilled Tuna with *Romesco*; and always a fine soup such as smoky Roasted Red Pepper Soup. Grilled fish dishes in the assertive garlic sauce are superb, and the accompanying potatoes are often zested with orange shavings and a dark tapenade of anchovies, capers, and black olives. The Roasted Chicken, enhanced only by olive oil and accompanied by a vegetable ragout, is highly satisfying.

Two of the several desserts stand out: *Crema Catalana*, a runny version of *crème brûlée* in which the crackling caramelized sugar tops a lemony custard, and Chocolate Mousse, very creamy and stocked with liqueur-soaked currants and toasted pine nuts. The restaurant is quite small, but its intimacy and subdued lighting, along with the handsome breakfront displaying brightly colored folk pottery, impart warmth and make for conviviality. La Catalana fully justifies the ancient Catalan proverb: *Pecat de gola Deu el persona* ("God pardons the sin of gluttony").

Couvron

1126 S.W. 18th Avenue, phone: 225-1844. Open Tuesday through Thursday, 5:30 p.m.–10 p.m.; Friday and Saturday, 5:30 p.m.–11 p.m. Credit cards accepted

Chef Tony Demes and his wife, Maura, named their restaurant after the French town where Maura was born. The charming space is a cozy dining spot, a small stage to showcase Tony's creativity. His presentation style is very hip New York: tall architectural constructions that are painstakingly executed and focused on drama. His culinary style is country French, dominated by his whimsy and imagination. The seasonal menu always includes a starter of rich and wonderfully indulgent Grilled Foie Gras, the preparation changing often, but sometimes including port and candied turnips. Successful entrées have included Seared Duck Breast with Braised Cabbage; Roasted Chicken Wrapped in Bacon with Spaetzle; and Grilled Maine Lobster atop crispy Capellini Cakes. A multi-course *degustation* (tasting) menu is a delightfully leisurely and indulgent meal, with the courses changing each evening.

From its opening last year, Couvron was besieged by Tri-Met light rail construction. Thankfully, access keeps improving. Couvron has settled into its own creatively dramatic rhythm.

Esparza's Tex-Mex Café

2725 S.E. Ankeny Street, phone: 234-7909. Open Tuesday through Saturday, 11:30 a.m.–10 p.m. Credit cards accepted

Get rid of your notions of Americanized Mexican food—excessive plates of boring cheese-stuffed tortillas, beans, and rice. Supress any thoughts of new wave Texas cuisine with cool ingredients, hip combinations, and dramatically arranged plates. This food is pure, goofy Joe Esparza: one part memory (of his Texas mama's cooking) and one part Joe's little smoker (his favorite culinary tool next to his salamander for top-glazing). Esparza knows how to smoke 'em: brisket comes out mildly toasty; lamb gets a woody essence. Esparza also throws chicken, buffalo, rattlesnake, shrimp, and turkey into the smoker, then combines them with mole, ranchero sauce, barbecue sauce, or cheese to create homey-good tacos, enchiladas, and burritos. Esparza's food is packed with heat and creativity, and his personality arrives on your plate—assertive flavors, warm generosity, and earthy fires.

We love the *Nopalitos*, skinny batons of cornmeal-dusted, pickled cactus, tender and crisp munchies that are absolutely addictive. Dunk them into the snappy house salsa (served with fresh warm chips at every table) for tangy wallop. Try the Pork *Asada*: three thin slices of nicely charred pork loin that have benefited from a pregrill bath of garlic, chili, and lime. Fresh *Chiles Rellenos* are superb: stuffed with stretchy cheese and batter-dipped, these fried chilies are exactly what they're supposed to be—crispy, oozing molten goo, with a hot bite. On Thursday night, we often make a pilgrimage for the special of Chicken-Fried Steak. Served with cream gravy and real mashed potatoes, it is retro road food at its best.

The "What's Available Today" list is handwritten on the boards near the kitchen. As the evening hours draw on, more and more dishes appear on the "sold out" side, so it pays to dine a little early. (The *Chiles Rellenos* typically run out by 8 P.M.) Esparza's doesn't accept reservations, so there's often a substantial queue, but turnover is pretty fast. Waiting at the bar can be a kick, especially for taking in the overdecorated space—hanging Mexican marionettes, stuffed snakes, animal skulls with flashing-light eyes—and enjoying a beer with the chips and salsa. This place always feels like a party, with plentiful, tasty food and prices that are very reasonable.

L'Etoile

4627 N.E. Fremont Street, phone: 281-4869. Open Wednesday through Saturday, 5 p.m.–9:30 p.m. Credit cards accepted

Charm radiates from every corner of this very French dining spot. The main dining room has a candle-lit glow, gold-flocked wallpaper, and a gracious ambience. The narrow bar—with its own menu of Confit of Duck, Duck Liver Terrine, and Lavender-Cured Gravlax—is made cozy by the large fireplace and intimate space that offers perhaps the most European feel of any restaurant in Portland. Edith Piaf—type music fills the room with a Parisian chic that comingles with Northwest casual. A private room at the back of the bar puts you in a small round space, more like a dining room in an elegant Parisian apartment. The crowning jewel to this lovely restaurant is the hidden rear garden: a formal landscaped parterre in which to wander before or after a lovely meal. In warm summer weather, dining tables are set out here, too. You have to walk through the kitchen to gain access to this magical space, and on the way you'll see just two people, owner John Zweben and his sous chef, scurrying to finish sauces, sear meats, and glaze vegetables.

Sweetbreads and foie gras are almost always on the menu at L'Etoile, a treat for us since we can't get enough of these delicacies. You'll also find Escargots in a Garlic and Walnut Sauce, and a terrific Leek and Goat Cheese Tart. Main course options range from a delicious thick Veal Chop buried in Fresh Morels to Roasted and Stuffed Quail, to Herb-Crusted Rack of Lamb. Restraint is unknown: cream, butter, or cheese adorn every morsel. Use the fabulous, flour-dusted rolls to mop up every last bit of sauce.

Desserts are also first-rate, and include a simple cookie plate, which arrives with a crown of spun sugar and flowers, and a single scoop of intensely flavored sorbet presented in an elaborate lacy cookie cup.

Fong Chong

301 N.W. 4th Avenue, phone: 220-0235.
Open Monday through Saturday, 11 a.m.–3 p.m. and 5 p.m.–10 p.m.; Sunday,
10:30 a.m.–3 p.m. and 5 p.m.–10 p.m. Credit cards accepted

It bustles every lunchtime, when the dim sum carts keep up a continuous circulation through the room and the little plates of steamed goodies—from shrimp enclosed in a wheat-starch wrapper to pork dumplings wrapped in rice noodles to steamed buns filled with barbecued pork—pile up on every table. The Chinese written characters for dim sum mean "to touch the heart," but these delectable appetizers will even more pleasurably touch your palate. The plates nestle under steaming bamboo baskets, and one is tempted to taste all of the many varieties that come around. Dim sum makes a great brunch, and Fong Chong is at its best late on Sunday morning, when Chinese families fill the brightly lit restaurant with contented chatter and voracious appetites. The mostly Cantonese cuisine is dependably good. Regardless of what you order, do not pass up the deep green Chinese Broccoli with Oyster Sauce—a burst of health and hedonism in each stalk—or the many homey (assuming home is Wuchow) claypot casseroles known as *po*, such as a Chinese grandmother might make. The bean-curd version startlingly includes shrimp and sea cucumber; for the utterly stouthearted, another version comes chock-full of duck feet.

Fong Chong's decor is strictly no frills: fluorescent lights, booths, foil-covered duct work. But keep your mind on the food. At dinner we tend to go for West Lake Beef Soup; Spice Salt Shrimp deliciously charred from the grill and encased in their shells; the many squid dishes, most of the slabs scored with elaborate geometric patterns to enhance tenderness; and Shrimp or plump Oysters with Fresh Ginger and Spring Onions, the scallions split open like a mandrake and lending a freshness to the dish.

You'll often see banquets served around large circular tables, the dishes spinning like vertiginous temptations. By all means ogle, inquire, and imitate the order. While you might do better in Hong Kong, Fong Chong is a welcoming place, and it's hard not to leave smiling.

Fuji Restaurant

2878 S.E. Gladstone Street, phone: 233-0577. Open Tuesday through
Saturday, 4:30 p.m.–9:45 p.m. Credit cards accepted

This may be the best sushi bar in the city. Fuji Handa's masterful way with the blades of his trade attracts a very loyal coterie of sushi devotees, many of whom show up nightly. We've often asked him to make whatever inspires him at the moment, and we're always enchanted, whether the offerings are gorgeously executed versions of the classics or such unusual trompe l'oeil creations as fish in the guise of birds, as when flying-fish eggs are placed onto a mound of rice into which a fan-spray of cucumber is inserted to resemble a fluted tail. Handa's work is delicately balanced and organized, intricate little worlds of refinement and bejeweled exuberance. He will shape fish to resemble flowers, diadems, even the geometry of a delicate escapement. No one works with greater virtuosity and more untrammeled imagination than he, and his creations often tease and startle.

You can assemble a splendid dinner from sushi and several appetizers, especially the creamy Soft Shell Crab, a miniature version that goes down in a couple of bites. For heartier fare, we recommend the *Yose Nabe*, a soup made and served in a clay pot that's perfect for a blustery winter evening. It's layered with shrimp, clams, whitefish, salmon, spinach, mushrooms, and potato noodles and looks like a pond with lily pads floating on it, each item easing into the harmonious pattern. Even a seemingly mundane dish such as *Sukiyaki* arrives looking like a brilliant lacquered sculpture, but the presentation never masks the food's vibrant taste.

There are only six or seven tables, and the decor is geometric black and white, with an elegant simplicity. One nice touch from the Old World comes with the sake boxes behind the counter, which bear customers' names in English and Japanese. These rustic containers impart a woodsy flavor to the rice wine much as oak barrels give a taste to Chardonnay.

Genoa

2832 S.E. Belmont Street, phone: 238-1464. Open Monday through Saturday,
5:30 p.m.–9:30 p.m. Credit cards accepted

Since the early 1970s, when pioneering restaurateur Michael Vidor changed the dining landscape in Portland, Genoa has presented serious Northern Italian food of outstanding quality. Vidor's Genoa was a hip haven, so focused on the kitchen that even sophisticates forgave the mismatched decor.

Employees Amelia and Fred Hard bought the place in the early 1980s and continued the traditions and upped the intensity of the kitchen with authenticity and well-researched recipes and menus. The newest regime—all veteran Genoa employees—has kept up the intensity, but they have also started to pay attention to other aspects of the restaurant. The clunky silverware has been banished, and the new spare white dishware does a better job of showing off pretty food. The once oppressively dark space has started to lighten up, and a comfortable parlor in the back offers a private pre- or post-dining refuge.

But it's the remarkable food that earns Genoa its real respect. It is arguably Portland's most ambitious restaurant. We have been dining here since its inception, and the food keeps getting better. The nearly $50 fixed-price menu changes every two weeks, offering creative possibilities not found elsewhere. In a seven-course meal that includes a fish, pasta, salad, entree, cheese, dessert, and fruit course, we've enjoyed silky Squash-Stuffed Ravioli with a Ground Nut-Butter Sauce; Fig-Stuffed Quail, honey-glazed and roasted to a wonderfully sticky finish; and Skewers of Veal, Sausage, and Herbs Served over Polenta. After six courses of lovely, filling food, it's hard to find room for dessert, but the effort is well worth it: from the *Boccone Dolce* meringue torte to a simple Lemon Tart, their desserts really sing.

Meals here are outstanding, but seven courses can be a frightening prospect. When we dine at Genoa, we starve ourselves all day (and on the following day) in order to eat all the delicious food set before us. (Four-course dinners are now available on weeknights.)

The Heathman Restaurant and Bar

1001 S.W. Broadway, phone: 241-4100.
Open daily, 6:30 a.m.–11 p.m. Credit cards accepted

Well into his third year at The Heathman, chef Philippe Boulot has settled in comfortably and impressively. The restaurant continues to be wonderfully reliable, and Boulot's enthusiasm about Oregon ingredients is evident in all his dishes. Many of them bear the stamp of Boulot's Norman heritage and his long training with the best in France, including Joel Robuchon, whom some consider the greatest chef in the world. One of the important aspects of Boulot's tenure at the hotel is that he is a magnet for superlative chefs and purveyors from New York and France. The chefs come to Portland to cook with Boulot or to showcase their individual expertise: last year, Philippe Groult—owner of Amphyclès, a Michelin two-star restaurant in Paris and a friend of Boulot since both men studied with Robuchon—came to town, and for several days cooked spectacular dinners as guest chef. As for the purveyors, Boulot hosted the largest American producer of fresh foie gras, and in no time The Heathman and several other restaurants in town were featuring it to raves.

Boulot has designed the menu so that The Heathman can be either a fine but simple bistro offering uncomplicated *cuisine bourgeoise* (stews, roasts, gratins, chops), or a luxurious restaurant offering refined dishes. He does a stunning charred rare Ahi Salad Bedded on Tuscan Beans, and he'll play textures off against one another in pairing broiled foie gras with young Oregon green beans, or in a Wild Mushroom Salad where the juice from the chanterelles laces the accompanying arugula. He has a great eye for textures and colors, melding a tawny Braised Rabbit, Red Chard, and Sautéed Potatoes. Elegance reigns in other dishes, such as a luscious slab of Swordfish with bosky Porcinis that comes with Chanterelle Whipped Potatoes and a Honey-Coriander Confit of Carrots. The simplest preparations, such as a marvelous free-range veal chop, maintain their integrity with minimum fussing and yet are intelligently accompanied, in this instance by richly satisfying Potato Gnocchi in a Light Sage Cream. In every instance, the dish is beautifully orchestrated. The menu greatly prizes such Oregon bounty as wild mushrooms, greens, fava beans, and berries.

Susan Boulot presides over the pastries, and her creations complement her husband's work. Look for a Calvados-infused *Tarte Tatin*, or her *Tiramisu* loaded with coffee flavor. Dinner is always a pleasure here, but don't forget the superior breakfasts—without question The Heathman is the finest place in town to greet the day.

Higgins Restaurant

1239 S.W. Broadway, phone: 222-9070. Open Monday through Friday, 11:30 a.m.–2 p.m. and 5 p.m.–10:30 p.m.; Saturday and Sunday, 5 p.m.–10:30 p.m.; bar menu daily, until 12 midnight Credit cards accepted

Sometimes we prefer Higgins's bar, which is dark, brooding, and masculine, the kind of place where you feel happy knocking back a good single-malt Scotch before consuming one of the better steaks in town. But sometimes we prefer the tasteful main dining room, which is arranged on several levels, brighter than the bar but still with plenty of atmosphere. Especially given its central downtown location, Higgins is a great spot for after-theater late suppers and an equally good place to have an efficiently served but not rushed meal before the show.

Greg Higgins's menu is colorful and spanking fresh. It's a bit hard to classify, but if we must we'd say traditional French country without orthodoxy. There are touches of Burgundy and Gascony, melded with respect for ingredients grown in local soil. Higgins's motto is "Our body clock follows the seasons," and so, too, does the menu, which changes every fortnight. Hence, a salad of Duck Confit, Toasted Rosemary Brioche and Fall Greens might appear as the weather begins to cool, along with Risotto Infused with Autumn Squash. Roast Loin of Pork Stuffed with Herbed Sausage is a treat. Vegetarian diners are respected, too: you might find a Meatless Chili with Tamale Dumplings, Forest Mushrooms, and Red Lentil Pancakes—hearty and bold. Desserts are usually splendid: a warm Plum and Cardamom Cake with fresh plums on the side makes for luscious fall fare.

Higgins insists on free-range chickens, organic greens, line-caught wild salmon, and as many local ingredients as possible from a sustainable agriculture. He regards the restaurant as his home writ large: just as he decides on his home menu after looking in the garden, so he develops the restaurant menu spontaneously from market availability, insisting that "the volatility of the supplies enhances our creativity." It's a fine place, equally unpretentious and sophisticated.

Indigine

3725 S.E. Division Street, phone: 238-1470. Open Tuesday through Saturday,
5:30 p.m.–10 p.m.; Sunday, 9 a.m.–2 p.m. Credit cards accepted

Indigine has long featured some of the most creative cooking in Portland, every dish strongly marked by Millie Howe's personal vision and sense of bounty. In a small, simple room, softly lit and dedicated to leisurely dining, Indigine can be counted on to meet the high expectations its loyal flock has maintained over the years. Things are at their heated best on Saturday night, when an all-Indian fixed-price menu offers a daring mix of entirely homemade ingredients, even the Indian cheeses and spectacular chutneys are created on-site. The Indian dinner at Indigine normally begins with tandoori drumsticks, pastries of phyllo filled with goat cheese, a glistening seafood salad keyed to the season, and a range of astonishing entrées: the imaginatively inflammatory Satanic Verses (pork sausage and prawns in a fiery vindaloo); Lamb Shanks Braised in Yogurt-Almond Sauce; Roast Chicken Stuffed with Cashews and Raisins; and an impressive Vegetarian Sampler including a Baked Masala Banana Sprinkled with Cardamom. Some items may never have appeared in Delhi or Bombay, but if you order Razor Clams with Curried

Vegetables, you'll begin to experience Howe's fantasy of the West Coast nuzzling up to the sub-continent..

Weeknights see a menu of many international entrées, including a classic Pesto Chicken and a great Seafood Enchilada, which are always preceded by a huge composed salad of greens and gorgeously arrayed raw vegetables and followed by a dessert tray of immense proportions. Indigine is famous for its groaning board dining (the line between generosity and excess is a fine one here), and you'll inevitably hear moans of pleasure and moans of satiety. Few places in Portland have maintained such exacting standards for so long.

Jake's

401 S.W. 12th Avenue, phone: 226-1419. Open Monday through Friday, 11:30 a.m.–4 p.m.;
Sunday through Thursday, 5 p.m.–11 p.m.; Friday and Saturday,
5 p.m.–12 midnight Credit cards accepted

To many Portlanders, Jake's is *the* place to bring visiting relatives and *the* spot to go for all things that swim in sea or stream. Over 100 years old, Jake's is really an institution: a reliable fish house with dark, turn-of-the-century ambiance. The fish offerings are wonderfully varied and fresh—a blackboard by the door lists the impressive daily availability. (Warning: Request your fish to be slightly undercooked; be silent at your own risk.) The signature dishes —Bouillabaisse, Clam Chowder, Crab Cakes, Crawfish—are consistently prepared and very good. Seasonal specials such as a King Salmon with Honey Glaze and Fried Leeks marries rich and sweet together. Fresh Maine Lobster is reasonably priced: just a simple one-and-a-half pounder served with melted butter is only $11.95 from 2 P.M. to 5:30 P.M. and a bit higher at other hours. Sometimes we dine here just to have the steamed bivalves, which are treated with simplicity and respect. Desserts include Jake's famous Chocolate Truffle Cake, a dense flourless affair now also available in flavors of mint or peanut butter. The warm Three-Berry Cobbler is another reliable favorite.

Jo Bar and Rotisserie

715 N.W. 23rd Avenue, phone: 222-0048. Open Tuesday through Thursday,
11:30 a.m.–12 midnight; Friday and Saturday, 11:30 a.m.–1 a.m.;
Sunday, 9 a.m.–11 p.m. Credit cards accepted

One of the brightest places on N.W. 23rd Avenue, Jo Bar is connected to Papa Haydn both by ownership and by a passageway. But Jo Bar is decidedly its own place, specializing in grills and rotisseries. The wood-burning oven looks as if it came from an eighteenth-century French château, but it is framed by plaster rather than real stone. Nevertheless, that oven produces dishes that are pretty to look at and often superb. The composed salads are first-rate, and, when amplified by an individual pizza, any one of them can make a fine light meal. A stew of meaty wild mushrooms, carrots, pearl onions, and celery root is one of the town's best vegetarian dishes. The menu shifts frequently, but look for an occasional Thai-inspired dish, such as a Fish Stew with Curry and Ginger. The Roast Chicken satisfies in a very primal way, and the Jo Potatoes are spectacular: baked and roasted in duck fat to a crispy brown. Jo Bar makes its warm desserts in the wood-burning oven, and while that may seem curious, the *Tarte Tatin* is as good a version as we've had outside France (expect homemade Cinnamon Ice Cream in lieu of crème fraîche). If you're a party of two, try sitting at the wide marble bar—it's more relaxing and comfortable than you might imagine, and you can keep an eye on the lively goings-on.

Lemongrass Thai Restaurant

5832 N.E. Glisan Street, phone: 231-5780. Open Monday and Tuesday, Thursday and Friday, 12 noon–2 p.m.; Sunday through Tuesday and Thursday 6 p.m.–10 p.m.; Friday and Saturday, 6 p.m.–10 p.m. (closed Wednesday). Credit cards not accepted

Ever since it opened in 1994, Lemongrass has been one of our favorite Thai restaurants in Portland. The cooking is very consistent, and Shelley Siripatrapa's energy at the stove never seems to flag. The place is fairly small, so it can sometimes be difficult to get a table immediately. And because everything is cooked to order by Siripatrapa alone, the service can sometimes be painfully slow. But the spectacular food is worth the wait.

Don't miss the Steamed Mussels with Fresh Shallots and Basil, or the soups —either light Tomato or Coconut Milk and Chili, set off by kaffir lime leaves. The spices are brilliant, the colors lively, the flavors clean and astonishingly fresh. The tastes just keep coming at you. You'll be asked to choose your degree of heat, on a scale from 1 to 10: don't be too macho, for 6 is hellish. Main courses are all made with chicken, fish, or vegetables; there is no beef or pork on this menu. For lovers of the national dish, Lemongrass does the best *Pad Thai* noodles around. You'll enjoy the bistrolike atmosphere of this sparkling little restaurant. The chef trained with her very accomplished mother, who owns one of our longtime favorites, the formidable Bangkok Kitchen. This restaurant introduced Thai cooking to Portland over a decade ago, in the very spot where Lemongrass now stands and to which the talented daughter has serendipitously returned.

Montage

301 S.E. Morrison Street, phone: 234-1324.
Open daily, 6 p.m.–4 a.m. Credit cards not accepted

There's a cartoon-mural of The Last Supper on one wall of Montage. If you worry that a supper of alligator pâté and green eggs and Spam will be *your* last, you'll have to try other picks from the vast southern-cum-Cajun good ol' boy menu. There's a wealth of good eating here, including more varieties of Jambalaya than any road house in the bayou could dream up. Try the version with spicy andouille sausage and scallops; the crawfish tail and the catfish versions taste mighty fine, too. All the ingredients that fortify the Jambalayas—frog's legs, mussels, chicken, rabbit sausage, and that big scary river beast—appear in the pastas, but the Louisiana rice dish is superior to the linguinis. A Kentucky Pie that's really a dense candy bar with whipped cream is the star of the desserts, and you'll feel like wearing a white suit and drinking a julep after eating this one. The scene is hip, full of frisky colts feeling the first pleasures of freedom. Dining is at long tables, cheek-by-jowl with who knows who, but don't fret: Montage is chock-full of good cheer. Lines after midnight are not uncommon, and the restaurant really does get lively at the Sinatra hour—three o'clock in the morning—when night birds and workers from the swing shift rumble for gumbo.

Paley's Place

1204 N.W. 21st Avenue, phone: 243-2403. Open Tuesday through Thursday,
5:30 p.m.–10 p.m.; Friday and Saturday, 5:30 p.m.–11 p.m. Credit cards accepted

Few Portland restaurants in recent memory have taken off so quickly and beautifully as Paley's Place or are run with such a sure hand. To begin with, it reflects Kimberly and Vitaly Paley's great aesthetic instincts. He studied piano in the Soviet Union and at Juilliard before deciding to become a cook; she was a professional dancer with Alvin Nikolai before gaining a diploma from the Sommelier Society of America and joining her husband at a two-star Michelin restaurant in southwestern France. Each of them learned the Gallic respect for food and the earth, a sense of fine cooking as an integral part of our lives, and the necessity of treating ingredients with loving and serious perfection. Between them they have worked in some of New York's best restaurants: Bouley, Union Square Café, and Chanterelle.

The simple dining room seats an intimate thirty-two diners with another eight on the porch in good weather. There are always baskets of produce near the entrance—wild mushrooms, strawberries, pears, tomatoes—and the unpretentious but tastefully decorated space is instantly inviting. Hostess Kim Paley makes every diner feel like a special guest.

The Paleys' idea was to create a subdued neighborhood bistro. Early menus included a spectacular salad of black mission figs surrounding a cluster of arugula, with a dressing of balsamic vinegar and dried cranberries; Sweetbreads with Polenta in a Morel Sauce; Braised Lamb Shank and White Beans; and Horseradish-Crusted Salmon on a Bed of Fennel, Red Cabbage, and Walnuts. Paley's Place specializes in solid, homey fare, something like what the French call *cuisine de grand-mère*.

As Vitaly Paley learned about the richness of Oregon products—quail, portobello mushrooms, marionberries, pears, mussels, crab—he felt challenged to create new dishes and became a bit more ambitious with his menu by treating classics in new ways. Recent visits have turned up a gorgeous, intensely flavorful Tambourine (ring) of Morel Mushrooms with Hazelnut-Thyme Vinaigrette, and Ravioli Stuffed with Ricotta and Purple Spinach and sauced with a bath of tomato and a sharp pecorino. What Vitaly's grandmother might have called a chicken pot pie turns out to be a spectacular dish of chicken first browned and then baked under a lofty Brunelleschi dome of golden puff pastry. The inspiration for this creation is the famous Truffle Soup Elysée made by Paul Bocuse for the president of France.

Among the desserts, the Crème Brûlée is impeccable—a crackling crust and a rich custard that has substance and lightness at once. A warm individual Chocolate Soufflé Cake—oozing liquid chocolate at its center—is a rich yet airy extravagance.

What we feel here is the devoted concern for getting things right, for cooking and serving with unfussy elegance, and, above all, a sense of creativity blended with discipline.

Pazzo's

627 S.W. Washington Street, phone 228-1515. Open Sunday through Thursday, 7 a.m.–10 p.m.; Friday and Saturday, 7 a.m.–11 p.m. Credit cards accepted

Chef David Machado is one of the senior members of the informal chef's club in Portland. He promotes Italian products and area chefs with equal enthusiasm and teaches classes on Italian cooking at every opportunity. He's a real chef's chef. His restaurant, the hotel kitchen at the Vintage Plaza Hotel, is somewhat more corporate in feeling than most Portland restaurants, with a crowd-pleasing menu and the requisite olive oil on the tables. The space is dark and clubby, heavy on wood and tile, and sports an open kitchen. The menu changes daily, and has a strong regional Italian influence. Wood-oven pizzas are terrific and pastas tend to be tasty, especially when Machado uses butternut squash, whether stuffed into little pasta pillows or blended into meltingly tender gnocchi. We're very fond of the Grilled Raddichio with Goat Cheese as a starter. We tend to confine ourselves to the appetizer selections, as the main courses can be a bit inconsistent, but the chops—veal and pork—are reliable and give off a heady, wood-seasoned perfume. Breads are first-rate as well, from focaccia with an oily glaze to crumbly rustic loaves. And desserts, such as a baked-to-order fruit tart, leave us very satisfied.

Pho Van

707 N.E. 82nd Avenue, phone: 253-2694.
Open daily, 9:30 a.m.–8 p.m. Credit cards accepted

Pho Van lingers in your tastebuds after your first visit. Even though it is a bit out of the way, you'll find a way to return to this bright and bustling Vietnamese noodle soup stop. The menu is small but choice and delivers a rich, complex, and exotically seasoned taste. Service is family-friendly.

Seven versions of Beef Noodle Soup are offered—the basic rich and flavorful broth and skinny rice noodles with the addition of your choice (or a combination) of round, flank, brisket, tripe, tendon, or meatball. A plate of herbs and greens accompanies each huge bowl for added punch; add drops from the bottle of hot sauce on each table to custom-heat your brew. You can't slurp the stuff fast enough, and the flavors are dynamite.

Other menu items worth exploring include a duck version of the exotic chicken soup your mother never made: it warms and soothes but bites back subtly. Another great discovery is No. 12: two crispy rice flour crepes, big half-moons stuffed with shrimp, pork, mushrooms, onions, and loads of bean sprouts. You eat it like traditional springrolls by tearing off a piece, wrapping it in lettuce with a cilantro sprig, and dipping it in the clear sweet-hot sauce. Heaven.

Restaurant Murata

200 S.W. Market Street, phone: 227-0080. Open Monday through Friday,
11:30 a.m.–2 p.m. and 5:30 p.m.–10 p.m. Credit cards accepted

Weekday crowds of dark-suited businessmen from Tokyo tell it all: here is the most authentic, sophisticated Japanese food in Portland. In this small but charming establishment, with a few handsome tatami rooms, you feel as if you're in another world. A blackboard notes several specials in Japanese characters, but the waitress will cheerfully translate. Don't be put off if she tries to dissuade your Western appetite from something too foreign; in fact, that's your cue to jump on the bullet train to gastronomic adventure.

The best way to experience the delicacy and artistry of Murata's executions is with a sample of à la carte offerings, many of which look as exquisite as tracery. From the sea-smacking freshness of the sashimi (the yellowtail is extraordinary) to the filigree tempura, everything is pleasing to the eye and the tongue. Try Oregon *Dofu*, chilled tofu enveloping oyster and crabmeat, the dish dripping with delicate noodles representing, as our server noted, "Oregon's water." Raw oysters, rice, and vinegar combine with chopped scallions, mint, and a touch of hot chili for a briny treat. Check for a special cold Sautéed Eggplant, crunchy with sesame seeds. Adventurous diners will enjoy strips of squid laced with sticky, fermented soy beans that pull apart with just the right tensile strength. Finish up with ice cream thickly powdered with ground jade tea leaves, a rare treat.

Even the serving bowls are an aesthetic delight. Try the sake, not only for its high quality but also because the cups have tiny ceramic faces of folk characters at the bottom; you're supposed to keep these little countenances under wine at all times. Murata is a bit more expensive than other Japanese restaurants, but it's worth every last yen.

Ringside

2165 W. Burnside Street, phone: 223-1513. Open Monday through Saturday, 5 p.m.–12 midnight; Sunday, 4 p.m.–11:30 p.m.
14021 N.E. Glisan Street, phone: 255-0750. Open Monday through Friday, 11:30 a.m.–2:30 p.m.; Saturday, 5 p.m.–11 p.m.; Sunday, 4 p.m.–10 p.m. Credit cards accepted

The reliable Ringside opened in 1944 and hasn't changed much since D Day. Veteran waiters, some here for three decades, provide quiet and efficient service. The steaks and prime rib are first-rate and the onion rings, thick crispy inner tubes, are enormously popular. The burgers are terrific, too, but you shouldn't stray too far; unfortunately, the salads and desserts are unimpressive.

While excellent chicken livers, fried chicken, and halibut are offered, beef is king. And beef is what Ringside does best, so the quality is high and each order cooked exactly as you request. Steaks make a dramatic arrival at your table on hot, oval metal platters that sizzle with the meat juices. Baked potatoes are the usual accompaniment—this is a meat-and-potatoes kind of place.

The original westside location has the air of an English gentleman's club. Seating is mostly in red leather booths. The addition of a wine room-cum-dining room was not an improvement, since sitting there feels like a banishment from the warmth of the main restaurant. If you can't get a seat in the main rooms, head for the bar, a great little hideaway. (It's the place where Lisa's husband, Kirk, popped the big question over a burger and fries.)

Ron Paul Charcuterie

See listing on page 16 for locations. Credit cards accepted

Everything that's available for take-out (see page 139) may be had in these pleasant, informal restaurants. No other establishment shows off its productions with such seductive arrangements in the deli cases, and patrons tend to spend more time surveying the display than the menu. Scrutiny will be rewarded. The simple breakfasts— mostly freshly baked goods and fruit— are a fine way to greet the day. At lunch, popular items include the excellent individual pizzas, the salads galore (try the Szechuan Noodles in Peanut-Ginger Sauce; the Wild Rice with various fruits and nuts; the good Caesar; or the Wild Gathered Greens with Oregon Blue Cheese and Hazelnuts), a wonderful, flaky Mushroom Strudel, and a great Southwest Casserole with Pork and Chile Verde. (Ron Paul hails from Tucson, and is true to his roots.)

Dinner items change weekly. There's often an interesting ravioli dish as well as another pasta such as Gnocchi with Wild Mushrooms; a spicy Braised Lamb Shank with Onion Confit; and an Herb-Roasted Loin of Pork. Great desserts are always available, especially the killer chocolate cookies and éclairs, Bread Pudding, Apple Walnut Cake, a tart or two, and the best rugelach around. These places are ideal if you're in the mood for excellent American food in relaxed surroundings.

Shakers Café

1212 N.W. Glisan Street, phone: 221-0011. Open Monday through Friday, 6:30 a.m.– 4 p.m.; Saturday and Sunday, 7:30 a.m.–4 p.m. Credit cards not accepted

Owners Jeani Subotnick and Bruce Bauer took a one-year hiatus from their beloved Shakers Café when they thought they had sold this popular spot. While they missed the Shakers scene, the two were perfectly happy running their eastside Irish pub, until the new owner of Shakers couldn't make the place work and gave it back.

Sunday hours are the only change in the new Shakers. The great old-fashioned diner atmosphere still prevails, and most customers are regulars whose food tastes are well known by the friendly staff. All the old roadhouse breakfast favorites are part of the menu magic, including big, beautiful Blue Corn Pancakes slathered with paddle-beaten butter and roasted pecans, and Huevos Rancheros, a spilling-over plate of tortillas, eggs, black beans, and a punch-packing salsa loaded with chilies.

Each table is set with jars of homemade preserves, and the lovely house-baked scones—huge triangles studded with dried fruit or nuts—accompany most egg entrees. Make sure to pay attention to the blackboard for specials that might include pancakes laden with the freshest fruit of the moment.

Lunch is the secondary meal here, but no less comfortable or homey. Options include BLTs, big bowls of chili, turkey burgers, and a few salads. Familiarity is the draw here. After your first visit, you'll be a friend of the house forever. Just make sure to have a good explanation when you're asked, "Where have you been?" on your next visit.

La Sirenita

2817 N.E. Alberta Street, phone: 335-8283.
Open daily, 10 a.m.–9 p.m. Credit cards not accepted

Though it's in a pretty dilapidated neighborhood, La Sirenita——"the little mermaid"—is the best and most authentic Mexican taqueria in Portland. Forget the linoleum floor and the counter case stocked with candy that looks as if it's been here since Zapata's Revolution. Note the Mexican flags and other decor in the national colors of red, green, and white; make your way to the kitchen window, where you can scan the sign board and place your order; then get a table and wait until your dish is called. This place is jammed with Latino workers at lunchtime, when you may not hear a word of English. Lunch is the best time for visiting this funky establishment, especially if you've got a hearty appetite. Prices are geared more to a peso than a dollar economy.

La Sirenita is a meat-eater's paradise, what with such ingredients for tacos and burritos as spicy sausage, pork and chilies, tongue, goat, and steak picado. The $1 tacos are steamy-fresh and soft, and you'll find the main ingredients mixed with chilies, onions, and cilantro. If you like things sizzling, there are plenty of bottles of extra hot sauce. The burritos are very filling and delicious, the tortillas chewy, and the beans properly plump. The tamales are scrumptious, the corn husks ripe with pungent flavor. A large bowl of cut limes sits on the counter. If you want great refreshment, have a briny Shrimp or Octopus Cocktail served in a large glass. The restaurant dishes up two great soups as well, one laden with shrimp, the other, called 7 Seas, overflowing with other shellfish of the day. There's no beer, unfortunately, but several drinks are worth ordering: bottled nonalcoholic sangria and two fresh beverages: *tamarindo*, a fruity, slightly bitter drink made from the tamarind seed, and a sweet, cinnamon-flavored rice drink from the Yucatán called *horchata de arroz*.

No other place in town is so like a local cantina, where the cooking's done by a family who loves making good food. Although the English of some of the employees is limited, everyone's friendly and helpful. La Sirenita is the real thing.

Swagat

4325 S.W. 109th Avenue, Beaverton, phone: 626-3000. Open daily,
11:30 a.m.–3 p.m. and 5 p.m.–10 p.m. Credit cards accepted

A large Indian community dwells in the suburbs of Beaverton, which helps explain the area's increasing number of subcontinental restaurants and grocery stores. Best among the crop is Swagat, the first *south* Indian dining spot in Oregon and consistently the most flavorful and well-executed Indian dining in Portland.

Located in a small ranch house (with awfully bright lighting), Swagat offers some of the most interesting and unusual Indian food around. The most characteristically southern dishes on the large, regional menu are vegetarian: crisp *Masala Vada* patties, thick disks of crunchy beans that taste like exotic corn fritters; and gargantuan crispy crepes called *Dosas*, singularly the best item on the menu, which come in seven very different varieties. The *Masala Dosa* is the house favorite: an enormous crepe envelope that hangs over the plate as if the china were from a child's toy set and is stuffed with a mild vegetable curry. Lisa often gets a craving for the chili-spiked *Utapam*, a stack of thin crepes topped with melted butter and minced onions.

The other regional food is top-notch, including an array of plain and stuffed naan breads baked on the side of the tandoor, curries, fiery *vindaloos*, and tandoor-baked meats. You'll get the best range of foods by ordering à la carte and sharing your bounty with others at your table. Be sure to ask for the special condiment rack, loaded with chutneys, pickled citrus fruits, and other intriguing jars for dipping and dabbing your food. The goal with Indian food is to make each mouthful a different combination of sweet, salty, hot, and sour.

Each day, an abundant midday buffet offers some fifteen different regional dishes for an amazingly low price of $5.95. On weekends, Indian diners in large groups use Swagat as a virtual community center, and the lunch buffet tends to have a better selection of more unusual foods: one can assume that the restaurant knows its clientele better on Saturday and Sunday. Box lunches are also available for those who want to take back to the office or home a very different and very delicious lunch.

3 Doors Down

1429 S.E. 37th Avenue, phone: 236-6886 . Open Tuesday through Saturday,
5 p.m.–10 p.m.; Sunday, 5 p.m.–9 p.m. Credit cards accepted

3 Doors Down has matured into a very confident, well-run restaurant. The menu is essentially Italian, but it stretches the boundaries of the cuisine to encompass other Mediterranean influences. The menu changes with some frequency, but certain classics remain, including the flavorful pasta *Fra Diavolo*, with its intense seafood broth and mound of mussels, scallops, shrimp, scampi, and squid tucked in and around ribbons of fettucini. We recently had a splendid Halibut Sauteed with Fennel, which was then baked in a very delicate but pungent saffron-infused fumé and perked with tasty cherry tomatoes. Saffron marries happily with the blandness of the plump, white fish. One of the satisfying starters consists of fresh Green Beans warmed in a Creamy Gorgonzola Sauce studded with Smoky Pancetta and Roasted Red Peppers, good for sopping up with the Grand Central Como bread. One nice touch: instead of the ubiquitous dish of olive oil, 3 Doors Down offers a chunky mash of warm white beans and oil to spread on the country bread. While the restaurant does nicely with its fish, the *Penne* with Sausage, Onions, Cream, and Vodka makes for a hearty yet subtle dish. The Basque Chicken smothered in plum tomatoes on creamy polenta is also excellent. The restaurant usually does well by its chicken entrées, including a robust order of what amounts to a chicken *puttanesca* made with cream instead of tomatoes. There's a good selection of desserts as well; try the whisky-soaked Bread Pudding, a rustic creation with white chocolate and raisins that is warm and soothing.

The staff couldn't be friendlier or more attentive. Unfortunately, this casual neighborhood bistro takes no reservations, and on weekends it is usually full by 6:15 P.M.—but it's worth persevering.

Tina's

760 S.W. Highway 99W, Dundee, phone: 538-8880. Open Tuesday through Friday,
11:30 a.m.–2 p.m.; daily, 5 p.m.–9 p.m. Credit cards accepted

David Bergen and Tina Landfried operate Tina's, our other favorite spot in the wine country (see Café Azul on page 218). The small blue box of a building along the main drag is always festooned with small lights, giving it a Christmas package appearance year-round. Inside, ten tables are available for David and Tina's inspired country cooking. Their sophisticated roots always shine through—they both cooked at L'Auberge for years, and David was Ron Paul's partner when their Charcuterie first opened—and attention is paid to local ingredients: silken oysters poached in a Troisgros sauce of crème fraîche, shallots, and white wine; local lamb that's always moist and luscious, especially when cooked with a local Pinot Noir; a lusty Mushroom Risotto studded with hunks of grilled rabbit. Soups can be velvety wonders, and desserts simple and lovely, such as fruit tarts or an Espresso Pot de Crème. At lunch, the Grilled Pork Loin Sandwich, piled on a homemade bun and slathered with mustard and onions, is a standout. The generous wine list has a definite Yamhill Valley orientation, as it should.

28 East

40 N.E. 28th Avenue, phone: 235-9060. Open Tuesday through Thursday,
11:30 a.m.–2:30 p.m. and 5 p.m.–10:30 p.m.; Friday, 11:30 a.m.–
2:30 p.m. and 5 p.m.–11 p.m.; Saturday, 5 p.m.–11 p.m.; Sunday,
10 a.m.–3 p.m. and 5 p.m.–9 p.m. Credit cards accepted

Amidst a sea change of eastside renovation, 28 East anchors the beginnings of neighborhood gentrification just off Burnside. This attractive storefront bistro sports a vaguely industrial interior (it plays against the sleek deco-era Coca-Cola bottling plant across the street), and its wood-burning oven and rotisserie turn out hearty dishes. The Mussels in Garlic-Rosemary Butter are quite fine, and so are Roasted Portobello Mushrooms with Roasted Garlic on herbed toast. In the French mode, a Lamb Shank with White Bean Ragout is a homey treat, and we've also become fans of a Grilled Rib-Eye Steak served with a soul-satisfying Garlic Potato Cake. Want a wonderful old favorite? Try Marinated Pork Chops with Homemade Applesauce and a mouthful of hot ginger. There's a formula-perfect *Crème Brûlée* and an even better *Tarte Tatin*. This pleasant hangout is perfect when you want nothing more elaborate than a wild green salad, some wild mushrooms, and a glass of Burgundy. It's nice to see such an inviting place on the eastside.

The Food Lover's Companion to Portland

822 S.W. Park Avenue, phone: 227-1845. Open Monday through Saturday,
11:30 a.m.–2 a.m. Credit cards not accepted

The Vat just goes on and on without missing a beat. The beat you'll hear is the downbeat of a conductor's baton, for this restaurant provides the best classical music in town. And the wine list, at twenty-five pages, is legendary. It's one of the cheeriest places to come just for wine and music, but the food is also a treat in an utterly unpretentious way. The cooking is strictly home-style: unadorned, dependable, and comforting (though there's no obviously trendy "comfort food" like garlic-ginger smashed potatoes). While the menu is limited, the offerings are like old, reliable friends: Smoked Salmon and Bread, a well-executed Cold Artichoke with Homemade Mayonnaise, a fine Roast Cornish Game Hen, Smoky Pork Chops, a Fennel and Tomato Salad, and a *Crème Caramel* (the sole dessert). This dark, moody restaurant has deep booth sitting, both in the main room downstairs and along a narrow open corridor upstairs, where the arias lightly waft. The Vat is a cozy place for lunch (in winter, the Goulash or the Moussaka will set you up for the rest of the day), a chummy place for a dinner rendezvous, and an ideal late-night spot.

2310 N.W. Everett Street, phone: 243-7557. Open Monday through Thursday, 11 a.m.–
2:30 p.m. and 5 p.m.–9 p.m.; Friday, 11:30 a.m.–2:30 p.m. and 5 p.m.–10 p.m.;
Saturday, 12 noon–10 p.m.; Sunday, 10 a.m.–2 p.m. Credit cards accepted

Within days of Typhoon!'s opening, Thai fans began forming a queue to dine in one of the most unusual and delicious Thai dining spots around. The food here is more complex and interesting than any other Thai restaurant we've ever visited—anywhere in the United States. Bo Kline's inspired cooking takes its cues from such diverse sources as pushcarts and palaces in her native Bangkok. Not only can you find familiar and intriguing new dishes at this small cafe, but multilayered taste combinations explode in your mouth.

The must-have starter is *Miang Kum,* a pretty presentation that includes a mountain of spinach leaves surrounded by little hills of flavorings: minced ginger, shallots, jalapeños, lime, peanuts, and dried shrimp. Two accompanying small bowls hold a thick ginger-honey sauce and toasted shards of coconut. This dish is a hands-on effort: you spread some sauce on a spinach frond and sprinkle a little bit of each of the flavorings on top, finally dusting the leaf with toasted coconut. Fold the leaf over on itself and you've got a two-bite package of remarkably complex and bright tastes. Another winner is *Hor Muk,* which arrives at your table like an exotic spacecraft. The terra cotta plate is outfitted with six small, domed lids, each concealing a single shrimp barely suspended in a delicate eggy coconut custard. You'll want to lick the dish.

Spicy Shrimp with Crispy Basil is a lively toss of crustaceans, garlic, chili sauce, and crispy basil leaves. The flavors sing in light counterpoint. (It's also offered with ground chicken in place of the shrimp.) Larb chicken (or shrimp) is another standout. Cold cooked meat gets tossed with a tangy, dynamite sauce. Place a mound of the salad on a romaine lettuce canoe and enjoy.

Green Curry Chicken offers buttery slices of chicken breast afloat in a delicate, creamy sauce flecked with bits of fresh basil. The harmony of ingredients is amazing. Even the classic Phad Thai has a slightly different twist here: *thin* soft noodles mingle with ground peanuts, tofu, chunks of your choice of chicken or shrimp, and a (happily) limited number of bean sprouts. All are bound in a delicate tamarind sauce. The contrasts between sweet and sour, tender and crisp are delicious.

The space is also a cut above the expected: a gracious room is decked out with simple rough-hewn wood trim, and large photos of Thailand are framed as if they were views from picture windows. Nothing is too elegant, just tasteful, spirited, and interesting—just like the food.

Wildwood Restaurant and Bar

1221 N.W. 21st Avenue, phone: 249-9663. Open Monday through Saturday, 11:30 a.m.–11 p.m.; Sunday, 10 a.m.–8:30 p.m. Credit cards accepted

Chef Cory Schreiber has native roots (his family owns Dan and Louis Oyster Bar) and an impressive San Francisco resume (he was the opening chef at the glitzy Cypress Club), but it's his love of the Northwest, his interest in promoting local products, and his creativity with a wood-burning oven that have earned him more national press than almost any other chef in town. When folks outside of Portland think of Portland restaurants and Oregon cuisine, Wildwood is likely the reason.

The restaurant's namesake is the Forest Park trail and its muse is James Beard. A glass mural in the entry pays homage to both. This place has always been a real scene: the hippest and hottest tend to congregate here. The bar always hops, and the restaurant itself, with tables packed so closely together that no conversation is private, is usually overflowing with happy diners.

The best food to come out of the kitchen is the simplest. Wood-roasted or clay oven meats and fish are great: generous portions, clean flavors, and a slight char taste. The ovens also produce the best roasted bivalves in town. Mussels or clams are piled in a bowl atop a delicious broth for dunking; the murky brew redolent of onions and saffron begs for bread to absorb its fabulous flavors. Pizzas are thin, chewy as naan bread, and topped with wild mushrooms and cheese or creative vegetable combos. The signature salad is an odd, yet tasty combination of a thin crepe, greens, and cornmeal-fried oysters, topped with a rasher of applewood bacon. The contrasting textures and tastes complement rather than compete to pull the dish together.

Most items on the menu reflect the seasons and local availability. Pears, figs, tomatoes, peppers, and game show up each fall. Spring brings forth Copper River salmon, sturgeon, morels, and asparagus. Berries are featured all through the summer. You can chart the year with Schreiber's menus, using them as a calendar of what's grown when in Oregon.

The bar menu sports the wood-roasted shellfish, pizzas, and a good burger among the options handwritten on big blackboards flanking the bar. Brunch on Sunday is a low-key affair, with burnished nut-based pancakes, wood-oven fritattas, and bountiful breads.

Yen Ha

6820 N.E. Sandy Boulevard, phone: 287-3698.
Open daily, 11 a.m.–11 p.m. Credit cards accepted

With more than 140 dishes on the menu, a full panoply of Vietnamese cuisine is at your disposal at Yen Ha. When Roger took Calvin Trillin here for dinner some years ago, before Vietnamese cooking had fully arrived in the writer's hometown of New York, Trillin said, "Now I know why, when I saw the famous photo of the helicopter hovering above the roof of the U.S. embassy during the fall of Saigon, I shouted 'Save the chefs! Save the chefs!'"

Yen Ha will give you pause, simply because the many dishes on the menu necessitate making a well-thought-out plan for your meal. If any single dish cries out for sampling, it's the Salty Cracked Crab in Black Bean and Garlic Sauce, messy but delectable. We also find ourselves frequently craving *Bo Noung Vi*, a classic assemblage of sliced marinated beef you dip into an island cooker at your table and then wrap in rice paper along with assorted fresh herbs; the Shrimp and Peanut Salad; and the Game Hen with Sweet Rice in Coconut Milk. There are both Eel and Frog's Legs on the menu, and they're wonderful. Among the basics, the spring rolls are first rate, a fresh mixture of chopped chicken, shrimp, mint, green onions, and lettuce wrapped in a rice pancake, to be dipped in a sweet sauce based on a condiment with salted anchovies. But what makes Yen Ha so special, aside from the abundant variety, is the absolute freshness of its mint, cilantro, carrots, and various greens. The French influence on this cuisine is evident, and the produce plays nicely against the crispness of, say, a whole charred fish.

We always feel a sense of gusto at Yen Ha: the dishes pile up, we're immersed in serious feasting, the food generates real excitement, and the prices are astonishingly reasonable.

Zefiro

500 N.W. 21st. Avenue, phone: 226-3394. Open Monday through Thursday, 11:30 a.m.–2:30 p.m., 5:30–10 p.m.; Friday, 11:30 a.m.–2:30 p.m., 5:30 p.m.–10:30 p.m.; Saturday, 5:30 p.m.–10:30 p.m. Credit cards accepted

Restaurants in Portland can be classified Before Zefiro and After Zefiro. When Bruce Carey and Christopher Israel opened this pretty spot in September 1990, the standards for Portland dining radically changed. Overnight, any new restaurants to appear competed not against the pack, but against Israel's kitchen, with its team that continues to produce the most interesting and consistently superior food in town.

Israel's creativity combines sophistication and simplicity, wrapped around the flavors of the Mediterranean, Mexico, and the Far East. Presentations never outshadow taste, and the menu changes often enough (every two weeks) to keep both chef and diners challenged and excited. Israel's inspirations reflect his California training: Alice Waters and Joyce Goldstein, with a little Giuliano Bugialli thrown in. When boredom hit the restless Israel, he spent a six-month sabbatical doing culinary research in Asia, tasting the street food and home cooking, and the flavors he found there have recently made their way to the menu.

Zefiro's offerings are built around four categories: warm appetizers, cold seafood, cold plates, and entrées. This is not a place that pressures you to order an appetizer, main course, and dessert. You can build a delicious meal by sticking with the top half of the menu, wandering around the smaller plates. Supplemented by a frequently replenished plate of breads (excellent pocked levain and grainy corn-based Broa) and marinated olives and oil, even a single salad—like the best Caesar in Portland, served whole-leaf—can make a first-rate modest meal.

The selection of about six entrées might include a Catalan treatment of duck legs braised to fall-apart tenderness and mingled with spiced pears, pine nuts, raisins, and sautéed greens. Or an Asian Mixed Grill of Marinated Quail and Barbecued Ribs, accompanied by house-brewed, lethal kimchee. There's always a grilled fish or two and usually a pasta.

Service is up to the kitchen's standards—Carey makes sure of that. The dining room has a big city buzz and feel, and Zefiro feels alive. We eat here when we tire of places that try to impress, combine too many ingredients, or fuss over food, and when we want just a simple, flavorful bite to eat. The spirit of the restaurant always brightens our mood.

INDEXES

Alphabetical

Geographical

PORTLAND

DOWNTOWN
Bread

Cheese
Chocolate, Candy, and Nuts
Coffee and Tea

Cooking Classes and Caterers
Ethnic Food

OUTSIDE PORTLAND

The Food Lover's Companion to Portland